Praise for

IKE'S
GAMBLE

"This book is subversively revisionist history with sharp relevance to the present. . . . [A] deeply researched, tightly argued and accessibly concise book. . . . [Doran] writes with the authority of a scholar and the familiarity of a senior policy adviser."

—David Frum, *New York Times Book Review*

"Mr. Doran illuminates a narrative with which very few non-specialists will be familiar. . . . A thoroughly researched, closely argued work of traditional diplomatic history."

—James Traub, *Wall Street Journal*

"The failure of the British-French invasion of Egypt in 1956 was one of the seminal events of the second half of the twentieth century: it marked the end of Britain's and France's aspirations to world leadership. America's involvement is brilliantly described in *Ike's Gamble*, a thoughtful and articulate account of the evolution of America's role in that fateful period."

—Henry A. Kissinger

"Richly researched, brisk, and insightful. . . . Offers a forceful and challenging interpretation of the Suez crisis that no student of Middle Eastern history can afford to ignore."

—*Foreign Affairs*

"Deeply researched, well-written, and powerfully persuasive, this book revises everything we've come to accept about America's role in the Middle East in the 1950s. This highly readable and remarkably forthright book explains how America changed from being a mere 'honest broker' in Middle Eastern affairs to being a committed player."

—Professor Andrew Roberts, Lehrman Institute
Distinguished Fellow, New-York Historical Society

"This is a story that has been told many times, but seldom with the depth and stylistic elegance of *Ike's Gamble*. Michael Doran does not just challenge the prevailing historiography, he turns it on its head."

—Ray Takeyh, *Weekly Standard*

"*Ike's Gamble* is a brilliant and fascinating story, compellingly told, of American politics, government, and foreign policy. Doran paints a fascinating portrait of how American foreign policy is designed, how mistakes are made, and how Eisenhower came to understand the errors that had strengthened America's enemies."

—Elliott Abrams, Senior Fellow for Middle Eastern
Studies, Council on Foreign Relations

"A riveting account of President Dwight Eisenhower's conduct in [the] Middle East. . . . Superb."

—Omri Ceren, *Commentary*

ALSO BY MICHAEL DORAN

Pan-Arabism Before Nasser

IKE'S GAMBLE

America's Rise
to Dominance in
the Middle East

MICHAEL DORAN

FREE PRESS
New York   London   Toronto   Sydney   New Delhi

Free Press
An Imprint of Simon & Schuster, Inc.
1230 Avenue of the Americas
New York, NY 10020

First Free Press trade paperback edition October 2017

FREE PRESS and colophon are trademarks of Simon & Schuster, Inc.

For information about special discounts for bulk purchases, please contact
Simon & Schuster Special Sales at 1-866-506-1949
or business@simonandschuster.com.

The Simon & Schuster Speakers Bureau can bring authors to your
live event. For more information or to book an event, contact the
Simon & Schuster Speakers Bureau at 1-866-248-3049
or visit our website at www.simonspeakers.com.

Manufactured in the United States of America

1   3   5   7   9   10   8   6   4   2

Library of Congress Cataloging-in-Publication Data

Names: Doran, Michael Scott, 1962–author.
Title: Ike's gamble : America's rise to dominance in the Middle East/
Michael Doran.
Description: First Free Press hardcover edition. | New York : Free Press, 2016. |
Includes bibliographical references and index.
Identifiers: LCCN 2016019471 | ISBN 9781451697759 | ISBN 1451697759 |
ISBN 9781451697858 (ebook)
Subjects: LCSH: Eisenhower, Dwight D. (Dwight David), 1890–1969. |
Egypt–History–Intervention, 1956. | United States–Foreign relations–
Middle East. | Middle East–Foreign relations–United States. | United States–
Foreign relations–1953–1961.
Classification: LCC E836 .D67 2016 | DDC 327.7305609/045–dc23
LC record available at https://lccn.loc.gov/2016019471

ISBN 978-1-4516-9775-9
ISBN 978-1-4516-9784-1 (pbk)
ISBN 978-1-4516-9785-8 (ebook)

For Melanie

CONTENTS

IKE'S GAMBLE

CHAPTER 1

A New President

Picking a fight was an odd way to say good-bye. In January 1953, Prime Minister Winston Churchill crossed the Atlantic to bid farewell to President Harry Truman, who was just two weeks away from retirement. At a dinner in Truman's honor at the British embassy, the guests included Secretary of State Dean Acheson, Secretary of Defense George Marshall, and a handful of other top American officials. No sooner had dinner begun than Churchill launched into a passionate diatribe in favor of Zionism. According to his right-hand man, Jock Colville, Churchill's position aroused "the disagreement of practically all the Americans present, though they admitted that the large Jewish vote would prevent them disagreeing publicly."[1]

The choice of subjects was impolite. It forced Truman to relive a bitter dispute that had placed him at loggerheads with some of the men around the table—George Marshall in particular. Back in May 1948, Marshall, then secretary of state, nearly resigned in protest over Truman's intention to recognize Israel. In an especially heated exchange in the White House, Marshall accused the president of pandering to the Jewish vote, and of endangering U.S. national security as a result. If the United States did recognize Israel, Marshall said, then he would cast his vote against Truman in the upcoming election.[2] The president, of course, did not follow his secretary of state's advice, and Marshall somehow made his peace with it, but raw feelings persisted.

After dinner, the argument continued, but Truman drifted away from the group, sat down at the piano, and began playing. When Churchill noticed, he instructed Colville to corral everyone around the piano. Truman performed for the group for about a quarter of an hour, and then made an exit, followed swiftly by Marshall. All the others remained behind, and the debate kicked up again, continuing uninterrupted until one in the morning.

In sidelining his guest of honor, Churchill had not acted alone: an invisible accomplice helped him usher Truman out the door. Dwight D. Eisenhower, the president-elect, was spending the evening in New York, planning his new administration, but even from afar he managed to dominate the party. He had already tapped three of Churchill's dinner guests for jobs in his administration. One of them, Walter Bedell Smith, the director of the CIA, had served as Ike's chief of staff during the war. Churchill, who had been on familiar terms with "Beetle" for years, could confidently assume that he would enjoy easy access to the new president. Truman may have had two more weeks in the White House, but his power was already gone.

Saying farewell was a good excuse for Churchill to come, but his true purpose was to begin influencing the new team, not to honor the old. Picking a fight was his way of doing it.

Fatuous Churchill

Once Truman had gone off to bed, the argument focused on two main issues, the European Defense Community (EDC) and the Middle East. On the surface, the issues seemed utterly disconnected, but for Churchill they were two parts of the same challenge: persuading the Americans to accept his vision of the special relationship between Britain and the United States. In both Europe and the Middle East, he argued, the United States should put the alliance with Britain ahead of all other interests. His American guests, however, were not having any of it.

Originally proposed by the French, the EDC was a plan for an integrated, pan-European army—an idea that Churchill hated. In its place he proposed a grand coalition, like the one that had defeated Germany and Japan in World War II. The Cold War alliance should be a pyramid, with the Anglo-American partnership at its apex. Emphasizing the Anglophone bond, he dismissed the multilingual EDC as nothing but "a sludgy amalgam."[3]

In the Middle East, the primary threat to Churchill's vision was the growing friendship between the United States and local nationalists. Particularly disturbing to Churchill was the warm attitude of the Americans toward Egypt's young military rulers, who had toppled King Faruq in a bloodless coup on July 23, 1952. The Free Officers, as they called themselves, had come to power in the midst of a breakdown in Egyptian-British relations, and they were now publicly demanding nothing less than an immediate and unconditional evacuation of the 80,000 British forces who occupied the base along the Suez Canal. Outwardly, General Muhammad Naguib was in charge of the movement, but behind the scenes, a young colonel, Gamal Abdel Nasser, was the one truly calling the shots. Shortly after taking power, Nasser had quietly reached out to the Americans, whose welcoming response was unsettling to the British. The Americans believed that Egypt, as the largest and most influential Arab country, was the key to delivering the entire Arab world to the West in the Cold War. Moreover, they saw nationalists like the Free Officers as the wave of the future.

"Our last hope" was how Acheson described Naguib to Churchill that night. The phrase was poison to Churchill, who believed that the abandonment of the British position in Egypt would spell the end of empire. Courting the Free Officers was not on his agenda; cutting them down to size was—and he sought American support in doing so. But the Americans were disinclined—so unreceptive that Colville feared his boss had pressed the point too hard for his own good. "I had an uneasy feeling," he wrote in his diary, that the "remarks—about Israel, the E.D.C. and Egypt . . . had better have been left unsaid in the presence of the three . . . who are staying with Ike and the Republicans."[4]

This was not the first time on his trip that Churchill had encountered strong resistance to his message. Only the day before, in New York, he had held a series of meetings with Eisenhower himself. Hoping to build on their wartime association, Churchill described his notion of the special relationship and, in the process, floated the idea of an early bilateral conference. He was prepared, he said, to return to Washington two weeks after the inauguration. What better way for Eisenhower to jump-start his foreign policy than to remind the world of the wartime summit conferences that Churchill had conducted with Roosevelt and Truman?

Eisenhower pretended to mull over the idea. He told Churchill that he certainly agreed that the two leaders should use their warm personal relations for mutual benefit, but on the specific question of whether to convene an early summit, he deferred to the man whom he had tapped to be the next secretary of state, John Foster Dulles. He suggested that the three of them—Eisenhower, Dulles, and Churchill—discuss the issue over dinner that night. Churchill left the meeting ecstatic. Eisenhower was entertaining his plan!

Or was he? At dinner, Dulles was a wet blanket. He called Churchill's suggestion "most unfortunate." The American people, he explained, believed that Churchill had the ability "to cast a spell on all American statesmen." The new administration, therefore, had to find its footing before organizing a summit conference. Churchill, according to Colville, "sat up and growled." That night in the privacy of his hotel room, he unleashed a tirade "about the Republican Party in general and Dulles in particular. . . . He said he would have no more to do with Dulles whose 'great slab of a face' he disliked and distrusted."[5]

Churchill blamed Dulles, but in truth he had fallen victim to an old Eisenhower trick. Ike preferred to have his subordinates deliver bad news. During the war, it was Bedell Smith who served as his hatchet man. Late in life, Beetle looked back on the role with bitterness. "I was just Ike's prat boy," he complained to Vice President Richard Nixon over a whiskey in 1959. "Ike always had to have a prat boy, someone who'd do the dirty work for him. He always had to have someone else do the firing, or the reprimanding, or give any orders which he knew people would find unpleasant to carry out." Tears were streaming down his face. "Ike always has to be the nice guy."[6]

Eisenhower played the nice guy with Churchill, but afterward he recorded his true feelings in his diary. "Much as I hold Winston in my personal affection and much as I admire him for his past accomplishments and leadership," he wrote, "I wish that he would turn over leadership of the British Conservative party to younger men."[7] Churchill was, Eisenhower continued, "trying to relive the days of World War II," when "he had the enjoyable feeling that he and our president were sitting on some rather Olympian platform with respect to the rest of the world and directing world affairs from that point of vantage." The British statesman's vision of World War II leadership was a myth, but even if it had been accurate, it was no model for the Cold War. "In the present international complexities," Eisenhower explained, "any hope of establishing such a relationship is completely fatuous."[8]

Felix Leiter

Eisenhower's reservations about Churchill's ideas were well founded, and he was hardly alone in entertaining them. If there was anyone who shared his belief that the prime minister should

make way for younger men, it was Anthony Eden, the British foreign secretary and Churchill's heir apparent.

Dapper and polished, Eden was known in his early days for his
"Noel Coward glamour and style."[9] But he was also an experienced
professional. He first became foreign secretary in late 1935, at the
age of thirty-eight. After just two years in office, in February 1938,
he clashed with Prime Minister Neville Chamberlain over British policy toward Mussolini and resigned. Six months later, when
Chamberlain reached the Munich Agreement with Hitler, Eden
took a stand against it, putting himself on the same side with Churchill, who soon became prime minister. In 1940, Eden again became foreign secretary, remaining in office at Churchill's side for
the next five years.

Having managed the international relations of Britain during
World War II, he was a seasoned diplomat, a highly experienced
politician—certainly one who was prepared to become prime minister. But Churchill was not ready to quit. When the duo returned
to power in 1951, they fell back into old patterns, with Churchill
taking the lead on the issues that mattered to him—relations with
America, first and foremost. On that score, Eden was often closer
in spirit to Ike than to his own prime minister. In contrast to Churchill, who still believed in the British Empire, Eden was a mod-
ernist, believing, like Eisenhower, that it was important to find an
accommodation with the rising generation of Middle Eastern nationalists. But agreeing with the Americans on general principles
was one thing; devising policies that harmonized the interests of
the two countries was another one altogether.

In June 1952, Eden had presented the Cabinet with a paper,
titled "British Overseas Obligations," which presented his basic
ideas about how to forge a common Anglo-American approach to
the Middle East. It opened with a stark admission of economic
weakness. "It is becoming clear," the paper stated, "that rigorous
maintenance of the presently-accepted policies of Her Majes-

ty's Government at home and abroad is placing a burden on the country's economy which it is beyond the resources of the country to meet." Consequently, some British obligations had to be "transferred to others' shoulders"—meaning, of course, those of the United States. The goal of British policy was to create international structures, such as a Middle East Defense Organization, which the Americans would bankroll, "while retaining for ourselves as much political control—and hence prestige and world influence—as we can."[10]

Call it the James Bond strategy. The Americans would provide the money and the muscle, while the British would supply the savoir-faire. This vision of Anglo-American partnership had a deep impact on the first novel in the Bond series, *Casino Royale*, which author Ian Fleming completed just a few months before Eden presented his paper to the Cabinet. The success of Bond's mission depended on defeating the Soviet agent, Le Chiffre, at a single game of high-stakes baccarat. A series of unlucky hands, however, stripped Bond of all of his money. As he stood at the table stunned, with no options left, his American friend, CIA agent Felix Leiter, miraculously appeared with a solution. Leiter passed Bond an envelope "as thick as a dictionary." Inside was a wad of cash and a note: "Marshall Aid. Thirty-two million francs. With the compliments of the USA." Resuscitated with American funds, Bond continued to play and, of course, trounced Le Chiffre.[11]

Bond's creator, Ian Fleming, was a personal friend of Anthony Eden, and he successfully channeled the emotions of the British elite into a satisfying myth. In the view of Eden and his colleagues, the British were hardly coming to the Americans cap in hand. Like James Bond, they were bankrupt, but they were placing uniquely valuable assets at the disposal of the United States. This, they believed, was especially true in the Middle East, where they brought to the table an established regional security system and years of deep experience in the region. The hub of their network was the

base along the Suez Canal, which contained workshops, supply warehouses, and training grounds that serviced British forces
not just in the Middle East but in East Africa as well. Britain also
maintained bases in Aden, Iraq, Jordan, Cyprus, and Malta. The
sheikhdoms of the Persian Gulf were protectorates, whose foreign
relations were conducted entirely by a British official, "the Resi-
dent," who sat in Bahrain. The commander of the Jordanian army,
the Arab Legion, was British, as were most of his top commanders. Thanks to this informal empire, American strategic planners
could confidently assume that, in the event of a war with the Soviet
Union, the British would be prepared to take the lead in defending
the region.

Eden, then, hardly considered himself to be a beggar. And if
ever there was an American president open to playing the role of
Felix Leiter, it was Ike—or so Eden hoped. In 1945, the British
made General Eisenhower an honorary citizen of London. The
address that he delivered on the occasion is as moving an expression of Anglo-American unity as any American leader has penned.
Eisenhower presented himself as a product of Abilene, Kansas, a
place as distant as one could imagine from sophisticated London.
Yet he and the Londoners were united by their common values.
"To preserve his freedom of worship, his equality before the law,
his liberty to speak and act as he sees fit . . . ," Ike proclaimed, "the
Londoner will fight! So will the citizen of Abilene!"[12] His audience
melted.

But the very love of liberty that Eisenhower celebrated in his
speech made it impossible for him to accept the idea of forging a
common Anglo-American front in the Middle East. Like many of
his fellow Americans, Eisenhower was uncomfortable with imperialism. He had registered his qualms clearly when Churchill visited
him in New York—if only to his diary. With respect to problems
like the Anglo-Egyptian conflict, he explained, Churchill had taken
an "old-fashioned, paternalistic approach." Because Britain and the

United States were "required to support and carry the heavy burdens of decent international plans, as well as to aid infant nations towards self-dependence," Churchill felt that "other nations should recognize the wisdom of our suggestions and follow them." [13]

In Ike's view, the problem was not so simple. Churchill's approach, he believed, would only benefit the Soviet Union. "Moscow leads many misguided people to believe that they can count on communist help to achieve and sustain nationalist ambitions." It was vitally important, therefore, to avoid policies that made it seem as if the West, as a bloc, had set its face against nationalism. The implications for the James Bond strategy were dire. There was a "great danger," Eisenhower wrote, "in the two most powerful free nations banding together to present their case in a 'take it or leave it' fashion." [14] Eisenhower was no Felix Leiter.

The Honest Broker

But who was he, exactly? Eisenhower saw the United States as an honest broker—a mediator helping nationalists seek fair redress from the British. In no way idiosyncratic, this view of the American role was by far the dominant perspective in Washington—and it was a perspective that the American elite's attitudes toward Israel strongly reinforced. Like Britain, Israel was a country inextricably linked to the United States but which also stirred up deep hostility among the Arabs. The desire to escape the stigma that American officials believed came from an association with the Jewish state led them to distance the United States from Israel and to establish the United States as a mediator between Arab nationalism and Zionism.

In short, Eisenhower and his top advisors, especially Dulles, saw Israel as a liability. The strategic goal of American policy was to reclaim as much Arab goodwill as possible by demonstrating, in the terminology of the Eisenhower administration, "impartiality"—a word that implied tacking away from Israel. This attitude expressed itself in the flowering, under the Eisenhower administration, of the American Friends of the Middle East (AFME), a CIA front organization, whose goals included countering the support for Zionism in domestic American politics. The organization had direct ties to the president and secretary of state through Reverend Edward L. R. Elson, who, in addition to being a leading officer in AFME, was the pastor of the National Presbyterian Church, which both the president and the secretary of state attended.[15]

It is impossible to exaggerate the impact that the image of America as an honest broker had on Eisenhower's thought. Words like *idea*, *concept*, and *strategy* mischaracterize the nature of the vision. Terms like *paradigm*, *worldview*, or *belief system* are more apt. The notion that the top priority of the United States was to co-opt Arab nationalists by helping them extract concessions—within limits—from Britain and Israel was not open to debate. It was a view that shaped all other policy proposals. In fact, the concept was so pervasive that Eisenhower and his colleagues regarded it not as an intellectual construct but as a description of reality itself.

This book examines the influence of the honest broker paradigm on American relations with the Arabs. It is a tale of Frankenstein's monster, with the United States as the mad scientist and the new regime in Egypt as his uncontrollable creation.

From among the young officers around General Naguib, Colonel Gamal Abdel Nasser would soon emerge publicly as the true leader of the Free Officers and as a charismatic figure in the wider Arab world. In keeping with the honest broker approach, Eisenhower identified him as a strategic partner, as the only leader capable of ushering in a new era of cooperation between all of the Arabs and the West. With this goal in mind, Eisenhower helped Nasser oust the British from Egypt. While doing so, he also allowed the CIA to equip Nasser with a powerful, state-of-the-art broadcasting system, which beamed his radical pan-Arab ideology, in all its anti-Western and anti-Zionist glory, into every Arab household. The Americans assisted Nasser in the expectation that, in the end, he would use this equipment to help unify the Arabs behind the United States in the Cold War. Instead, he gravitated toward the Soviet Union and worked assiduously to undermine the Western position in the Middle East.

What went wrong? The literature on the question is vast, but a major theme runs through much of it. Eisenhower and Dulles, so the tale goes, came into office with the right ideas and good intentions, but, in the end, they followed in the footsteps of empire. Against their better angels, they alienated Nasser and, along with him, much of the rest of the Arab world; by the time that they realized their mistake, it was already too late. The precise cause of Nasser's alienation differs from account to account—in some versions, a ham-fisted America undermines itself; in others, it is a belligerent Israel that drives Egypt into the arms of the Soviet Union. In still others, both factors conspire together.

This book tells a different story. Imbued with the honest broker ethos, Eisenhower and Dulles prioritized the settlement of the Anglo-Egyptian and Arab-Israeli conflicts over all other issues—in order to eliminate the obstacles to strategic partnership with the Arabs. This approach suffered from a severe defect: it turned a blind eye to the conflicts between the regional, Muslim powers, and to the hegemonic aspirations of Egypt. Nasser used the American fixation on peacemaking as a means of deflecting the attention of Washington from his revolutionary pan-Arab program, which screamed about Zionism and imperialism, but which also sought to eliminate Arab rivals to regional leadership.

It was the long-term impact of the 1956 Suez Crisis that finally brought home to Eisenhower the deficiencies of the honest broker approach. The crisis came to a head when Britain, France, and Israel attacked Egypt simultaneously. Eisenhower took a strong position against the three attackers, even going so far as to side with the Soviet Union against his allies in the United Nations. He believed

that if the United States would publicly demonstrate firm opposition to the Europeans and the Israelis, it would receive a strategic payoff in the form of widespread Arab goodwill. But the payoff
never came. Instead, Eisenhower handed Nasser yet another political victory—the greatest of his career. He helped transform the
Egyptian leader into a pan-Arab hero of epic proportions.

The consequences for the United States were profound. When
Eisenhower took office in 1953, the Arab world was still tied to
the West, thanks in no small measure to the continued influence of
British and French imperialism. The Soviet Union had been successfully locked out of the region for three decades, and the American goal was to keep it out. By the end of his second term, however,
a wave of revolution had swept the region. It did its greatest damage in Iraq, where revolutionaries, modeling themselves on Nasser,
toppled the Hashemite monarchy. The new leaders quickly looked
to Moscow for support, and the Middle East became a major arena
of Cold War competition.

In the aftermath of the Suez Crisis, as Eisenhower watched
these results unfold, he discarded, once and for all, his fundamental assumptions about the Middle East. He no longer believed that
helping the Arabs balance the power of the Israelis and the Europeans was the key to a successful regional strategy. In fact, he
dispensed altogether with the notion of making policy toward the
Arabs collectively. The key challenge before the United States, he
now realized, was to manage inter-Arab conflict, to help one network of Arab states balance the power of a rival network. In later
life, he expressed regret for having treated his allies so harshly at
Suez, and he came to see Israel as a strategic asset.

Then and Now

"History does not repeat itself but it often rhymes," Mark Twain
supposedly said. There is no period in twentieth-century Middle

Eastern history that rhymes more powerfully with the present than the Eisenhower era. Today, as then, we are witnessing the fall of a discredited old order and the rise of something new. Transnational Islamist movements are shaking the region in a manner similar to Nasser's pan-Arabism. While Nasser had Radio Cairo to spread his message, today's revolutionaries have Facebook and Twitter.

To be sure, there are also big differences. Vladimir Putin's Russia might be a thorn in the side of the United States today, but it does not pose as grave a threat as the Soviet Union did, and there is certainly no contemporary Arab figure analogous to Nasser. The role that Egypt played in the international system in the 1950s is somewhat analogous to the role that Iran plays today, but the differences between the two are almost as great as the similarities. Nevertheless, many of the key questions that plagued Eisenhower continue to challenge us. Should Washington make policy toward Arab and Muslim public opinion generally, or should it focus on the narrow interests of specific elites? Is Israel a liability or an asset? In a region so riven with conflict, how much support does America owe its allies? Indeed, what criteria should the United States use to distinguish between allies and enemies?

The story of Eisenhower's relations with Nasser is nothing if not a lesson in the dangers of calibrating the distinction between ally and enemy incorrectly. Eisenhower was the first American president to formulate a comprehensive strategy for the Middle East, and he was one of the most sophisticated and experienced practitioners of international politics ever to reside in the White House. Thanks to his military experience, he was accustomed to reviewing his actions and assessing their effectiveness; when he made mistakes, he paused and thought deeply about them. The lessons he learned from the Suez Crisis were weighty, and they have an enduring quality. They may not provide us with a detailed route out of the Middle Eastern labyrinth today, but they will certainly make us wiser about how to negotiate it.

CHAPTER 2

Collision

What gift do you give an Egyptian leader? You can't go wrong with a silver-plated Colt .38—especially when that leader, Muhammad Naguib, happens to be a general in the army. Eisenhower saw the gun as an innocent gesture, a token of respect from one military man to another. The last thing he expected was an international incident.

On May 11, 1953, a smiling Foster Dulles presented the pistol to Naguib on behalf of the president. A photographer snapped a picture of the ceremony, and the next day it appeared in newspapers across Britain. "What could Eisenhower possibly be thinking?" the British public wondered. At that moment, Egyptian forces were surrounding some 80,000 British troops in the Suez Canal Zone. Naguib and his top officials were publicly threatening to unleash rivers of blood. Behind the scenes, Egyptian military intelligence had launched a covert guerrilla campaign, recently killing or wounding some twenty British soldiers.[1] Was Eisenhower signaling support for Egypt?

While officials in London knew the revolver was just a gaffe, it still symbolized a worrying trend in American policy. Before departing for Cairo, Dulles had warned London that, in fact, he was inclined to begin arming the Egyptian military—not in order to support attacks against Britain but to tie Egypt to the West in the Cold War. When Eisenhower learned of the bad impression the revolver had made in London, he sent a soothing letter to Churchill, assuring him that "one Colt .38 . . . did not presage a flow [to Egypt] of planes, tanks and guns."²

That was certainly welcome news, but Churchill knew full well that Eisenhower was eager to solve the Anglo-Egyptian conflict—that he expected to see a spirit of compromise from the British. Churchill, however, was hardly in a position to make concessions. Defense of the empire ran through his life like a crimson thread in a tapestry. In November 1942, when announcing British war aims, he famously stated that he had "not become the King's first minister in order to preside over the liquidation of the British Empire." Electoral defeat in 1945 allowed him to escape responsibility for the grinding retreat from empire that ensued after World War II—retreat from Palestine, Malaya, Burma, and, most painfully, India. As the leader of the opposition, Churchill blamed the government of Clement Attlee for "scuttling" imperial positions of strength. "It does not matter where you look in the world," he thundered in June 1948, "you will see how grievously the name and prestige of Britain have suffered since the British Nation fell flat upon the moment of its greatest victory." In 1951, Churchill was returned to power.

The dispute with Egypt was one of the most emotive issues in British politics, and it mattered greatly to Churchill's political base. It was a rallying point for "the Suez Group," a band of Conservative members of parliament who vehemently opposed concessions to the Egyptians. The military base in the Canal Zone was the hub of the defense system in the Middle East, the last region where Britain was still dominant. The loss of the base meant the end of Britain as a great power—the definitive end of empire.

Churchill could not back down, and Ike could not support him. The two titans were not just on a collision course; they were already colliding. Eisenhower's gift to Naguib was a fitting end to a strenuous effort by Churchill to forge a joint Anglo-American approach to the Egyptian question. That effort began three months earlier, in mid-February, when Churchill sent Eisenhower a very puzzling letter.

Churchill Asks for Help

The letter confidently asserted that the British had the situation in the Canal Zone fully under control. "There is no question," Churchill wrote, "of our seeking or needing military, physical, or financial aid from you." At the same time, however, it also implied that all hell could break loose at any moment. The British forces in the Canal Zone, he assured Eisenhower, "are in ample strength to resist any attack, and even if necessary, in order to prevent a massacre of white people and to rescue them, to enter Cairo and Alexandria."[3]

Churchill proceeded to reference an understanding that the British government had reached with the Americans in the final days of the Truman administration. The agreement called for Washington to support the British on three key issues: the terms of the withdrawal of the occupying forces, the status of the Canal Zone base after the evacuation, and the establishment of a Middle East Defense Organization, which would tie the Arab world to NATO through the two organizations' common partners, Britain and Turkey.[4] The Truman administration had accepted the idea of a package deal: no agreement on any one component was valid until agreement on all three had been reached.

The package-deal concept was sacrosanct to Churchill. The moment Britain would evacuate the troops, it would lose its greatest source of influence over the Free Officers: coercive power. In addition, Churchill also understood just how eager the junta was to establish a strategic relationship with the Americans, the gatekeepers of Western economic and military aid. The British wielded a temporary stick, but the Americans held permanent carrots. If Washington and London were to work at cross-purposes, then Churchill would never get the deal that he needed from the Egyptians.

The Free Officers, for their part, understood Churchill's calculations perfectly. They therefore sought to split the Americans from
the British and to negotiate over one issue and one issue only: the
evacuation of the British troops from Egypt. Once the British troops
were gone, Churchill's leverage would evaporate and Egypt would
be free to ignore Britain and work directly with the Americans.

To Eisenhower, these details were not immediately obvious
from the text of Churchill's letter. At a meeting of the National Security Council in mid-February, Eisenhower turned to Dulles and
asked what exactly "Churchill was concerned about and why a solution was so urgent." Dulles was not at the top of his game. He said
the matter was not urgent. He outlined the differences between the
Egyptian and British positions, and noted that Churchill had made
two requests: to affirm the agreement with the Truman administration; and to appoint an American military man to work as the
partner of Field Marshal William Slim, whom Churchill had put in
charge of the British negotiating team. Dulles closed his remarks
by repeating that he "didn't think the problem very important."

The president flatly disagreed. It was, he said, "a matter of great
significance." He was concerned lest the urgent tone of Churchill's
letter "should be the means of securing this administration's agreement to something more than had been agreed to last January." He
feared that Churchill "was trying to tie our hands in advance to
something about which we were not very clear."[5]

Eisenhower knew the wily Churchill all too well. They had
worked together closely, during the war. As Supreme Allied Commander, Eisenhower had planned D-Day from Telegraph Cottage,
located just outside London, and there Churchill would meet him
twice weekly. As a man accustomed to being dressed by servants,
Churchill did not hesitate to emphasize rank and status when it
suited him. With Ike, however, he always played the amiable friend.
His behavior toward Kay Summersby was typical. During the war,
Summersby was Eisenhower's driver, a trusted member of his war-

time "household." Rumors of an affair between Ike and his attractive driver spread among the British. While some clucked with disapproval, Churchill was not among them. He perceived an opportunity to forge a bond of intimacy with Ike. Whenever he came for dinner, he would ask that Summersby be seated at the table, too. "Now tell Kay to come," he would say to Ike. "I want to see her."[6]

In its own way, the letter about Egypt was also a way of establishing a more intimate bond. Churchill had requested that Eisenhower appoint a military officer to run the negotiations in order to cut out the diplomats on both sides. He distrusted Britain's Foreign Office, the State Department, and, especially, Dulles. If Eisenhower would appoint an American general to work with Field Marshal Slim, Churchill calculated, then he and Ike could manage the negotiations on their own, executive to executive.

Once Dulles gleaned the depth of Eisenhower's distrust of Churchill, he reminded the president that Anthony Eden was scheduled to visit in a few weeks. "[I]t was easier to deal with Mr. Eden than with Mr. Churchill," Dulles observed.[7] Eisenhower agreed. He resolved to tell Churchill that the new administration would honor the agreement with Truman. Any decision on the details, however, would await the foreign secretary's visit. The devil, Eden would soon learn, was in the details.

The Heir Apparent

Though Churchill was nearly eighty and had already suffered at least one stroke, he could not bring himself to retire. Three months before Eden flew to Washington, he spent an infuriating weekend with Churchill at Chequers, the prime minister's country retreat. Upon his return, he confessed his frustration to his private secretary, Evelyn Shuckburgh. Aching to take power, Eden mustered the courage to ask Churchill about his retirement plans. The prime minister assured Eden that his time would soon come. He delivered, Shuckburgh wrote in his diary, "a solemn Winstonian speech to the effect that his intention was, when the time came, to hand over his powers and authority with the utmost smoothness and surety to Anthony."

Eden asked when that time might be. Churchill sat silent for a full minute. "Often," he said, "I think there are things I could say, speeches I could make more easily if I were not Prime Minister." Another long and uncomfortable silence followed. Then Churchill moved on to other topics and never answered the question.[8]

Throughout 1952, Eden was the uncontested heir apparent, but his political fortunes were beginning to dip—mainly due to Egypt. In late 1952 and early 1953, the foreign secretary launched a negotiation with the Free Officers over the Sudan, whose disposition was intimately bound up with the fate of the Canal Zone base. The Suez Group feared that Eden's Sudan initiative, which entailed concessions to Egypt, signaled an impending retreat from the Canal Zone. The newspapers of Lord Beaverbrook, a conservative press magnate and close ally of Churchill, harshly criticized Eden.

On occasion, Churchill himself would add his voice to the criticisms. On January 29, 1952, he met with Eden for lunch. While the two were dining alone, Jock Colville, Churchill's private secretary, took a moment to confer with Shuckburgh. Colville feared that Churchill and Eden would soon be at each other's throats. Only the day before, Churchill had worked himself into "a rage" over the Sudan, labeling Eden's policy "appeasement," and saying that "he never knew before that Munich was situated on the Nile." Churchill described Eden "as having been a failure as Foreign Secretary and as being 'tired, sick and bound up in detail.'" Colville warned that the prime minister "would never give way over Egypt. He positively desired the talks on the Sudan to fail, just as he positively hoped we should not succeed in getting into conversations with the Egyptians on defence, which might lead to our abandonment of the Canal Zone." In the end, the lunch went smoothly, without the slightest hint of bad feeling. "These two," Shuckburgh wrote in his diary, "always shy away from a quarrel at the last moment."[9]

Eden and his staff in the Foreign Office saw Churchill as a magisterial figure, but one who was over the hill, stubbornly clinging to outmoded ideas—a wondrous relic. They saw themselves, by contrast, as realists and modernists. They were dedicated to bringing British policy into alignment with the main contours of the age: nationalism, anti-imperialism, and the global dominance of the Soviets and the Americans, neither of whom were favorably disposed to European notions of empire. On February 16, Eden distributed to the Cabinet a paper that encapsulated the Foreign Office viewpoint. "In the second half of the 20th century," the document argued, "we cannot hope to maintain our position in the Middle East by the methods of the last century. . . . Our strategic purposes in the Middle East can no longer be served by arrangements which local nationalism will regard as military occupation."[10]

Churchill detested these sentiments and he fought a vehement but haphazard campaign against them. Typical was an episode in January 1953. After traveling to Washington to bid farewell to Truman, Churchill took the *Queen Mary* to Jamaica for vacation. While relaxing in the sun, he suddenly and inexplicably became convinced that Eden was making unwarranted concessions to the Egyptians. According to Shuckburgh's diary, he "started telegraphing and telephoning from his ship" in an effort to prevent the transfer of "four jet fighters, now due for Egypt under an old contract, from proceeding." It later became clear that Lord Beaverbrook had sounded the alarm from London and spurred Churchill to action.

For Eden, to be second-guessed from the middle of the Caribbean was demoralizing. "If he has so little confidence in me," the foreign secretary lamented to Shuckburgh, "I had better go."[11]

Mr. Eden Goes to Washington

But Eden did not leave the government; instead, he left for Washington—as planned. In early March he arrived for five days of discussion with Dulles and Eisenhower, primarily over the Middle East. His first progress report to Churchill was disappointing. "We had a long and at times difficult discussion this morning about Egypt," he wrote on March 6. The Americans had two principal reservations concerning the impending Anglo-Egyptian negotiations—one on process, the other on substance. Regarding process, they "feel reluctance to enter these discussions," unless invited by the Egyptians to join. Eisenhower, himself, "was emphatic that he could not gate-crash." Eden consoled himself, however, with Eisenhower's attitude toward substance. The president, he wrote to Churchill, "is fully alive to the importance of having a base available in Egypt in time of war" and "for that reason he wants to get as near as he can to A." [12]

"A" was a shorthand reference to the first of three possible outcomes to the negotiations—Cases A, B, and C. Case A envisioned a base along the Canal under British control, servicing imperial positions around the Middle East and in East Africa. Under A, British troops would remain on the base and run it. By contrast, Case B outlined a base that would not service the British defense system in the Middle East but would remain in a state of perpetual readiness, in case of another major war. It called for prepositioning supplies and maintaining military workshops that the British could reactivate in time of crisis. The Egyptians would be in charge of the base, but some number of British technicians would remain behind to ensure its readiness. Case C called for the complete surrender of the base to the Egyptians, who would maintain it themselves but guarantee the British the right to return in wartime.

For Churchill, Case A was the only acceptable option—but getting Eisenhower to commit to it was proving to be a thornier challenge than expected. If the British would accept the American refusal "to gate-crash," Eden reported, then Eisenhower would immediately appoint General John Hull as Field Marshal Slim's American counterpart. "Much more difficult," Eden continued, "was the American reluctance to commit themselves in advance not in any circumstances to go beyond Case A." Eisenhower said the British "must not doubt" the Americans' "sincere determination to get A. . . . If, however, A was unobtainable, they did not wish from the start to exclude B, and later to be told by us that they were pressing us to concessions we did not want to make." Eden explained to Churchill that they stood before a clear choice. Either they could go into the negotiations alone in a determined effort to get Case A, or they could partner with the Americans in pursuit of Eisenhower's more flexible goals. "My own judgment," Eden offered, "is that on balance we should be infinitely better placed with full American participation." [13]

Churchill detested his options, and he penned a harsh note of protest to Eisenhower. He strongly implied that if the Americans refused to support Case A, then he would withdraw the British forces from the Korean War. He cabled the note to Eden, asking him to pass it on to Eisenhower. When Eden read the note, he called it "foolish and bad tempered"—but only to his trusted staff.[14] To Churchill himself, he reacted more politely. He suggested that the British should approach Eisenhower in a less confrontational manner, and he had a concrete idea about how to do so. He proposed to ask the president to promise not to deviate from Case A unless both the American and the British military advisors agreed. Churchill assented, but also did not retract his threat regarding Korea, which, however, Eden refrained from delivering to Eisenhower.

Eden came away delighted from his next meeting with the president—but only because he was unfamiliar with Eisenhower's habit of letting subordinates deliver bad news. The foreign secretary reported to Churchill that the president had agreed to strive for a base that was "workable in peacetime"—Case A. If that proved impossible, then he agreed that "we must have a base which can be reactivated as soon as possible after the outbreak of war"—Case B. Even if Case A could not be fully achieved, Eisenhower recognized the necessity of keeping some installations under direct British supervision. He also agreed that the military representatives, Slim and Hull, would work as a team and would have the latitude to make modifications to which they both agreed.[15]

The discussion with Eisenhower left Eden with the belief that General Hull would be fully in charge of the American team. The moment he returned to London, however, he learned that the State Department had informed the Foreign Office that Jefferson Caffery, the American ambassador in Cairo, would lead the negotiations. The news hit Eden like a punch in the nose. Caffery was the very embodiment of American anti-imperialism—and he reported to Dulles, not the White House.

Eden was certain this news was a mistake. "Caffery's name was never mentioned," Eden protested to Roger Makins, the British ambassador in Washington. "You know our lack of confidence in Caffery."[16] Makins double-checked, then confirmed that, indeed, Caffery was in charge of the American delegation, with General Hull serving only as his advisor. Eden was in a state of disbelief. He wrote to Makins again, saying "the President, I know, shares my view about Caffery. I should therefore like you to have another go with Bedell Smith," who had proved helpful to Eden in maneuvering around Dulles.[17] Makins followed his instructions and received the same answer from Bedell Smith: Caffery was in charge.

A Friend of Egypt

Before serving in Cairo, Caffery had been ambassador to France. Another man might have seen the posting to Paris as the capstone to a successful career, but Caffery had his sights set on one more job: Egypt. In terms of professional prestige, a posting to Cairo was a step down from Paris, but Caffery, as an amateur Egyptologist, relished the idea of scampering around the pyramids for a few years before retirement. His hobby was Britain's misfortune. Eden found himself saddled with an American ambassador who was respected in Washington and who, being at the end of his career, didn't care whether he made enemies. The British had no leverage over him.

Nor did they have influence inside Caffery's team. William Lakeland, a young American political officer in the embassy in Cairo, had developed a close relationship with Gamal Abdel Nasser, who was the secret leader of the junta, the true power behind Naguib. Nasser was a regular visitor in Lakeland's apartment, where he would eat hot dogs and watch Hollywood films that Lakeland would borrow from the embassy and project on his wall. (Nasser had a soft spot for Esther Williams.) The British were well informed about Lakeland's special relationship with Nasser—and livid about it. Their dispatches from Cairo described the young American diplomat as "more Egyptian than the Egyptians," and "notable for his youthful enthusiasm and idealistic, even sentimental, approach to the Egyptians, untempered by realism and uncoloured by any feeling of solidarity with us." Lakeland, they claimed, gave Nasser and his colleagues the impression that they "could get what they wanted if they pushed the British a little further still."[18]

Only thirty-four years old, Nasser had the experience of a man twice his age. He had led men into battle in the 1948 Arab-Israeli War, organized a clandestine revolutionary movement, and toppled a king. Soon he would be famous the world over, a leader of the Non-Aligned Movement in the Cold War. Recognizing that his youth, obscurity, and relatively low rank of colonel were political disabilities, he let Naguib serve as the face of the Egyptian revolution. It was a mark of Nasser's genius that Naguib did not realize that he was more a figurehead than a leader. Nasser had a gift for making older men feel that they were counseling him, when, in fact, they were doing his bidding.

Nasser's charms certainly worked on Caffery, who was thoroughly convinced that the Egyptians would settle down nicely in the American sphere of interest—if only the United States would first help them oust the British. Caffery, therefore, was highly displeased with the outcome of Eden's meetings in Washington. On the basis of the Eden-Eisenhower understanding, Dulles instructed Caffery to proceed together with his British colleague, Ambassador Ralph Stevenson, to inform the Egyptian government of the American willingness to participate in the negotiations. Caffery chafed at these instructions. He cabled back to Dulles, arguing that it would be better if the negotiations proceeded in a strictly bilateral, Anglo-Egyptian, fashion. The United States, he explained, would have more leverage if he could "intervene 'behind the scenes,'" which he had already done to wrest concessions from Britain for Egypt in the Sudan negotiations. If he were forced to work together with Stevenson as part of a formal team, his influence would be minimized. "If we are to get anywhere, it will be by my 'behind the scenes' talks," he advised.

Caffery also feared that working closely with the British would tar America with the brush of European imperialism. He urged Dulles to bear in mind the possibility that the negotiations might fail. In that case, he argued, the Egyptians and Arabs would identify the United States with the British demand to occupy the Canal Zone "against the wishes of the Egyptians." [19]

Dulles was easily convinced. A former Wall Street lawyer, he found it easy to erase the substance of Eisenhower's commitments to Eden while respecting their form. He explained to Caffery that the Eisenhower-Eden agreement required Caffery to participate in a joint Anglo-American approach to the Egyptians. However, it did not require him to work *solely* within that framework. "You have our authority," Dulles explained, "to make such additional informal approaches as you consider wise. The President was very clear in his remarks to Eden that we would participate in the negotiations only upon Egyptian concurrence and invitation."[20]

Put plainly, Dulles told Caffery to inform the Egyptians that the Americans were free agents, and that Eisenhower would not be offended if they rejected his offer to participate in the negotiations.

On March 14, 1953, Caffery complied with the letter of the Eisenhower-Eden agreement. Together with his British counterpart, he met with Naguib and the Egyptian foreign minister, Muhammad Fawzi, and conveyed to them Eisenhower's willingness to participate in the Anglo-Egyptian negotiations. The next day, however, he informed Dulles that the Egyptians had angrily rejected the American offer. "I have previously on several occasions warned that the joint approach might be unhappily received," Caffery wrote. He did not so much as hint that he told the Egyptians that their anger would be without consequence. Caffery also reported that he won for himself the coveted position of mediator. The Egyptians "particularly asked that I continue during the Suez negotiations the same role that I played during the Sudan negotiations. 'We believe,' they said, 'that you can accomplish more in your behind-the-scenes role than you could have accomplished as an active negotiator.'"[21]

Relations Deteriorate

With Caffery now firmly in their corner, the Egyptians proposed to the British that the two sides begin talks on the phased withdrawal of British troops. "This is quite unacceptable," was Eden's immediate response. He fired off an indignant cable to Ambassador Makins in Washington, complaining about the American position. "To begin negotiations on this basis would be to abandon our package proposal and could only result in the defence vacuum which the President agreed with me could not be accepted. Moreover, it appears to be the Egyptian intention to use the Americans as mediators at a moment that suits them. This is exactly what I do not (repeat not) wish."[22]

Eden failed to realize that Caffery enjoyed strong support from Dulles and, no doubt, from Eisenhower himself. "It seems to me fantastic," he wrote to Makins on March 18, "that when we and the Americans are agreed upon what we want to achieve, how to achieve it and even upon the personalities for handling the negotiations, we should fail to get into the talks together. It is hard to believe that the Americans . . . cannot persuade the Egyptian Government to make some arrangement whereby they could take part in the negotiations."[23]

Makins again turned to Bedell Smith for help—and again to no avail. "Caffery is a cross which we shall have to bear," he informed Eden.[24] The foreign secretary, however, was in a state of utter disbelief. A week later, he urged Makins to press the issue one more time, but the ambassador advised against another approach to the Americans. When all was said and done, he told Eden, the British faced a simple question: could they trust Eisenhower? "If we trust him, as he has asked us to do, we may be let down. But if we let him see that we do not trust him, we shall not get anywhere."[25]

Meanwhile, Churchill adopted a more combative approach. Writing directly to Eisenhower, he expressed disappointment "that you do not feel that you can do much to help us about the Canal Zone." Then he issued the threat to pull the British troops from Korea that Eden, during his Washington visit, had kept from Eisenhower.[26] Eden's moderating influence would probably have been useful at this moment of severe tension, but a botched medical operation had incapacitated him. While the foreign secretary was undergoing surgery for gallstones, the surgeon accidentally severed his bile duct. The injury required additional operations and a long convalescence. Eden never entirely recovered, and he remained incapable of performing his professional duties for some

six months, during which Churchill seized the portfolio of foreign
secretary, taking on the additional responsibilities while continuing
his duties as prime minister.

The threat to withdraw from the coalition in Korea generated
a testy exchange with Eisenhower, who countered with a threat of
his own—to provide military aid to Egypt. Just after receiving this
news, Churchill paid a visit to Eden, who was recuperating at home
after his operation. The prime minister, Shuckburgh wrote in his
diary, "was raging against the Americans. He said, 'If they give le-
thal weapons to Egypt, I shall take the British brigade away from
Korea.'"[27]

In the end, however, an act of pure petulance in Korea proved
unnecessary, because Churchill soon identified a way to stick a
more statesmanlike thorn in Ike's side. At that moment, Eisenhower was in the final stages of drafting a major speech, titled
"Chance for Peace," which would define his policy toward the Soviet Union. When Eisenhower shared a draft of the address with
Churchill, the prime minister strongly objected to Eisenhower's hard-line attitude toward Moscow. Churchill recommended
shelving the speech as written. Instead, he argued, Eisenhower
should announce his intention to meet with the new Soviet
leaders.

This was not the first time Churchill had made such a suggestion. Shortly after Joseph Stalin died, in early March, he began advocating outreach to Moscow, in order to test whether the change
in leadership might lead to a change in policy. Eisenhower had
consistently rejected the advice in the past, and this time was no
different. In his "Chance for Peace" address, the president set un-
realizable preconditions for a summit with the Soviets. The leaders in Moscow, he declared, must prove themselves first before the
Americans would engage with them directly. "We care nothing for
mere rhetoric," he proclaimed. "We are only for sincerity of peaceful purpose attested by deeds."[28]

Tacking Away from the United States

Churchill did not let the Soviet matter drop; on the contrary, he turned it into a major disagreement.[29] As he tacked away from Eisenhower on Cold War policy, a desire to modify the American position on Egypt undoubtedly influenced his thinking. To be sure, his desire to reach out to the new leaders in Moscow was based on much more than just a desire to gain advantage in the Egyptian conflict. Searching for an accommodation with Russia was a major theme throughout Churchill's long career. Nevertheless, he was now weaving his Soviet and Egyptian policies together.

A week after Eisenhower delivered "Chance for Peace," Churchill wrote to inform him that there was strong feeling in Britain in favor of a summit meeting with the Soviets. "How do you stand about this?" he asked, as if he had never before exchanged views with the president on the subject. Churchill then escalated the conflict between the two—by threatening to meet with the Soviet leaders on his own. "If nothing can be arranged [by you], I shall have to consider seriously a personal contact," he wrote.[30]

Eisenhower expressed firm opposition, but Churchill played deaf.[31] In his next letter, on May 4, he pretended that Eisenhower was in total agreement with him. He forwarded the draft of a letter that he was thinking of sending to Vyacheslav Molotov, the Soviet foreign minister. "I wonder whether you would like me to come to Moscow," the letter to the Russian said, "so that we could renew our own war-time relation and so that I could meet monsieur Malenkov and others of your leading men."[32]

This proved too much for Eisenhower. If Churchill were to go to Moscow alone, the press on both sides of the Atlantic would recognize the event as a major rift in the Western alliance. Eisenhower dropped all pretense of polite disagreement. "You will pardon me, I know," he wrote to Churchill, "if I express a bit of astonishment that you think it appropriate to recommend Moscow to Molotov as a suitable meeting place."[33] Churchill continued undeterred. "It is only by going to Moscow," he responded, "that I can meet them all." In the same letter, Churchill now saw fit to inject Egypt into the conversation. "I have also today telegraphed as acting Foreign Secretary to Foster Dulles about the United States offering arms to Egypt at this critical juncture."[34]

The juncture was indeed critical. Churchill was writing on May 7, the day after direct Anglo-Egyptian talks broke down. Having begun on April 27, they were over before they started. The two sides deadlocked immediately over a key question: was the base along the Canal to include any British army personnel? The British negotiators took their stance on Case A—the base should be British-run. The Egyptian delegation, by contrast, demanded that the base be entirely under Egyptian control, with almost no foreign advisors. Foreign Minister Fawzi, who led the Egyptian negotiating team, insisted that if the British government refused to accept these core principles, then they should simply leave Egypt "bag and baggage."[35]

No sooner had the negotiations broken down than Churchill received very disturbing news from Washington: the Americans were preparing to supply Egypt with military aid. In his message to Dulles on the subject, Churchill complained that the delivery of arms would harden the Egyptian negotiating position. "We hope indeed that the negotiations may be resumed," he wrote, "and I am sure you would greatly regret it if your intervention with an offer of arms contributed to a complete breakdown and this was followed by bloodshed on an indefinite scale."[36] Upon receiving this message, Dulles took a step back. He informed Churchill that he would refrain from passing the list of arms to the Egyptians—but only for the moment. He was about to leave on his major tour of the Middle East, a trip that would begin in Cairo. He and the president would reassess their position after he gained an understanding of the situation on the ground.

On May 9, just as Dulles was preparing to leave the United States, Churchill informed the Americans that he was preparing a major speech on foreign policy. He implied that some of his remarks might put Dulles on the spot. "I propose to mention," he wrote, "that the basis on which we were willing to discuss a solution to the defence problem with the Egyptians was agreed with the United States Civil and Military authorities last January and endorsed by the present administration."[37] The proposed statement would prove particularly embarrassing for Dulles during his trip, because it would suggest to the Egyptians that the Americans had been negotiating with the British behind their backs.

Dulles received the heads-up from Churchill just as his plane was readying for takeoff. With no time to draft a response personally, Dulles instructed Bedell Smith to transmit an angry reply. "Your proposed statement," Bedell Smith wrote, "would imply that the United States and the United Kingdom had fully agreed upon the tactics of negotiation on which, as you know, we have never fully reached a meeting of the minds."[38] If Churchill were to go through with it, he risked forcing the Americans to break publicly with the British. "If you make your statement, which would coincide with the date of Foster's arrival in Egypt, I do not see how we can avoid mentioning, under the close questioning to which he will inevitably be exposed while in the East, the alternative cases which were discussed at the same time."

Churchill's reply was a study in passive-aggressive diplomacy. "I am doing all I can to meet your and the Secretary of State's wishes in my speech tomorrow," he wrote. "I will refer to the conclusions reached between us and the Truman Administration and not commit your Government in public to any definite programme." This new suggestion still signaled collusion against the Egyptians. Churchill, however, gave the Americans no more opportunity to propose edits to the text. He brought the exchange to an abrupt close by forwarding the final draft and stating that there

was no time for further discussion. "I hope that you will be satisfied and relieved by the efforts I have made to meet your views,"
he wrote.[39]

Eisenhower was far from being satisfied. If discussions with
Churchill "were not held completely confidential," he grumbled to
Bedell Smith, "they would have to cease."[40]

The Egyptian Argument

In the Anglo-Egyptian contest to influence American policy, Churchill had a number of unique assets. The Free Officers, however,
were not without their own special advantages. For one thing, they
controlled the situation on the ground—a factor they exploited effectively. The quick failure of the negotiations, for example, was
entirely their doing. They scuttled the talks on May 6, less than
a week before Dulles arrived in Cairo, timing the breakdown to
invite further American mediation. On the day before Dulles arrived, Naguib all but stated the point in public. "We entered the
talks with Britain," he said, "knowing what we wanted and determined to say it shortly and clearly and to demand it firmly, so that
the other side would know that we would not tolerate any bargaining." He also promised extreme violence if the British did not
meet Egyptian demands. "[I]ndependence cannot be granted by a
piece of paper," he said. "It can be achieved only by sacrifice and
blood."[41]

Naguib's speech was the culmination of an extended campaign
designed to bring the Anglo-Egyptian conflict to the brink of
war. In the preceding months, the regime had opened some thirty
training camps for "Liberation Battalions," guerrilla units trained,
according to Radio Cairo, "in the use of all kinds of arms and ex-
plosives, in the tactics of night operations, destruction and demo-
lition."[42] On March 31, Abdel Latif Baghdadi, a close associate of
Nasser, had delivered a speech typical of that period, commemo-

rating the battle of 1807, when Egyptian forces lured British units into an ambush inside the walls of Rosetta, a port city in the Nile Delta. After recounting the details of the victory, al-Baghdadi explained its contemporary lesson. "We will not resort to negotiations under any circumstances. Leave our country, occupiers! . . . Get out of our homeland—otherwise every village in Egypt will become another Rosetta."[43]

The Free Officers did more than just make bellicose speeches. In mid-April, they began a quiet redeployment of forces from the Israeli border. Their intention, according to a British intelligence report, was "to offer the best possible resistance to British military intervention in the Delta . . . and, if necessary, harass British troops in their present position in the Canal Zone."[44] The Egyptians moved units to strategic intersections, smuggled thousands of guerrillas into the Canal Zone, and placed anti-tank batteries and commandos in the Delta. In the event of war, these preparations ensured that there would be a conflagration in the most densely populated part of the country. On top of all of this, the Free Officers also conducted harassing attacks against individual British soldiers. Nasser, however, calibrated the violence with meticulous care. He knew that in the event of an all-out conflict, the British would occupy Cairo and Alexandria and topple the regime.[45] His goal was to stage a spectacle of defiance for Dulles, not to set the Nile Valley ablaze.

Dulles arrived on May 11. He presented Naguib with the Colt .38, and then began a series of meetings with the Egyptians. Nasser and his colleagues stressed that they did not want war but would certainly fight the British if given no alternative. Appealing to Dulles's critical evaluation of Truman's Middle East policies, they stressed that the reputation of the United States was at low ebb among the Arabs as a result of past support for Britain and Israel. America, they warned, risked losing the support of all the Arabs if it failed to force the British to withdraw. Other partners, they said, were certainly available to them. "Perhaps," Foreign Minister Fawzi said, "we are not Communists now. We do not want to be, but this situation might change."[46]

Churchill's Rebuttal

While Dulles was meeting with Nasser and his colleagues, Churchill appeared before Parliament and delivered a major speech on foreign policy. Ever the showman, he had postponed his address several times, building up an air of expectation in Parliament. Can it be a coincidence that he finally scheduled the address for May 11, the very day Dulles arrived in Cairo? Regardless of the answer, the speech was definitely his way of projecting his voice to Dulles and Nasser in distant Cairo, and to Eisenhower in Washington.

His performance more than satisfied the expectant crowd. On the question of engaging the Soviet Union, the prime minister blatantly contradicted the position that Eisenhower had taken in "Chance for Peace." "I believe," Churchill said, "that a conference on the highest level should take place between the leading Powers without long delay." At stake was nothing less than world peace. "It might well be that no hard-faced agreements would be reached," he said, "but there might be a general feeling among those gathered together that they might do something better than tear the human race, including themselves, into bits." Churchill devoted a good portion of the speech to the history of the Anglo-Egyptian negotiations. Uncompromising, he prepared the public for the possibility of going to war—and of going it alone. He made a special point of emphasizing that Britain was entirely capable of defending itself "without requiring any physical assistance from the United States."[47]

According to the American ambassador, Churchill managed to touch on the "whole range of emotions of [the] British people." One of those emotions was anti-Americanism.[48] Some of Churchill's references to the United States were obviously hostile; for the first time ever, he did not so much as mention the Anglo-American alliance.

On May 11, 1953, Churchill delivered a speech, Dulles delivered a Colt .38, and Anglo-American relations descended to their lowest point since the outbreak of World War II.

CHAPTER 3

A Patient Sulky Pig

Ralph Stevenson, the British ambassador to Egypt, fell ill in May 1953, and Churchill temporarily replaced him with Robin Hankey, a professional diplomat but also the son of a political ally and famous supporter of empire. As Hankey prepared to leave for Cairo, Churchill coached him on his role as lead negotiator in the Anglo-Egyptian talks. The diplomat's notes reveal that the prime minister spoke disparagingly about the Americans. Churchill was fairly convinced that Eisenhower and Bedell Smith supported Britain. "Of Mr. Foster Dulles," however, "he seemed to despair."

Churchill disapproved of "our always running to the Americans for help. It was undignified and did not increase their respect for us." Likewise, it was a mistake to "run after the Egyptians." They desperately needed an agreement, and if confronted with a determined British opposition, they would eventually come around. The key to success in the negotiations was to preserve "an attitude of patience and composure." The prime minister would be satisfied if Hankey did nothing except avoid making concessions. He should, Churchill said, "be a patient, sulky pig."[1]

Dulles Responds

Dulles recognized the sulky-pig policy for what it was even before Churchill had given it a name. Ten days earlier, while still in

Cairo, he wired Bedell Smith, informing him that when the Anglo-Egyptian talks broke down, on May 6, the British negotiators in Cairo turned to Churchill for new guidance. Churchill replied that they already had their instructions: they should hold pat. Dulles feared that British stubbornness would lead to war. The Egyptians, he told Bedell Smith, "will choose that alternative rather than make concessions to the British. . . . Their emotions are so great they would rather go down as martyrs than concede."[2] The United States, therefore, must mediate. Dulles sent Bedell Smith a new plan for mediation, and was anxious to have it approved as soon as possible, because he would be on the road for two more weeks. Bedell Smith should begin discussions immediately.

Dulles's plan had Caffery's fingerprints all over it. The initiative called for significant British concessions leading to a wholly Egyptian base. But instead of following Dulles's instructions, Bedell Smith tried to kill the plan while the secretary of state was still on the road. At a meeting of the National Security Council on May 20, he briefed Eisenhower on Dulles's ideas but encouraged the president to support Britain, even if doing so angered the Egyptians. With Anglo-American relations now "worse than at any time since Pearl Harbor," he said, it was the anger of Britain that should be the greatest concern to America. Churchill's new, independent line on the Soviet Union was providing Moscow with an opportunity to sow dissension between the Western allies. "[W]e might well be confronted in the next few weeks," he warned, "with a Soviet invitation for high-level talks including the French as well as the British and ourselves."[3]

Technically, Bedell Smith was Dulles's subordinate, but he enjoyed an independent stature. After serving as Ike's chief of staff during the war, he was appointed by Truman in 1946 as ambassador to Moscow, and then in 1950, as director of the CIA. With such a distinguished résumé, he chafed in the relatively lowly position of undersecretary in the State Department. His greatest ambition was to be appointed chief of staff of the army. His hopes soared when Eisenhower was first elected, but his old comrade in arms disappointed him—and doubly so. Not only did Ike deny Bedell Smith his dream job; he also passed him over for a cabinet-level position.

In the discussion on Dulles's new plan, Eisenhower deflected Bedell Smith's dire warnings with a facetious comment. The Americans, he said, should consider preempting a Soviet-orchestrated summit by organizing a four-power conference themselves, hosting it in Iceland or Greenland, where the temperatures "would moderate the heat of the meeting."[4] And with that, he closed the discussion, leaving no one the wiser as to whether he agreed with Bedell Smith or with Dulles.

Later that night, Eisenhower received a request from the French prime minister, René Mayer, who indeed asked for help in convening a summit conference (without the Soviets) that would include Britain, France, and the United States. Mayer's political opponents were using Churchill's May 11 speech as a weapon against him. Churchill had called for a summit conference that "should be confined to the smallest number of Powers and persons possible," and the French opposition seized on the words to claim that Mayer was too insignificant to be a member of this elite club. To refute the accusation, Mayer sought Eisenhower's help in orchestrating a tripartite conference.[5]

Eisenhower jumped at the idea. A demonstration of Allied solidarity would blunt the force of the potential Soviet initiative that was worrying Bedell Smith. At the same time, it would tamp down speculation in the press, which Churchill's speech had generated, about a growing rift between the United States and Britain. Eisenhower immediately relayed Mayer's proposal to Churchill, who, too, was delighted. The next day the three powers simultaneously announced their intention to hold a conference on June 29—not in Iceland or Greenland, but in sunny Bermuda. It was Churchill who chose the venue. Ike had proposed Maine, but Churchill insisted on a British territory, subtly signaling that he would not run after the Americans; they would come to him. He was playing the sulky pig, not just on the Egypt question, but on everything.

Caffery Wins

After Eisenhower dodged his invitation to kill Dulles's latest proposal, Bedell Smith had to take up the fight against it by more direct means. In an outward show of compliance with the secretary of state's directive, he drafted a concept paper and distributed it to all concerned parties. In a sop to the Dulles-Caffery viewpoint, he conceded that the British plan for the settlement of the Canal Zone conflict "seems unobtainable," but he identified the attitude of the Egyptians as the biggest problem, and the one that required an immediate solution. The Free Officers, Bedell Smith wrote, were offering only "vague assurances" regarding Middle Eastern defense. It was necessary, therefore, to smoke them out—by demanding that they produce a written commitment, up front, to place the Canal Zone base at the disposal of the West in time of war, and to allow Western personnel to oversee its maintenance in time of peace.[6]

Caffery penned a sharp rebuttal, arguing that Bedell Smith failed to recognize basic facts. The reputation of the West was at a dangerous low point in the Middle East, and Dulles's trip had rekindled hope among the Egyptians for a more productive relationship—hope that Bedell Smith's plan would snuff out. The key task now was to prove to the Free Officers that the United States would act independently of Britain. "I believe," Caffery summed up, "the only productive course will be . . . to persuade [the] British [to] accept [the] principles contained in [the] Secretary's original formula."[7]

It took gumption to oppose Bedell Smith, a surly martinet with a fearsome reputation. Caffery, however, was formidable in his own right, and, what is more, he knew Dulles was on his side. Indeed, on June 1, the secretary of state, now back in Washington, briefed the president on his trip, saying that the British might resist American mediation, but it was vitally important to change their minds. The only alternative was war. "General Naguib," he warned, "had agreed to wait only two or three weeks . . . before taking action." Eisenhower chided Dulles for being "too rough on the British," but gave him a green light to mediate.[8] That settled it. The debate was over. Bedell Smith and Churchill had lost.

Ten days later, Ike broke the news to the prime minister. "From my discussions with Foster about the findings of his recent trip," he wrote in a letter, "I am particularly concerned about Egypt. While I will wish to talk to you personally about this matter in Bermuda, there seems to be a real danger that the situation there will not hold that long without further action." He encouraged Churchill to show greater deference to "the very strong nationalist sentiments of the Egyptian Government and people."[9] Case A, he said, was simply unattainable. Churchill should recognize as much and make "concessions" that would "permit a quick start on withdrawal of UK troops and produce an adequate if not ideal arrangement for maintenance of the Base."[10]

Concessions? The word made Churchill's blood boil. The British, he replied, were "disappointed not to receive more support . . . in spite of the numerous far-reaching concessions which we made in our joint discussions with you." The stalemate in the negotiations, he protested, was entirely the fault of the Egyptians. It was they who had broken off the talks, "timing it no doubt to fit in with Mr. Foster Dulles' visit." As for next steps, the British would simply stay the course. "We propose to await developments with patience and composure"—the exact words he had used a few weeks earlier in his instructions to Hankey.

Churchill was now pinning his hopes on the conference in Bermuda. To stave off American mediation until then, he warned Eisenhower that if the Americans were to signal to the Egyptians any divergence from the British position, then "we should not think we had been treated fairly by our great Ally, with whom we are working in so many parts of the globe for the causes which we both espouse."[11]

Churchill was playing a losing hand—and, to make matters worse, his health was giving out. Serving simultaneously as prime minister and foreign secretary was taking a toll. On June 23, less than a week before the Bermuda conference, disaster struck as he hosted a dinner in honor of the Italian prime minister. According to Jock Colville's diary, Churchill captivated his guests with "a little speech in his best and most sparkling form, mainly about the Roman Conquest of Britain!" As he led his guests from the dining table to the drawing room, however, he suffered a stroke. Remarkably, he managed to avoid disrupting the evening. Slumping down into a chair next to Lady Clark, the wife of historian Kenneth Clark, he took hold of her hand.[12] She was unaware that he had suffered a stroke. "I want a friend," Churchill told her. "They put too much on me. Foreign Affairs . . ."[13]

The Indigenous Approach

In early July, Churchill sent to Eisenhower a frank explanation for postponing the Bermuda summit. "I had a sudden stroke which . . . completely paralyzed my left side and affected my speech." He was much less forthcoming with the British people—and even with some members of his own government. For the next three months, Colville led a small team of loyalists who hid the prime minister's infirmity from the world, running interference between him and those who were out of the loop.

The postponement of the conference was especially disappointing to the prime minister, because it prevented him from engaging Eisenhower directly—without, that is, interference from Dulles, whom he regarded as Eisenhower's brain. It was Dulles's anti-imperialism, he mistakenly believed, that was turning the president against the British in Egypt, and it was his militant anticommunism that was preventing constructive engagement of Moscow. Dulles, Churchill grumbled to Lord Moran, his doctor and confidant, was "clever enough to be stupid on a rather large scale."[14]

During his convalescence, Churchill fixated on an initiative to engage the new Soviet leaders. The thought of participating in a summit meeting with Georgy Malenkov, the new Communist Party leader, gave him the motivation to get well. As he grew stronger, it also gave him a justification for soldiering on as prime minister. Just a month after the stroke, he told Moran, "I don't like being kicked out till I've had a shot at settling this Russian business." At that point, his walk was still unsteady, his speech slurred. "You realize," he said, "I'm playing a big hand—the easement of the world." The grandeur of the project allowed him to imagine that once again he might stride the globe as one of the Big Three. "Roosevelt and Stalin are both dead. I only am left," he told Moran.[15]

Meanwhile, however, the Americans were hatching plans to diminish Churchill's role in the world. A memo by John Jernegan, the deputy assistant secretary of state for the Middle East, described the mood in Washington. "For a long time," he wrote, "we have been trying to follow policies in the Near East which were 'jointly agreed' with the British." This policy, however, had proved unworkable. As a consequence, the Eisenhower administration was now looking to increase its freedom of action. "To tie ourselves to the tail of the British kite in the Middle East . . . ," Jernegan continued, "would be to abandon all hope of a peaceful alignment of that area with the West."[16]

This anti-imperialism stamped an indelible imprint on the Eisenhower administration's first comprehensive Middle East strategy, known, according to its bureaucratic designation, as NSC

155/1. On July 9, 1953, the National Security Council met to approve the policy, which had been revised to reflect the secretary of state's conclusions from his Middle East trip. Dulles emphasized two points for special consideration. First, he explained, "Egypt must be discounted as a strong point for the foreseeable future, because it was so engrossed in its own problems that the free world could not depend upon it as the cornerstone of a Near East structure." Second, he directed attention to "the so-called northern tier of nations, stretching from Pakistan to Turkey," who felt "the hot breath of the Soviet Union on their necks, and were accordingly less preoccupied with strictly internal problems or with British and French imperialism."[17]

The new strategy was formally approved in July, but Dulles had actually started unveiling it much earlier—in May, while he was still on his trip. To the Pakistani prime minister, for example, he explained that a new approach to regional defense was necessary, and that it was important to avoid creating collective security structures that appeared as if imposed by powers from outside the region—an obvious reference to Britain. "It was better," Dulles argued, "to start with something more indigenous to the area and, at least initially, countries strangers to the area should not participate."[18] The logic of this "indigenous" approach was clearly stated in NSC 155/1, which identified "unfavorable trends" that offered opportunities to the Soviets.

One of these trends was the taint of European imperialism. Due to the rise of nationalism, the document stated, "some of the distrust of the United Kingdom and France has devolved upon the United States." A second unfavorable trend was the fact that "the Arab nations are incensed by what they believe to be our pro-Israel policy." The popular hostility to the imperial powers and to Israel made "the possibility of cooperation with the Arab states . . . in a formal defense organization" highly unlikely. The immediate goal of the United States, therefore, was, just as Caffery had been arguing, to "convince the Arab states that it is capable of acting independently of other Western states and of Israel."

Eisenhower, Dulles, and most of their key advisors shared a common picture of the Middle East. The United States, as they saw it, was caught in the middle. On one side were the Arabs and other "indigenous" nationalities; on the other, the Europeans and the Israelis. Each side had hold of one arm of the United States, which they were pulling like a tug rope. This picture was so obvious to almost everyone in the Eisenhower administration that it was understood as an objective description of reality. It was, in a word, a paradigm, a set of core assumptions about the nature of the world that shaped all other discussions.

If the United States was caught in the middle, then the only sensible thing for it to do was to become a mediator, an honest broker. In public, Eisenhower and Dulles labeled this policy "impartiality," especially in reference to the Arab-Israeli conflict. In private, however, they admitted that their goal was to help the "indigenous" nationalists seek redress from Israel and the European imperial powers. Did this mean that Eisenhower was consciously seeking to supplant the British? No, was the formal answer. NSC 155/1 recognized that "the UK retains substantial interests, experience, and security positions, so that the United States will need to act in concert with the United Kingdom to the greatest extent practicable."[19]

In truth, however, the honest broker approach made close cooperation impractical.

Preparing for Guests

NSC 155/1 represented a tectonic shift in America's Middle East policy. Churchill, however, had yet to realize how far the ground under his feet had shifted. Eisenhower and Dulles quickly devised a method to bring him up to speed.

On July 1, 1953, Churchill wrote to Eisenhower introducing the Marquess of Salisbury, who, after the prime minister's stroke, took on the role of acting foreign secretary. Salisbury was due to arrive in Washington for tripartite talks with the Americans and the French—a meeting organized in lieu of the Bermuda conference. He had a reputation as a hard-liner, an old-fashioned imperialist. "I am sure you and Foster will like Salisbury," Churchill wrote. "He holds all my views on Egypt . . . very strongly."[20] Churchill no doubt chuckled to himself as he penned that line, but Eisenhower was not amused. His response warned Churchill that he expected Salisbury to come with a new British policy. "[W]e shall certainly be ready to talk to Lord Salisbury," he wrote, but also demanded that "concessions would have to be made to Egyptian pride and spirit of nationalism."[21]

Meanwhile, Dulles was implementing a sly plan to extract those concessions. "It is becoming increasingly clear," he wrote to Caffery, "that Salisbury will present Churchill's stand on [the Egypt] problem," and, therefore, it was necessary to inject a "new element" into the conversation. "If," he told Caffery, "Naguib were to send [a] message to me just prior to our talks we would have something on which to work."[22] Leaving nothing to chance, Dulles composed a detailed draft of just the kind of message that he would like to receive from Naguib. He then cabled it to Caffery along with the suggestion that the Egyptians should return it to him as if it were their own proposal. Caffery worked his magic, and three days later Eisenhower received an official letter from Naguib presenting a new "Egyptian" offer, which contained few changes to Dulles's script. The paper envisioned an Egyptian-run base, which the British would be permitted to use only in wartime. "These proposals," Naguib's letter stated, "do not represent a bargaining position and any attempt to treat them as such will only convince us that Egypt's earnest desire for a prompt, honorable and peaceful settlement is not reciprocated."[23]

The letter arrived on July 10, the day before Lord Salisbury and Georges Bidault, the French foreign minister, began their meetings in Washington with Dulles. On the morning of July 11, Dulles opened the meeting with his European guests by briefing them on his intention to bypass the difficulties posed by the Anglo-Egyptian and Arab-Israeli conflicts by focusing on building up the countries closest to the Soviet Union, the so-called Northern Tier—a loose term that, eventually, would refer to Iraq, Turkey, Iran, and Pakistan. Even if an agreement were reached over the Canal Zone, he argued, there would still "be constant friction" between Egypt and the West, so he saw nothing but problems "in making Egypt the military center of a defensive pact." Instead, the United States would now be focusing on the northern countries, which were more alert to the Soviet danger and "less preoccupied with the colonialism aspects of the past and the existing feud with Israel."[24]

That afternoon, Dulles and Salisbury met without Bidault in a bilateral, Anglo-American session that focused exclusively on the Canal Zone question. The session began with a lengthy briefing by Salisbury and his team on their thinking, which had changed little since Eden had come to Washington four months earlier. The moment they finished their pitch, Dulles handed Salisbury a copy of Naguib's offer, praising it as "a considerable advance."[25] Later, when Salisbury cabled Churchill with an update, he complained bitterly about American trickery. It was, he wrote, "very tiresome of the Americans to have taken this initiative without consulting us."[26]

But Dulles was not finished with his shock treatment. A few days later, at another Anglo-American session, he delivered a sermon on the evils of British imperialism. "Some people," he informed his guest, "have the impression that the U.K. . . . has reverted to the old-type, hardboiled approach formerly employed in dealing with Arab States." The Americans, however, were of the strong belief that "this old type of policy will not succeed." If the British were to persist in their uncompromising approach, "it will only create a wave of anti-Western feeling affecting all of our interests adversely." Salisbury attempted to defend the British postwar record, noting that it was defined by the granting of independence to former colonies. Dulles responded that he "appreciated all of that" but he still "sensed a tendency to swing back to the old methods."[27]

Salisbury filed a report to Churchill after the sermon, which he called "a tedious lecture." The Americans, he said, felt that the British still believed that the best way to deal with colonized peoples "was to be completely stern and firm and to deliver a well-placed kick when they made difficulties. They felt times had changed, etc., etc. I found this hard to bear."[28] But bear it he did. When Salisbury met Dulles again that afternoon, he avoided any further debate. Instead, he focused on trying to influence the practical steps that the Americans would now take moving forward. His two main goals were to convince Dulles to refrain from further mediation, and to permit the British to help draft Eisenhower's response to Naguib's offer. On both points, he succeeded, thanks in no small measure to the surprisingly supportive attitude of Dulles, which had brightened markedly in just a few short hours.

What happened between the morning sermon and the afternoon discussion to change Dulles's disposition? Salisbury met with Eisenhower, and he also tried to enlist the aid of Bedell Smith. "I suspect," Salisbury explained to Churchill, "that it was a personal intervention by the President" that brought Dulles around. Whatever the reason, Dulles's attitude did change. "He accepted our view," Salisbury reported, "as to the nature of the reply to Naguib, and he agreed in so doing that we should play the hand."[29]

Working together, Salisbury and Dulles drafted a reply to the Egyptian offer, which Eisenhower then sent to Cairo as a personal message to Naguib. The letter welcomed the Egyptian proposal

as "a significant step forward." But it also stated that key issues remained unsolved. One line was notable for its harshness. "I must
state to you in all candor," Eisenhower wrote, "that I find certain
points adversely affecting the security interests of my own country. These points deal with the future availability of the Base and
the duration of any agreement." The admonishment must have angered Nasser, especially the part about the availability of the base.
After all, he had simply copied the formula that Dulles had passed
to him with a wink and a nod. Suddenly and with no explanation,
Eisenhower was demanding new terms. In addition, he was also
urging the Egyptians to resume direct talks with General Brian
Robertson, who was now the British military representative to the
negotiations. "Sir Brian Robertson," the president wrote, "should
be returning to Cairo shortly and . . . will be available to discuss the
situation."[30]

However irksome Nasser may have found the Americans, they
were nevertheless invaluable to him. Eisenhower had extracted
concessions from the British that the Egyptians could not have
attained on their own. When Salisbury entered the doors of the
State Department on July 11, he had come carrying papers that
described a unified Anglo-American approach, an operational British base along the Suez Canal, and a regional defense organization.
When he departed several days later, he left those papers behind in
the trash.

Blaming Britain

In accordance with Eisenhower's wishes, Nasser resumed talks
with the British in Cairo. The negotiations began in late August
and lasted two months, until October 21, when they broke down
in acrimony. Formally, they were a bilateral, Anglo-Egyptian affair,
and most historians have treated them as such. In reality, however,
they were a three-sided exercise, with both the Egyptians and the

British consulting the Americans on all details and at every stage. American influence worked to the decided advantage of the Free Officers. To be sure, Eisenhower and Dulles did not support the Egyptians on every detail, but they saw the British Empire as a relic of a bygone era. Egypt, in their eyes, was the rising power, the state that held the keys to Arab friendship with the West. The longer the negotiations wore on, therefore, the more frustrated the Americans grew with the British.

The talks took a turn for the worse on September 23, when General Robertson asserted that the British technicians who would help manage the base in peacetime would wear military uniforms. His statement sparked a heated argument. Nasser, who led the Egyptian negotiators, insisted that the technicians wear only civilian dress. Robertson claimed that, at an earlier meeting, the Egyptians had already given their assent to uniforms. Nasser contradicted him. When Robertson persisted, Nasser, according to Cafferty's report, "lost his temper and stalked out."[31]

The dispute over uniforms looked petty, but it was fundamental to both sides. To convince his hard-line allies that the Canal Zone was still a British military asset, Churchill needed a base that was populated with soldiers. Nasser, by contrast, was eager to convince the Egyptian people that, after some seven decades, he had finally brought the British occupation to an end. To do that, he needed a base that was stripped of all British military trappings.

Dulles sympathized with Nasser. He sent a letter of protest to Eden, who had now returned to his post as foreign secretary. "Our information," he wrote with studied irritation, is that the Free Officers "are prepared to meet [the British] substantially" on core concerns. "Now we learn somewhat to our dismay that the negotiations may collapse on the issue of what kind of uniform the technicians should wear." Dulles pointedly reminded Eden that, during Salisbury's visit, the Americans had adopted the "British thesis," meaning that they agreed to refrain from further direct mediation.[32]

This threat of renewed American intervention had no impact. When the negotiators returned to the table on October 21, the Egyptians made a slight concession on the duration of the agreement, hoping, no doubt, to elicit a reciprocal concession on uniforms. The British, however, refused to budge. The negotiations broke down and did not resume again for months. Caffery reported to Washington that the Egyptians now had their backs to the wall. The Americans had pressed them for so many concessions, he informed Dulles, that "our coin . . . is pretty well exhausted."

In London, the breakdown coincided with the return of the sulky pig. On October 10, 1953, Churchill, whose recuperation from his stroke was remarkable, passed a crucial test of competence by delivering an hour-long address to the Conservative Party Conference at the seaside town of Margate. The high point of his delivery was a recapitulation of the major thesis of his May 11 speech, namely that "informal, personal talks" with the new leaders in the Soviet Union "might do good and could not easily do much harm."[33]

Julian Amery, a prominent member of the Suez Group, the imperialists in Parliament who demanded that Britain must forever retain the military base along the Suez Canal, delivered the second most notable address at Margate. Amery electrified the crowd with demands that the government break off talks with the Egyptians. When he informed his audience that he had heard reports that Britain might agree to pull its fighting troops from Egypt, the audience cried, "Shame!" "None of us could believe for a moment," he said, "that a government led by Sir Winston Churchill or Mr. Eden would ever contemplate such a surrender."[34]

The obvious resurgence of the Suez Group created the distinct impression in Washington that Churchill was negotiating in bad faith. Dulles therefore turned up the heat. On November 13, he warned Eden that the United States was again on the verge of providing aid to the Egyptians.[35] Dulles had been holding up the assistance, he said, to further the Canal Zone agreement, but "this settlement has dragged out to a point where we cannot continue much longer without very grave effect upon our Arab relationships. If you felt that it was likely there would soon be new moves . . . which might produce agreement, we could still hold up briefly but our time is fast running out."[36]

Anglo-American relations had reached a standoff, similar to the one that had developed in July, on the eve of the postponed Bermuda conference. It was only fitting, then, that Churchill now suggested rescheduling the conclave. Eisenhower and the French agreed, and the conference took place in the first week of December 1953—in Bermuda, as originally planned. The event, however, failed to live up to Churchill's dreams. Twice during the conference, Eisenhower revealed strong personal opposition—*hostility* might be a better word—to Churchill's ambitions.

On one occasion, Churchill sent Colville on an errand to Eisenhower's room. Over the years, Colville had spent many hours in Ike's company, but the somber and cerebral figure who was now seated before him was thoroughly unfamiliar. Ike, Colville wrote in his diary, was "in his sitting-room, cross-legged in an arm-chair," editing a draft of a speech, called "Atoms for Peace," which he was due to deliver immediately upon his return to the United States. "He was friendly," Colville observed, "but I noticed that he never smiled: a change from the Ike of war days." Their conversation eventually turned to the rift between London and Washington over imperialism. "I told him," Colville wrote, "that a reference to the 'obsolete Colonial mold' contained in his draft speech would give offence in England."

When Eisenhower defended the phrase as "part of the American philosophy," Colville countered that many in England believed that India had been better ruled by Britain than by its own independent government. Eisenhower said that he, personally, shared that belief, but noted that for Americans, in general, "liberty was more precious than good government." He refused to delete the passage. Later that day, Churchill tackled Eisenhower personally over the issue, and the president retreated. He agreed, Colville wrote, "to remove the obnoxious phrase about colonialism."[37]

Expunging a line from a speech was one thing, but changing the underlying, anti-imperialist thinking was impossible. Bridging the gap between the Americans and the British over policy toward the Soviet Union was equally difficult. The second occasion on which Eisenhower flashed his opposition to Churchill came when the prime minister renewed his call for a meeting with Stalin's successors. After delivering an eloquent speech that pointed to outward signs of new behavior by the Soviets, Churchill asked whether these were indications of a "change of heart," or merely "an ingenious variation of tactics."[38] The question sent Eisenhower into a rage. The president, according to Colville, made "a short, very violent statement, in the coarsest terms." The Soviet Union, he said, "was a woman of the streets, and whether her dress was new, or just the old one patched, it was certainly the same whore underneath. America intended to drive her off her present 'beat' into the back streets." Ike laced his statement with profanity, which nobody recorded verbatim. "I doubt," Colville wrote, "if such language has ever been heard at an international conference. Pained looks all around." To ease the tension, Eden tried to change the subject, raising an innocuous question of scheduling. Did anyone know, he asked, when the next session would take place? "I don't know," Ike said. "Mine is with a whisky and soda." With that, he left the room.[39]

Due to the chasm that separated Eisenhower and Churchill, the conference generated no significant change on the Canal Zone question. The Americans and the British left just as they had arrived—deadlocked on Egypt, with Washington threatening to begin the unilateral delivery of aid to the Egyptians.

Despite his inability to get through to Eisenhower personally,

A PATIENT SULKY PIG

53

Churchill persisted in his view of Dulles as Eisenhower's Svengali. "It appears that the President is no more than a ventriloquist's doll," he lamented to Moran after being subjected to Ike's fury. He paused, and then resumed his grumbling about Dulles. "This fellow preaches like a Methodist Minister, and his bloody text is always the same: That nothing but evil can come out of a meeting with Malenkov." Once again he drew silent, then resumed his rant, his emotions now beginning to show on his face. "Dulles is a terrible handicap. . . . Ten years ago I could have dealt with him. Even as it is I have not been defeated by this bastard. I have been humiliated by my own decay." Tears flowed from his eyes.[40]

Churchill had it wrong. Eisenhower was every bit the man in charge, and he was in complete agreement with Dulles on both the Egyptian and the Soviet questions. The painful truth was that Churchill needed Ike much more than Ike needed Churchill.

CHAPTER 4

Ike's First Bet

Patience was never John Foster Dulles's greatest virtue, but when he sat down for lunch with Anthony Eden on December 15, 1953, it was in even shorter supply than usual. The two men were attending a NATO summit in Paris, and the Anglo-Egyptian talks had been suspended for two months. Dulles was intent on forcing the British back to the negotiating table, and with that goal in mind he insisted that Eden put into writing the last offer that the British had made to the Egyptians—to lock the British position in place, so that when the stalled negotiations resumed, they would begin again precisely where they had left off. Eden resented the implication that the British were slippery; behind Dulles's demand, he perceived the nefarious influence of the American ambassador in Cairo. "Caffery," Shuckburgh wrote in his diary, "now says that we must write down what we have so far agreed with the Egyptians. . . . Otherwise the poor Egyptians are not to know that the British will not raise all sorts of new issues."[1]

At the same time, Dulles renewed his threat to begin supplying Egypt with aid, which the Americans were still holding back pending a final settlement of the Canal Zone question. The underlying message to the British was clear: make new concessions or the United States will move closer to the Egyptians—and thereby reduce British leverage in the negotiations. "The Americans," Eden wrote to Churchill in a memo, "will have no friends left if they go on in this way."[2]

Eden's memo prompted Churchill to send an angry letter to Eisenhower. Three days before Christmas, the president telephoned Dulles in exasperation. "Have you seen the latest one?" he asked, referring to the letter.[3] Eisenhower said he felt obligated to acknowledge the message but was "getting tired" of the endless wrangling. He intended to put the Egyptian question "back in diplomatic channels."[4] On December 23, he penned a curt reply to Churchill. "We shall study [your letter] and you will hear further from us, probably through the State Department," he wrote. Before shutting down the Egypt conversation for good, he added a perfunctory, "Merry Christmas to you and yours."[5] Eisenhower had lost patience with Churchill on many occasions in the past, but this was the first time that he had simply brushed him off.

The Waterhouse Theory

Over the Christmas holiday, Churchill mulled his dilemma. Concessions to the Egyptians would please Eisenhower and Dulles, but they would enrage his domestic political base. Hanging tough would win him applause at home, but it would undermine relations with the Americans. Which option was the least bad?

He decided in favor of displaying independence from the Americans—by issuing an ultimatum to Egypt. On December 28, Churchill sent a memo to Eden outlining his ideas. The British government, he wrote, should notify the Free Officers that the October proposal was Britain's final offer. The window for acceptance of it would close in one month. If the Egyptians capitulated, Churchill explained, then it would "appear to the world and especially to other countries in the Middle East such as Iraq, that we had forced them to accept our terms." The appearance of victory "would also be of some value in Parliament and indeed throughout the country." Alternatively, if the Egyptians rejected the ultimatum, then the negotiations would end and the British would "act towards Egypt in accordance with what we think are our long-term interests." As for the Americans, if they decided to begin giving Egypt aid unilaterally, "a more difficult situation will arise, which we can judge when the time comes."[6]

This proposal was a version of what was known as "the Waterhouse Theory," a plan named after Captain Charles Waterhouse, the leader of the Suez Group in Parliament. Waterhouse believed that it was possible for Britain to remain in the Canal Zone by redeploying to a more defensible position and hunkering down. He based his views on the 1936 Anglo-Egyptian treaty, which had granted Britain the basing rights in Egypt that it was currently exercising, and which stipulated that those rights would remain in force until such time as both the Egyptian and British governments came to mutual agreement on new terms. As Waterhouse saw it, international law was clear: Britain had the right to occupy Egypt in perpetuity. There was, however, one catch. The current size of the force in the Canal Zone, some 80,000 soldiers, violated the terms of the 1936 treaty, which capped their number at 10,000. Bringing the numbers into compliance with international law therefore required redeploying to a smaller area within the Canal Zone—an area that 10,000 men could actually defend.

The Foreign Office read Churchill's scenario as a prelude to just such a redeployment, and it drafted a rebuttal of Churchill's proposal. Issuing an ultimatum to Egypt, the Foreign Office argued, would inevitably spark a war that would result in a more profound "scuttle" than would result from an unfavorable negotiated agreement. It would start "a fight which we can ill afford and from which we should emerge, though victorious in arms, without a friend in the Middle East."[7] Eden used these arguments in a Cabinet meeting on December 29, when the prime minister shared with the government his plan for issuing an ultimatum.

Much to Eden's dismay, his colleagues sided with Churchill. They took no firm decision about what to do, but the lack of support shook the foreign secretary, who even briefly entertained the Waterhouse Theory himself. Eden "seems to be toying with the PM's so-called alternative to an agreement with Egypt, i.e. break off negotiations and announce we will 'redeploy in our own time,'" Shuckburgh wrote in his diary. "But unless that means we announce that we will start moving our forces out at once, unconditionally, it is surely the equivalent of a straight break and show-down with Egypt and would lead to attacks on our base, bloodshed, the occupation of Cairo and all the rest."[8]

Eden's flirtation with the Suez Group's ideas, however, proved ephemeral. Within a few short weeks he managed to build a coalition around a more conciliatory policy. The key to the change was a decisive shift in the attitude of the uniformed military. The generals agreed with the Foreign Office about the ill-advised nature of a war with Egypt, especially because they were growing increasingly alarmed about an altogether new threat—namely, the American Northern Tier project.

Over the previous six months, the Northern Tier had started to take firm shape in the form of a bilateral pact between Turkey and Pakistan. The two countries formally ratified the treaty in April 1954, but it had neared completion by early January. While the Americans insisted on calling this alliance an "indigenous" organization, everybody knew that it was very much the fruit of American diplomacy. Dulles, however, had told the British next to nothing about it. On January 6, Eden signaled his displeasure at being left in the dark by instructing the British embassy in Washington to submit to the State Department a list of pointed questions about the Northern Tier. The American official who received the queries reported to his superiors that "the Foreign Office was not altogether happy."[9]

In fact, it was humiliated. Britain was still the dominant power in the Middle East, but American officials kept the British no better informed about American plans for the Northern Tier than the international press, which throughout the fall had regularly reported on the subject. In October, a particularly disturbing report appeared in the *New York Times*. General Ayub Khan, the chief of staff of the Pakistani military, told the paper about his intention to conclude "a Turkish-Pakistani mutual assistance pact as the nucleus of a Middle East defense organization including Iran and Iraq."[10]

The news that Iraq would be a part of the proposed organization was particularly disturbing to Eden and his colleagues. To be relegated to the role of bystander as the Americans brought Turkey and Pakistan together was bad enough, but to watch helplessly as they courted Britain's most important ally in the Arab world was intolerable. After all, the British had created Iraq, which, home to their most valuable energy interests, was second only to Egypt in importance to the British position in the Middle East. It was they, not the Americans, who were treaty-bound to guarantee the security of the country, yet as the Turks and the Pakistanis moved toward an alliance, Dulles began working to supply the Iraqis with military aid, which he saw as a means of enticing Baghdad to join the Northern Tier. Unlike the deep-pocketed Americans, the British expected the Iraqis to *buy* arms. If the Americans were simply going to give them away, what need would the Iraqis have at all for an alliance with Britain? In London, it appeared as if the Americans might be trying to supplant the British in Iraq.

This fear created a strong feeling among the uniformed military in favor of settling the Egypt question quickly. After that, the forces in the Canal Zone could redeploy to Iraq and Jordan, which would then replace Egypt as the foundation of what remained of the British defense system. On January 12, 1954, Eden moved to capitalize on the mood in the military, instructing his staff to prepare a paper for the Cabinet on Middle East strategy. He asked for the paper quickly, hoping that he could "enlist the support of [the]

Chiefs of Staff and service ministries." His goal was to present a common front in the Cabinet against Churchill's position. "If we are to have any position in [the] Middle East our authority must be based on close association with Jordan and Iraq," Eden wrote. "If we waver any more we shall be friendless."[11]

Britain Capitulates

Three days later, Roger Makins, the ambassador in Washington, alerted London to the perilous state of transatlantic relations. Failure to compromise on Egypt, Makins explained, would undermine the Anglo-American alliance.

"The Middle East," he wrote, "is the field in which our relations with the Americans are most likely to be difficult to handle in the coming year." Relations were complicated, on the British side, by "a very understandable suspicion that the Americans are out to take our place in the Middle East." Was this suspicion true? Makins was doubtful. "They realize that such a policy would involve the extension of their own military commitments, and it would be inconsistent with their general attitude towards the United Kingdom as their major ally." But it was also true that the Americans nurtured a number of grievances toward Britain. They were especially resentful of the fact "that we have cast them for a supporting role, which is to consist of switching on or off the powerful current of their diplomatic and financial influence at a word from us." Felix Leiter, it turned out, did not actually enjoy being James Bond's sidekick.

Makins then asked a second question: if the United States was not intentionally hostile to Great Britain, was the displacement of it simply an unintentional consequence of the rise of U.S. power? No, he answered. The Anglo-American alliance in the Middle East could still survive, but salvaging it would require Britain to make one very significant concession: it must come to an agreement over the Canal Zone. The Americans "do not really understand our present position in the defense negotiations with Egypt. The American conception of a negotiation does not provide for prolonged pauses of the kind which has now lasted since 21st October last, and this is beginning to be not only puzzling but irritating to the officials here who are anxious to go ahead with economic aid for Egypt." If, however, the negotiations were brought to a successful conclusion, then the Americans would develop "an added respect for our position in the region."[12]

Though no mention of Churchill's proposed ultimatum appears in Makins's cable, its arguments were a very cogent rebuttal of it, and they had a sobering effect on the debate in the government. Eden's ministerial colleagues began to recognize Churchill's idea for what it was—an act of desperation. For all intents and purposes, the fight was over, and Eden had won. Shortly thereafter, the British resumed negotiations and their position softened. Meanwhile, support for the Suez Group in Parliament swiftly eroded. Over the next five months, the British government had made a series of concessions that broke the logjam, clearing the way for a basic understanding that would eventually come at the end of July 1954.

To be sure, the negotiations between January and July were not all smooth sailing. Several rounds of talks were required before Cairo and London finally arrived at mutually acceptable terms. Churchill, throughout, remained a challenge for Eden, who was frequently exasperated by the prime minister's emotional resistance to compromise, and by his physical decline. "This simply cannot go on," Eden complained to Shuckburgh after one particularly exasperating meeting with Churchill. "[H]e is gaga; he cannot finish his sentences."[13] Nevertheless, Eden now held the upper hand. Churchill had no practical alternatives to offer—and the pressure from Washington was relentless.

When Eisenhower first took office he already believed that it was time for Churchill to leave public life, and nothing he had learned in the meantime had made him question that assessment.

In July 1954, Eisenhower told the prime minister, rather bluntly, how he felt. The occasion was a letter from Churchill renewing his campaign to organize a high-level summit with the Soviets. Refusing to engage on the substance of the matter, Eisenhower treated the proposal as nothing more than an attempt to stave off old age. "I am certain," he replied to Churchill, "that you must have a very deep and understandable desire to do something special . . . in your remaining period of active service" and "that some such thought of your conscious or subconscious mind must be responsible for your desire to meet Malenkov."

It would be far more constructive, Eisenhower proposed, for Churchill to begin planning his farewell address. The president even had in mind a theme for the speech: the right of colonial peoples to self-determination. "Colonialism," Eisenhower wrote, "is on the way out as a relationship among peoples. The sole question is one of time and method. I think we should handle it so as to win adherents to Western aims."[14] Churchill should therefore promise total independence for all subject peoples by a date certain. That was a promise, Eisenhower wrote, that "would electrify the world."[15]

Churchill rejected the idea—how could he do otherwise? A statement on decolonization would amount to a repudiation of his entire career. He explained politely that he was "not looking about for the means of making a dramatic exit"—and anyway, he was the wrong man for the job. "I am a bit sceptical about universal suffrage for the Hottentots even if refined by proportional representation." In addition, a promise to grant independence to colonized countries was unnecessary, because "as a matter of fact the sentiments and ideas which your letter expresses are in full accord with the policy now being pursued in all the Colonies of the British Empire."[16]

He had a point. Just five days after Eisenhower encouraged Churchill to begin planning his retirement, British and Egyptian negotiators in Cairo signed a statement of principles for the settlement of the Canal Zone conflict. The so-called "Heads of Agreement" outlined a simple deal. The British agreed to withdraw all troops within an eighteen-month period, and in return the Egyptians agreed to place the base at the disposal of the West in the event of another major war. The clock on the eighteen months would start ticking upon the signing of the final agreement, which, as it would turn out, would take place three months later, in October. Devoid of options, Churchill had completely capitulated, handing over the base to the Egyptians—lock, stock, and barrel.

Settling Scores

For the Suez Group, the Heads of Agreement was a funeral for the empire. "This is a day of triumph for all the timorous at home and the wicked abroad who want Britain to be small and weak and to count for little," Lord Beaverbrook's *Daily Express* wailed on July 29, the day Parliament debated the agreement. "Under our very eyes, by the hand of a Tory Government, the greatest surrender is taking place since the Socialists and Mountbatten engineered the scuttle from India."[17]

As the imperialists wailed in agony, the opposition went for blood. The Labor Party remembered all too well how, when it had been in power back in 1946, Churchill had vilified it for proposing a withdrawal from Egypt. The prime minister at that time, Clement Attlee, was now the leader of the opposition, and he seized the opportunity that the debate in Parliament afforded him to make Churchill eat his words. The highlight of Attlee's performance was a show of mock sympathy for the hard-liners in the Suez Group. Those gullible souls, he said, had taken Churchill at his word when he had attacked the Labor government's initiative to withdraw from Egypt. They had believed his "accusations, freely thrown about, of 'scuttle,'" and they had failed to recognize the "immense difference" between Winston Churchill in office and Winston Churchill in opposition. "When he comes into office he has to face realities; he has to take responsibility instead of indulging in merely factious attacks on those who are bearing responsibility."[18]

Churchill sat motionless on the front bench.[19] It fell to Antony Head, the secretary of state for war, to stand and defend the government's retreat from Egypt. Head cited a number of factors that had generated the decision to evacuate, including the development of the hydrogen bomb, which supposedly made huge military facilities like the Canal Zone base obsolete.[20] The opposition dismissed this line of argument. The hydrogen bomb was a very new development. If it was indeed the key factor that changed the government's calculus, then it absolved Churchill of guilt for having obstructed the evacuation from Egypt for the better part of a decade. Labor's rejection of Antony Head's presentation received support from a surprising source—Captain Waterhouse himself. The government's explanations for its decision to withdraw from Egypt were indeed disingenuous, Waterhouse said. "I do not believe that these are the real reasons at all." But Waterhouse strongly disagreed with the Labor Party's assertion that retreat from Egypt was inevitable. The true problem was flagging national resolve. "[O]ur burdens are becoming too irksome for us, and we are really losing our will to rule," he said.

Waterhouse also emphasized the hostile policy of the United States. "I am not one of those," he said, "who normally carp and criticize that great country." The Americans harbor a deep affection for the British Isles, he said, but they "actively dislike the British Empire," which they seek to destroy. "For many years," he continued, "we have had a little American lamb bleating in Cairo, not helping and if anything hindering in most things. Well, he has got his way."[21] That little lamb was, of course, Jefferson Caffery.

Churchill's doctor, Lord Moran, witnessed Waterhouse's speech from the gallery, then noted in his diary that it had wounded Churchill more deeply than the attacks of the opposition. Moran's heart

went out to the prime minister. "If Winston has believed in anything at all in the course of his long life," he wrote, "it has been in
the British Empire and all that it stands for."[22] Churchill did eventually rise from the front bench to defend himself, but he kept his
words brief. Pointing to the detonation of the hydrogen bomb, he
insisted that it indeed had brought about "tremendous changes"
that made "the thoughts which were well-founded and well knit
together a year ago utterly obsolete." A transformation in professional military thinking, not any political calculation, was what had
convinced him "of the obsolescence of the base."[23]

His short speech was a half-truth. The advent of the hydrogen
bomb was a secondary cause of the withdrawal. The obsolescence
of the base had been planned, and Waterhouse had it right: the
Americans were the ones who had done the planning.

America's Moral Standing

The key role that Eisenhower and Dulles played in brokering the
Anglo-Egyptian settlement has too often escaped the attention of
historians, probably because neither Churchill nor Eisenhower
saw any benefit in acknowledging the depth of their disagreement.
Both leaders found it advisable to deflect attention—and both were
supremely adept at misdirection. As for Churchill's skill, it was on
full display when he answered Eisenhower's letter urging him to
deliver a farewell address on decolonization. "I shall certainly have
to choose another topic for my swan song," he cheerily responded.
"I think I will stick to the old one 'The Unity of the English-Speak-
ing Peoples.' With that all will work out well."[24]

Anglophone solidarity was a song he sang loudly throughout
the early 1950s. Shortly before the Bermuda conference, for example, he delivered a speech in London that took note of the rising
public concern over tensions with the United States. "Some people say their worry is about Anglo-American relations," Churchill

stated. "I do not share their anxieties. After all we are both very free-speaking democracies and where there is a great deal of free speech there is always a certain amount of foolish speech." In order to overcome its detrimental effects, he advised, "Let us stick to our heroes, John Bull and Uncle Sam. They never were closer together than they are now; not only in sentiment but in common interest and in faithfulness to the cause of world freedom."[25] Even as he spoke, however, in the Middle East Uncle Sam was busy cutting John Bull down to size. By praising a fictive Anglo-American unity, Churchill was actually trying to mitigate the impact of disunity.

For all that the Foreign Office considered Churchill a political fossil, he never had any doubt about the power of Britain relative to the United States. He may have been bullheaded, but he was a realist, and he picked his battles carefully. A few weeks before the debate in Parliament over the Egypt agreement, he made a point of counseling Eden against unnecessary fights with the United States. "Up to July 1944," he reminded his protégé, "England had a considerable say in things; after that I was conscious that it was America who made the big decisions. She will make the big decisions now. . . . We do not yet realize her immeasurable power."[26]

When it came to skill at misdirection, Eisenhower was every bit Churchill's equal. In public he always took care to express deep admiration for the prime minister, and to avoid condemnations of British imperialism. A more accurate guide to his true feelings, however, was his letter urging Churchill to plan a farewell address about decolonization. More revealing still were the ideas that he never expressed but which deeply shaped his policies—ideas, for example, such as the anti-imperialism that guided him during the Dien Bien Phu crisis, which coincided with the final stages of the negotiations over the Suez Canal Zone.

Dien Bien Phu was a fortified French outpost in the northwest corner of Vietnam, on the Laos border. In March 1954, the communist Vietnamese laid siege to it and quickly gained advantage.

If the French were to lose, a good portion of Vietnam would inevitably fall to communism. As awareness of French vulnerability
grew, the key question was whether the United States would intervene to save the Western position. It was at this moment, at a press
conference in early April, that Eisenhower explained what subse-
quently became known as the "domino theory." "You have a row
of dominoes set up," he said. "[Y]ou knock over the first one, and
what will happen to the last one is the certainty that it will go over
very quickly." If Vietnam were to fall to communism, the countries
of Southeast Asia would follow in train. Therefore, Eisenhower
seemed to be saying, the United States must take whatever actions
were necessary to shore up the French position.

Eisenhower made out as if he were readying the American public for a military intervention. In fact, he was performing a head
fake. "Privately," the historian Jean Edward Smith writes, "Eisenhower was setting out the conditions for American involvement in
such a way so as to ensure that it did not happen."[27]

The president had at least two good reasons to avoid intervention in Vietnam. Victory, first of all, would have been very costly.
Eisenhower could never forget that he had won the presidency on
a peace platform. The American people had elected him to end a
war in Asia, not to start a new one. Second, he harbored a strong
strategic objection to American involvement in Vietnam—one that
he refrained from expressing until years later. In the early 1960s,
when he was out of office and writing his memoirs, he drafted the
following passage, which did not make it into the published text:

The standing of the United States as the most powerful of the
anti-colonial powers is an asset of incalculable value to the Free
World. It means that our counsel is trusted where that of others may not be. It is essential to our position of leadership in
a world wherein the majority of nations have at some time or
another felt the yoke of colonialism. Thus it is that the moral

position of the United States was more to be guarded than the Tonkin Delta, indeed than all of Indochina.[28]

To this final sentence, he might also have added that the moral position of the United States was more to be guarded than the Nile Delta and all of Egypt.

Convinced that European imperialism was damaging the American position in the Cold War, Eisenhower maneuvered Britain out of the Canal Zone. By July 1954, the hardest work was finished, but the British and the Egyptian governments did not sign a formal agreement until October 19—in Cairo. At the signing ceremony, Nasser and the British ambassador issued statements that relegated the conflict between their two countries to the past, and looked forward to a future of friendship and cooperation. Eisenhower shared these hopes. He had made a point of demonstrating to Nasser that the United States was eager to elevate both him and the cause of Arab nationalism. In so doing, he believed that he had laid the foundation for an Arab-Western alliance in the Cold War.

Even at the signing ceremony, however, there were already indications that these hopes might have been misplaced—or so reported Robert Doty, the *New York Times* correspondent in Cairo. As Nasser was proclaiming a new dawn of Anglo-Egyptian friendship, Doty noted, a pamphlet bearing Nasser's name was circulating on the streets of Cairo. Instead of looking forward to a hopeful future, the pamphlet dwelled on the troubled past, "assigning credit for the evacuation agreement to action by Egyptian 'commanders' who 'struck terror in the hearts of the British.'" Westerners sympathetic to Nasser dismissed the pamphlet "as a piece of internal propaganda designed to appease extreme nationalist elements that been attacking the agreement as a 'sell-out' because of the provision for [reoccupying the base]."

Eisenhower had placed his first big bet in the Middle East. He wagered that the evacuation of the British from Egypt would sate

Nasser's nationalist appetite. The Egyptian leader, having learned that the United States was willing and able to act as a strategic partner, would now keep Egypt solidly within the Western security system. It would not take long before Eisenhower would come to realize that Nasser's appetite only increased with eating.

CHAPTER 5

Anatomy of a Miscalculation

Anthony Eden met Gamal Abdel Nasser only once. Eden passed through Cairo on the way to Asia in mid-February 1955 and invited Nasser to dinner at the British embassy. The Canal Zone agreement had been finalized four months earlier; the British were busy evacuating the base; and the Anglo-Egyptian conflict seemed to be a thing of the past. The atmosphere at the dinner was, Eden reported to Churchill, "most friendly, especially on all that concerned Anglo-Egyptian relations." Little did Eden realize, but his charming Egyptian guest would soon destroy him.

In retrospect, one can see an ominous cloud hovering over the evening. After dinner, when the two men discussed the problem of Middle Eastern defense, a significant disagreement emerged. Even as Nasser and Eden were dining, the Turkish and Iraqi prime ministers, Adnan Menderes and Nuri al-Said, were finalizing a mutual security agreement between their two countries. The so-called Turco-Iraqi Pact was a companion to the Turco-Pakistani Pact, a step toward turning Iraq into a core member of Dulles's Northern Tier. Nasser, however, was adamantly opposed to the development, which he saw as, among other things, an effort to build up Iraq as the pillar of the Western position in the Middle East—a move that would diminish Egypt's regional clout.

Meanwhile, Eden had reached a modus vivendi with the Americans over British interests in Iraq. He supported the Northern

Tier and tried hard to change Nasser's mind, urging him to cease his propaganda attacks against the Iraqi and Turkish governments. Eden made every effort, he reported to Churchill, "to persuade [Nasser] at least to restrain his criticism and, if the agreement were reasonable in terms, to cease his opposition." His words fell on deaf ears. When Eden told Nasser "that he should not treat this pact as a crime," Nasser flatly contradicted him. "No, but it is one," he said.[1]

Indeed, for the last three months Nasser's propaganda machine had treated it as the crime of the century. When the pact was finalized, shortly after Eden left Cairo, the Egyptian campaign took an even more sinister turn. Voice of the Arabs, Nasser's most influential radio station, gave prominent airtime to Iraqi dissidents and called on the Iraqi people to rise up in rebellion against their government. "By rising against Nuri al-Said and his accomplices," one dissident said on the day the pact was signed, "you will destroy this imperialist plot."[2]

These broadcasts inaugurated a new era in Arab politics. They were the beginning of a campaign of aggressive subversion that targeted the Hashemite dynasty, which ruled both Iraq and Jordan through different wings of the family. Egypt's Voice of the Arabs was an outlet of unrivaled influence because it was at the forefront of the mass communications revolution made possible by the cheap transistor radio. Nasser was the first revolutionary leader in the postwar Middle East to exploit the technology in order to call over the heads of the monarchs to the man in the street. Suddenly, the Hashemite monarchy found itself sitting atop volcanoes. The threat to the British was direct and significant. Britain had created Iraq and Jordan after World War I, so Nasser's propaganda cast it as the evil puppet master pulling the strings of the Hashemites.

At the dinner in Cairo in February 1955, Eden might not have realized the full depth of his conflict with Nasser, but he did recognize that he, together with Eisenhower and Dulles, had miscalcu-

lated in at least one respect: they had all believed that settling the
Canal Zone conflict would usher in an era of coordination, possibly even overt cooperation, between Egypt and the West. Nasser
disabused Eden of that notion with blunt language. The Turco-
Iraqi Pact, he said, had done more than just damage relations with
Egypt; it had "seriously set back the development of effective col-
laboration with the West by the Arab states."[3]

The choice of words was telling. No longer speaking simply as
the representative of the Egyptian people, Nasser now saw himself as the leader of the entire Arab world. The ambitions of the
young Egyptian leader were boundless—a fact that the American
and British architects of the Canal Zone settlement had never entertained. They had assumed that Nasser would use his regional
influence in support of a connection between the Arabs and the
West, never imagining that, after the settlement of the Canal Zone
question, he would simply continue his campaign against British
imperialism.

The Anglo-Egyptian conflict had not ended; it had simply
moved to a new theater.

A Failure of Prediction

The announcement of the Turco-Iraqi Pact represented a major
turning point in relations between the United States and Egypt,
but most historians have failed to understand just how significant it
was. The pact simultaneously goaded Nasser and revealed the disturbing scope of his ambitions. Historians, however, have tended
to explain Nasser's disaffection from the West as a gradual process
spurred by a number of different factors, placing special emphasis on the border war with Israel, which heated up in the spring of
1955. However, in the opening months of the year, before the border with Israel was ever a factor in anyone's calculations, Nasser
spoke in clear and unambiguous terms about the depth of his op-

position to the Northern Tier, and about the centrality of it, not Israel, to his entire foreign policy.

Consider, for example, Nasser's conversation in February 1955 with G. Lewis Jones, the new American chargé d'affaires in Cairo. Jones was meeting Nasser on something else entirely, but the Egyptian leader hastened to steer the conversation to the Turco-Iraqi Pact and then spoke of little else. He was particularly angry with the Iraqi prime minister and deeply contemptuous of him. "Everyone thinks of Nuri as a British agent," he complained. "It is possible that you may get away with [the] pact and that Nuri may remain in power for a few months, but your pact will be only a piece of paper and will gain you nothing from [the] point of view of area defense."

Nasser told Jones in no uncertain terms that the pact was a turning point in relations between Egypt and the United States. "He feels," Jones reported, "that the US has let him down and is responsible" for the consequences. The United States, he said, "had decided to move independently by instigating [the] pact; he felt free now to move independently also."[4]

Four months later, William C. Burdett, the Egyptian desk officer in the State Department, presented the same assessment. "Looking back over US-Egyptian relations since the signature last October of the Suez Base Agreement," he wrote to a colleague, "it is clear that the turning point was the Turk-Iraq Pact." Burdett also admitted that at the time of the pact's announcement, Nasser's hostility had caught the Americans totally by surprise. "None of us anticipated the strength of the Egyptians' reaction," Burdett wrote, "and considering how irrational they have been, it is difficult to see how we could have done so."[5]

Nasser's response, however, was not irrational, nor should it have surprised the Americans. After all, they had been warned ahead of time—by, of all people, the British.

On January 11, 1955, a State Department official had approached Evelyn Shuckburgh, who had taken up a new position as the most senior official in the Foreign Office working on the Middle East, and urged the British to cajole Nuri al-Said to participate in the Northern Tier. After the meeting, Shuckburgh penned a memo to his colleagues that criticized the thinking in Washington. The Americans, he wrote, have "no desire to see a worsening of relations between Egypt and Iraq, or between Egypt and the West. They do not think, however, that either of these things is likely to occur as a result of Iraq joining the Northern Tier." To Shuckburgh, the American disregard for Egyptian attitudes was cavalier. "No Middle East defence arrangement," he wrote, "is likely to have much value unless it enjoys Egyptian support or participation, and we must therefore take account of Egyptian views as to how it should be organized." The Americans, he believed, were embarking on a very dangerous course. If they succeed "it may be a great success but I think it is risky and may well fail."[6]

This prediction was entirely correct. The British accurately forecast Nasser's reaction to the Turco-Iraqi Pact, which was not particularly difficult to do, because the Egyptians had never made a secret of their hostility. Although the Americans prided themselves on their sympathetic understanding of the Egyptians, they completely missed the significance of the Egyptian-Iraqi conflict. Why? The question goes to the heart of the Eisenhower administration's misreading of Middle Eastern politics.

The Flap of the Butterfly's Wings

Clearly, lack of information was not the problem. Washington had at its disposal all of the facts necessary to make an accurate assessment of Nasser's motivations. The problem stemmed from the distorting prism through which the Americans viewed the Middle East.

The prism had shaped Dulles's perceptions from the beginning. As he toured the region in May 1953, he grew increasingly convinced that British imperialism and Zionism were undermining the Western position. While still on the road, he sent a dire appraisal to Eisenhower, sounding an alarm about growing bitterness toward the United States, due to its support for Israel and British and French imperialism. Changing this perception, Dulles said, was the key to gaining the cooperation of the Arabs in the Cold War—and it was an urgent priority. The time frame in which the Americans had to act "must be measured in weeks, not months." The Arabs harbored high hopes for Eisenhower, but their optimism "will quickly dissolve unless our acts seem here to show [a] capacity to influence British and Israeli policies, which now tend to converge in what is looked upon as [a] new phase of aggression against Arabs."[7]

This dispatch represents a clear and concise statement of the honest broker paradigm that shaped not just Dulles's thinking, but the thinking of the vast majority of American officials working on the Middle East. In another communication with Eisenhower, a memo written just after his trip, Dulles emphasized the key assumptions of the paradigm. "The Israel factor," he wrote, "and the association of the United States in the minds of the people of the area with French and British colonial and imperialistic policies are millstones around our neck."[8]

As Dulles saw it in mid-1953, the first order of business was to lighten the burden of the British millstone, because of the immediate threat of war in the Canal Zone. In the process, however, he inadvertently subordinated Egypt to Iraq. The key decision was taken on June 1, 1953, at a meeting of the National Security Council—the same meeting, ironically, at which Dulles received Eisenhower's approval to tilt in favor of the Egyptians in the Canal Zone conflict. Reporting to the council on his trip, Dulles explained that he had arrived in Egypt "with the expectation that it would be the key to the development of strength in the Middle East." However, he left the country disappointed. For one thing, it was unclear who, precisely, was in charge. General Naguib, Dulles said, "turned out not to be the 'strong man' in Egypt, but merely a front." Nasser and his cohort, who were young and inexperienced, were the ones who actually ran the show. Second, the Canal Zone conflict, even if it were quickly solved, was destined to impede Western-Egyptian cooperation for a long time to come. Dulles concluded, therefore, "that we must abandon our preconceived ideas of making Egypt the key country in building the foundations for a military defense of the Middle East."[9]

And with that, Egypt was demoted, the abundant attention to the Suez Canal notwithstanding. In an interview many years later, Ambassador Parker Hart, a distinguished Foreign Service officer, reflected back on the implications of this decision. Hart would eventually go on to become ambassador to Saudi Arabia and an assistant secretary of state, but in 1955, when Eisenhower and Dulles were making the key decisions about Nasser, he was a junior officer in the State Department. Dulles, Hart said in an interview, "got a little too euphoric about the possibilities of a useful relationship between the United States and Egypt." During the period 1953–54, he had given Nasser every reason to think that the United States would build up Egypt as "the natural leader of the Arab world." When, however, it became apparent that Dulles was supporting the Turco-Iraqi Pact, the Egyptians felt betrayed and were "absolutely furious with the United States." Egyptian anger was unappeasable. As a consequence, Hart explained, a cloud came over the American-Egyptian relationship, which "never dissipated." The Egyptians "went to work immediately to make sure that no other Arab country could join the Pact, and they did their best to undermine Nuri Said's regime in Iraq."[10]

Nasser's hostility to the Northern Tier meant that Eisenhower's strategy suffered from a fatal flaw. On the one hand, he was pursuing a "pro-Egyptian" outcome in the Middle East. By forcing a British evacuation from Egypt, he inevitably increased the influence of Cairo in the Arab world more broadly. On the other hand, he simultaneously embarked upon the Northern Tier project, which entailed building up alternative centers of power: Karachi, Ankara, and Baghdad. Nasser, therefore, was bound to see the Northern Tier project as an objectively "anti-Egyptian" orientation, regardless of how the Americans themselves conceived of it.

At the crucial meeting of the National Security Council in 1953, however, Dulles's recommendation to demote Egypt elicited no objections from any quarter. No one in the room so much as hinted that the demotion might harm relations with Egypt. Like the proverbial flap of a butterfly's wings, the decision hardly disturbed the air in the room, but, over time, it generated a tornado.

A Bifurcated Policy

The unrealistic task that the Eisenhower administration set for itself was to change popular Arab perceptions of the United States. General hostility to the West, so the argument went, was constraining Arab elites, making it impossible for them to associate with the West in the Cold War. Consequently, it was insufficient for American officials to work quietly behind the scenes for Arab nationalist causes. Arab men and women on the street had to see American officials actively working for Arab nationalism. Thus Dulles, with the full support of Eisenhower, lost no time in sending a clear public signal that the United States was distancing itself from Britain, France, and Israel.

On the morning of June 1, 1953, Dulles demoted Egypt; in the evening, he delivered a prime-time television address in which he summarized for the nation the findings of his Middle East trip. He was remarkably frank about this desire to win over popular opinion in the Middle East—and about the keys for doing so. First, there was the problem of European imperialism. "We found," he said, that most of the peoples of the Near East and South Asia are deeply concerned about political independence for themselves and others. They are suspicious of the colonial powers and we of the United States, too, are suspect, because, they reason, our NATO alliance with France and Britain requires us to try to preserve or restore the old colonial interests of our allies. I'm convinced that United States policy has become unnecessarily ambiguous in this matter. The leaders of the countries I visited fully recognize it would be a disaster if there were any break between the United States and Great Britain and France. . . . However, without breaking out from the framework of Western unity, we can pursue our traditional dedication to political liberty.

After distancing the United States from European imperialism, Dulles sounded a retreat from Truman-era support of Israel:

The United States should seek to allay the deep resentment against it that has resulted from the creation of Israel. In the past we had good relations with the Arab peoples. . . . Today the Arab peoples are afraid that the United States will back the new state of Israel in aggressive expansion. They are more fearful of Zionism than they are of communism and they fear the United States, lest we become the backer of expansionist Zionism.[11]

Eisenhower and Dulles habitually described their policy toward the Arab-Israeli conflict as one of "impartiality," but in his prime-time address, Dulles was admirably clear in expressing his intention to shift support away from Israel and in the direction of Arab nationalism: "We cannot afford to be distrusted by millions who should be sturdy friends of freedom," he said.

The goal of the address was to establish the United States as the honest broker, mediating between Arab nationalism, on the one side, and the Europeans and Israel on the other. But this approach suffered from a fatal intellectual flaw: it imagined the Arabs and Muslims as a unified bloc. It paid no attention whatsoever to all of the bitter rivalries in the Middle East that had no connection to the British and Israeli millstones. Consequently, Nasser's disputes with his rivals simply did not register in Washington as factors of strategic significance.

Dulles was not the only American official to see the Middle East through this distorting prism; nearly all American officials saw it that way. Consider, for example, a 1953 National Intelligence Estimate (NIE) titled "Conditions and Trends in the Middle East Affecting US Security." Ominously, it describes "rivalries among the Arab states," which, despite a common religious heritage, suffer from "dynastic quarrels, narrow nationalistic politics, religious differences, and differences of economic interest." These factors "have interfered with efforts to solve common problems" and prevented the emergence of an effective regional leadership. Egypt, the prime candidate for such leadership, "has had little success in achieving positive united action."[12]

The Arabs were divided—deeply, bitterly, and hopelessly. On the basis of this NIE, American strategists of 1953 had within their grasp all the information necessary to predict that the United States could never organize all of the Arabs into a single pro-Western bloc, because American support for one Arab camp would inevitably provoke powerful opposition from rival camps. But no senior American official ever entertained such a proposition, and the NIE itself helps us understand why. The section titled "Obstacles to US Influence in the Middle East" identifies three such obstacles, and only three: the association of the United States with Israel; the American alliance with the British and the French; and the fact that the Soviet Union did not directly threaten the Arabs. For policy makers, the logic of the NIE led inexorably to a single conclusion: in order to win Arab goodwill, the United States had to distance itself from Britain, France, and, above all, Israel.

In short, American strategic thinking was oddly bifurcated. The State Department and CIA absorbed all manner of information regarding the Egyptian rivalry with regional powers, to say nothing of many other conflicts that beset the Arab world. This kind of information, however, had little influence on the formulation of major policy priorities, which focused, almost exclusively, on eliminating the millstones of Zionism and imperialism.

Promises, Promises

The blind spots and biases in the American worldview made American officials easy marks for Egyptian efforts at deception. Throughout 1953–54, the Egyptians had been consumed with ousting the British from the Canal Zone—a task that required borrowing power from the United States. To win American support, Nasser had to convince Washington that Egyptian nationalism was compatible with Western interests. In the context of contemporary American thinking, which emphasized the creation of collective security organizations, this challenge was particularly tricky. Nasser had to do the impossible: he had to convince Eisenhower and Dulles that they could remove Egypt from the British regional security system and yet still rely on it to side with the West against the Soviet Union.

When Nasser had met Dulles in May 1953, therefore, he stated that "the objectives of the US and Egypt are the same; Egypt, too, would like to see the defense of the area organized." The problem was the British occupation, which created, he said, "a psychological block to setting up an area defense arrangement. The Egyptian people think of a Middle East defense organization as a 'perpetuation of occupation.'" When Dulles asked how long it would take, after the evacuation of British troops, until Egypt could join a collective security organization, Nasser dodged the question. First, he said, "British influence must entirely disappear."[13] Then he promised that, if the British really did go, Egypt would participate in a Western-dominated system—even a British system.

Nasser was at his most dishonest when he promised to allow British troops to use the base in the event of another major war. The British insisted on inserting a clause into the final version of the Anglo-Egyptian agreement that granted the British the right to reactivate the base in the future. The demand enraged every self-respecting Egyptian nationalist. On two occasions in recent history—World Wars I and II—foreign soldiers had flooded into Egypt and dominated it. Nasser and his colleagues were adamant that there would not be another repetition of the experience. Their determination placed them directly at odds with Eisenhower and Dulles, who were staunch supporters of the British demand for reactivation rights.

To gain the American support that he desperately needed, Nasser had no choice but to capitulate on the question of reactivation. The memoirs of Khalid Muhi'l-Din, one of the original Free Officers, testify to the fact that Nasser never intended to honor his pledge. "Nasser understood that the evacuation was the dream of every Egyptian, and that it was very important for us to realize it for them," Muhi'l-Din writes. "He always emphasized that carrying out the evacuation would be an historic victory. If, after that, the British would want to return, we would prevent them, because, hopefully, we would have acquired the requisite strength."[14]

Nasser traded vague promises of Egyptian cooperation in the future for concrete concessions from Britain in the present. He understood—quite correctly—that once the British troops were gone, the rules of the game had changed, and Egypt could behave with impunity. If Jefferson Caffery, the American ambassador in Cairo, understood Nasser's tactics, he did not advertise the fact. His dispatches depicted the young Egyptian leader as nothing if not a straight shooter. Thus, when Bedell Smith raised doubts, in May 1953, about the Free Officers' sincerity, Caffery dismissed them with, among other arguments, this character sketch:

> We have an opportunity to do business with a group of men who will not easily give commitments because they believe in keeping their word. If we are going to do business with them, we shall have to take this into account and we shall have to move quickly. Admittedly such a course of action will involve a considerable gamble and a large measure of trust. Nothing breeds confidence like a display of confidence, however, and the vicious circle of Anglo-Egyptian recrimination and distrust must be broken.[15]

Typical of Caffery's dispatches, this sketch betrays no awareness of Nasser's cunning. In a few short months, he went from being an obscure colonel to ruling Egypt. A man with such skills was a born manipulator, a man who was never forthright with anyone—including the Americans.

The Unseen Hostility

The policies of Nasser that would soon shake the Middle East to its foundations were already visible in the first weeks of 1954, during the long deadlock in the Anglo-Egyptian negotiations, when the Free Officers unveiled what they dubbed Egypt's "New Foreign Policy." Its centerpiece was neutralism in the Cold War, and it openly expressed an intention to develop productive relations with the East Bloc. As part of the new policy, Nasser published a series of articles, which were later collected and issued as a book under the title *The Philosophy of the Revolution*. The

third installment in the series appeared on January 6, 1954, just
when the Free Officers were in the midst of unveiling their new
neutralism.

It opened by asking, "What is our role in the world? And where
must we play our role?" Nasser's answer is now famous. Egypt, he
said, occupied a position at the center of three concentric circles:
the Arab, African, and Islamic. Recalling Pirandello's play *Six Characters in Search of an Author*, he wrote that in the Middle East there
existed "a role which is awaiting an actor to perform it." Egypt had
no choice but to assume the role—which was one, he hastened to
explain, not of leader but of catalyst. But what kind of catalyst?

The people of the Middle East, he explained, were separated
from each other by international frontiers, but experienced a
shared fate nevertheless, especially the Arabs, who were united by
bonds of culture, religion, and history. "An event would take place
in Cairo," he wrote, "and a similar one would occur on the morrow
in Damascus, on the following day in Beirut, and later in Baghdad,
Amman, and other places. . . ." The entire region was politically
heterogeneous, but behind the scenes, identical forces were generating similar events. The most powerful of these, Nasser claimed,
was imperialism—"the greatest power that has laid a fatal and invisible siege to the whole zone under review."

Having diagnosed the disease, the cure was obvious. The Arabs
must band together in a united struggle. "So long as the whole zone
is one," Nasser wrote, "and its conditions and problems are alike,
and so long as the enemy is the same whatever guises he may don,
why do we scatter and waste our energy?"[16] Egypt's role, therefore,
was to catalyze a united front against imperialism.

Three days after the publication of this installment of "The
Philosophy of the Revolution," the Egyptians announced that their
new foreign policy would seek to establish an Arab bloc, based on
the Arab League, which at that time included Egypt, Syria, Lebanon, Iraq, Jordan, Saudi Arabia, and Yemen. Egypt dominated the

organization, which, founded in 1945, was located in Cairo and run by Abdel Rahman Azzam, an Egyptian diplomat. In principle, the League stood for promoting greater cooperation among independent Arab states, especially in confronting Zionism and imperialism. In practice, Cairo used it, with the support of the Saudis and the Syrians, as a tool for blocking the regional ambitions of their common adversaries, Iraq and Jordan.

As soon as the Northern Tier started to take shape, Nasser's propagandists denounced it as a menace to the Arab League—a plot to divide the Arabs in order to protect Israel and the British. In the first half of 1954, the denunciations grew increasingly shrill. By July, Prime Minister Menderes of Turkey was complaining to the American ambassador in Ankara about the personal attacks against him that were appearing in Egyptian propaganda, which, at the same time, was denouncing the Turco-Pakistani pact "as an instrument calculated to destroy the Arab League."[17]

Nasser was publicly announcing a policy of neutrality in the Cold War, attacking an American ally, and heaping scorn on Dulles's major foreign policy initiative in the Middle East—yet Washington lodged no protest in Cairo. Remarkably, the Americans were so confident in Nasser's commitment to the West that they actually furnished him with the tools to spread his revolutionary message across the Arab world. As the historian Kenneth Osgood has amply documented, it was with American aid, in the form of direct assistance from the CIA, that the Egyptians set up their formidable propaganda system. In addition to providing Nasser with the most powerful broadcasting equipment in the Arab world, the CIA loaned the Egyptians experts on psychological warfare, including the legendary Paul Linebarger, whom one admirer in the CIA viewed as "perhaps the leading practitioner of 'black' and 'gray' propaganda in the Western World." The Americans also provided audience analyses, training in all aspects of broadcasting, and grants for officials working in the media to travel to the United

States, where they toured broadcast facilities and learned trade-craft. The CIA has long been accused of facilitating the transfer of ex-Nazi intelligence officers to Egypt, some of whom contributed to Egyptian propaganda. Among them was Franz Bunsch, a for-mer aide to Joseph Goebbels best known for his anti-Semitic tract *The Sexual Habits of Jews.* Whether the CIA was truly responsible for the appearance of the Nazis in Egypt, the full-throttled cam-paign of incitement against Iraq that erupted upon the signing of the Turco-Iraqi Pact was certainly made possible, in part, by the generous assistance of the American taxpayer.[18]

Sarsank

The closer the Northern Tier project came to fruition, the stron-ger Egyptian opposition grew. In mid-August 1954, Nasser's rela-tions with Nuri al-Said, which were always bad, took a permanent turn for the worse. As the Americans increased their pressure on Baghdad to join the Northern Tier, Nasser dispatched Salah Salim, the minister for national guidance, to Iraq for talks. As voluble as he was peripatetic, Salim earned the nickname "the Dancing Major" after he was photographed dancing with Sudanese tribes-men, dressed only in a loincloth. Salim served as the point man in the effort to prevent Iraq—and, for that matter, any other Arab state—from joining the Northern Tier. This assignment would take him all around the Arab world agitating against association with the West in matters of defense.

The goal of his trip to Iraq, in August 1954, was a summit meet-ing with Iraqi Prime Minister Nuri al-Said in Sarsank, a resort in the Kurdish mountains. Salim made two major mistakes during the trip. The first was a simple slip of the tongue. At a press conference in Baghdad, a journalist asked him whether Egypt opposed the fed-eration of two or more Arab states. Salim tried a little too hard to please his audience. "Egypt," he said, "does not oppose any kind of union. If two or more Arab peoples wish to unite in some form, Egypt does not object."[19]

A storm erupted. Salim seemed to be signaling Egyptian support for Iraqi plans to federate with Syria—a long-standing Iraqi aspiration, which traditionally Egypt had bitterly opposed. Salim's statement sent a chill down the spine of leaders in Syria, who had always looked to Egypt and Saudi Arabia to balance the influence of the Turks and the Iraqis. To calm the fears of its Syrian allies, the Egyptian government issued an immediate clarification, denying the claim that Cairo supported Arab federation ideas. With that, the controversy subsided.[20]

Salim's second mistake is harder to explain. Contrary to established Egyptian policy, he reached an understanding with Nuri al-Said over Iraqi-Egyptian cooperation on regional defense. During their meetings, Salim suggested to al-Said that he should forswear new treaties with non-Arab states and that he should join together with the Egyptians in turning the Arab League Collective Security Pact (ALCSP) into a truly effective regional security mechanism. Al-Said countered that the circumstances of Iraq—its tense relations with neighbors, its proximity to the Soviet Union, and its general weakness—meant that it could not rely solely on its fellow Arab states. Relying exclusively on Arab solidarity was a laudable aspiration, but Iraq needed the weapons and diplomatic support that only the West could provide.

Al-Said suggested a compromise. Egypt and Iraq would work to strengthen the ALCSP; at the same time, however, they would also revise it so as to accommodate security relationships with the Western powers. Salim agreed. He issued a joint statement with al-Said that called for Iraq and Egypt to conduct discussions with the Western powers about revising the ALCSP.[21] Remarkably, Salim had undermined a basic pillar of Egyptian policy—the principle that Arabs must unite only with other Arabs.

When news reached Nasser that "an agreed plan" had emerged

from the meeting in Sarsank, he exploded in rage and confronted
Salim. The Dancing Major wept in shame for having let Nasser
down, and resigned. The next day, after Nasser's temper had died
down, he reinstated Salim, but the mistake had indeed been damaging.[22] The point of Salim's mission had been to place Nuri al-Said
on the defensive before the court of Arab public opinion by pinning him between two equally unpleasant options. Option One was
to announce that he was in total agreement with Egypt, thus revealing himself as the weaker figure, Nasser's subordinate. Option
Two was to reject the Egyptian stance—in which case he would lay
himself open to the charge that he was more dedicated to serving
the West than working to build Arab nationalism. For some inex-
plicable reason, however, Salim had allowed the wily Iraqi to wig-
gle free from the trap.

Nevertheless, Nasser held an ace in the hole: the Voice of the
Arabs. Nasser's propaganda machine passed off Salim's missteps as
the result of Iraqi trickery. The lies that it told were much more
persuasive than the truth. A few months after Salim returned from
Sarsank, the Turks and Iraqis announced their firm intention to
sign a pact, and the Voice of the Arabs intensified its campaign to
stop it.

The Missed Opportunity

Salah Salim's performance in Iraq called attention to more than
just the disagreement over Arab solidarity. It also exposed a second
major point of contention in inter-Arab politics: the controversy
over the Hashemite ambitions to annex Syria. For several years,
the issue had lain dormant—until, that is, Washington inadvertently stirred it awake with the Northern Tier project. In late 1953,
when Dulles began talking to the Iraqis about regional defense,
their greatest dream sprang to life after a period of dormancy—the
dream of taking over Syria. In January 1954, Iraqi Prime Minister

Muhammad Fadhil Jamali publicly unveiled a plan for Arab unification, which Arab public opinion immediately read, correctly, as
a new bid for Iraqi-Syrian federation. Six months after unveiling
his plan, Jamali took up the position of foreign minister in the new
government of Nuri al-Said, who was also well known as a staunch
advocate of Iraqi-Syrian federation. In consultations with Dulles,
Jamali asked whether "such a move would be tolerable from the
United States point of view after Iraq's joining with Turkey and
Pakistan."[23] In that case, Dulles replied, the annexation of Syria
might be "tolerable" from an American point of view.

Nasser took notice. He launched his Arab neutralism campaign at precisely the same moment as when Jamali called for his
new Arab federation. Egypt and Iraq were engaged in a bitter conflict over power and authority in the post-imperial Middle East—
a struggle that pitted two rival concepts of Arab unity against each
other. The first of these was integral unity, represented by the
Hashemites. Jordan and Iraq advocated erasing the borders drawn
by the imperialists and creating larger states, leading eventually
to the creation of a single Arab superstate in the Fertile Crescent.
By contrast, the Egyptians championed the idea of Arab solidarity, standing united against the imperialists. Their view enjoyed the
strong support of Saudi Arabia and the Syrian government, both of
whom feared the expansion of Hashemite power. For Nasser, then,
much was at stake in the fight with Nuri al-Said. His status as the
leader of the Arab world, the very currency that he traded for influence on the global stage, was based in large measure on his ability
to command the respect of his allies in Riyadh and Damascus. The
Saudis and Syrians, however, supported him only in proportion to
his ability to help them block the expansionist urges of the Hashemites. Thus the preservation of Egyptian status in the regional
order required active opposition to the Northern Tier, that is, lim-
iting the power of Iraq.

But for Nasser there was something even more important at

stake in his conflict with Baghdad and Amman. So long as Britain remained a military power in the Middle East, with basing rights in Iraq and Jordan, there was a risk that it would one day reoccupy Egypt. Because the Canal Zone agreement gave Britain the right to reactivate the base, the only way for Nasser to secure the permanent independence of Egypt was to strip Britain of that capability—by severing, once and for all, its security relationships with the Hashemites.

By giving Eisenhower and Dulles an opportunity to recognize the profound depth of the chasm that separated Egypt from Iraq, the controversy surrounding Sarsank invited them to recognize, before it was too late, that their policy was empowering a Hashemite expansion into Syria while simultaneously provoking the forces, led by Egypt, that were most hostile to that expansion. The Americans were speeding toward the Northern Tier. Sarsank represented the last off-ramp before it was too late. The British read some of the warning signs clearly and counseled the Americans to slow down. Dulles gunned it.

CHAPTER 6

The Alpha Contradiction

On February 5, 1955, Iraqi Prime Minister Nuri al-Said urged the Americans to join the Turco-Iraqi Pact—a step that would transform the bilateral agreement into the foundation of a pro-Western regional defense system, a Middle Eastern NATO. Two weeks later, Waldemar Gallman, the American ambassador in Baghdad, sent to Washington a very forceful recommendation in favor of formal American participation. "We are the originators of the northern tier concept," he wrote, "and it is we who gave the inspiration and encouragement which resulted in the Iraq-Turk pact. Indigenous interest has now been adequately proved. Yet the task of forging the paper northern tier into an effective northern tier defense organization has still to be accomplished, and we do not see how this can be done without US adherence."

Direct American participation, Gallman argued, would stiffen the courage of countries such as Jordan and Lebanon, which were incapable of standing up to Nasser alone. It would also shore up Nuri al-Said. He deserved American support, because he "showed great courage in taking the initiative to align Iraq with Turkey and the west, risking much at home and in relations with Arab neighbors."[1]

The American ambassador in Ankara, Avra Warren, also offered his personal support, but in even stronger terms. "Frankly," he wrote to Washington, "I feel our Turkish friends have demonstrated they have rather clearer eye-sight than some of the rest of us. I cannot avoid feeling that we are letting them down badly—and against our own interest. 'Northern Tier' is our concept, and in my mind, a sound one." Given the openness of Egyptian hostility to the American defense plans and to American allies, Warren argued, to show continued deference to Nasser "seriously undercuts the position we have encouraged the Turks to take by our support of the Turco-Pakistani and Turco-Iraqi pacts."[2]

But Egypt was strongly opposed. Vehemently. Dulles faced a simple choice: to support Egypt or Iraq? Without the slightest hesitation, he sided against America's avowed allies in the Cold War and with Egypt. Why? The answer can be summed up in one word: Palestine. Dulles was already deeply involved in plans to settle the Arab-Israeli conflict—and Nasser, he believed, held the keys to a settlement. Peacemaking, in his mind, trumped everything else.

Alpha

The planning for Arab-Israeli peace began the moment the Anglo-Egyptian conflict was put to rest. In early November 1954, a few weeks after the British and Egyptians signed the agreement on the Canal Zone, Anthony Eden informed Roger Makins, the British ambassador in Washington, that he was concerned about rising Arab-Israeli tensions and had a general idea about how to deal with them. He had in mind a joint Anglo-American initiative, and he had already dispatched Evelyn Shuckburgh on a tour of the Middle East in order to formulate a plan. Eden asked Makins to see whether Dulles "would consider sending one of his experts from the State Department to London to join forces with Mr. Shuckburgh."[3]

The next day, Makins delivered Eden's message to Dulles, who "was clearly interested and pleased."[4] Before long, Shuckburgh was teamed up with American diplomat Francis Russell, who had just returned from a posting in Israel. The two men put together a plan, code-named "Alpha," which was based on Shuckburgh's ideas. The plan was secret and tightly held. It was the highest-priority issue in American Middle East strategy from January 1955 until March 1956. It overshadowed every other major policy of the United States in the region. And it was an abject failure.

At the heart of the Alpha concept was an effort to reduce the weight of the Israeli millstone. Shuckburgh, the primary British architect of the project, described the essential idea as "a plan whereby in return for minimal Israeli concessions and with various forms of economic and material assistance from the West the Arabs might be induced to make peace with Israel and the US and UK would guarantee the settlement."[5] The description is accurate except for the word *minimal*. In 1955, when exchanging views with his Foreign Office colleagues, Shuckburgh was more candid. "[A]ny initiative, if it is to be realistic and to avoid damaging even more seriously our position in the Arab world, will have to be something which the Israelis will detest," he said.[6]

Shuckburgh wrote the first draft of the plan on his own, and his original version would certainly have met this requirement. Among other concessions from the Israelis, it called for the internationalization of Jerusalem and for Israel to withdraw from the Negev, the desert in southern Israel separating Egypt's Sinai from Jordan. The Americans adopted Shuckburgh's general outlook but they scaled back the demands on Israel. Even so, the joint Anglo-American documents state plainly, "Israel must make [territorial] concessions. The Arabs will not reconcile themselves to reaching a settlement with an Israel with the present boundaries."[7]

The British and the Americans concluded that Israel, in addition to ceding land to Jordan along the border, must also relinquish two triangles in the Negev: one would go to Egypt, the other to Jordan. The bases of the two triangles would fall, respectively, on the Egyptian-Israeli and Jordanian-Israeli borders. The apexes would meet at a single point on the highway from Tel Aviv to Eilat. Thus an hourglass-shaped corridor would link Egypt to Jordan. The meeting point of the triangles would form a crossroads. The north–south highway would be Jewish, providing Israelis access to their port on the Red Sea; the east–west highway would be Arab, offering Egypt a land connection, via an overpass, to the other Arab countries.

From the beginning, Egypt was identified as the primary Arab partner, both because it was the most influential Arab state and because Nasser was the only Arab leader, at that time, who seemed willing to entertain the idea of a peace settlement. The British and Americans therefore planned to preview Alpha to Nasser first. Only after gaining his approval would they then approach the Israelis. They would use tough pressure combined with a package of incentives, including Western security guarantees, to compel the Israelis to make the envisioned territorial concessions. Seen from Washington, this sequential process would not just solve the Arab-Israeli conflict but would also purchase goodwill from the Arabs in general, and especially from Nasser. Washington and London agreed that Eden should test Nasser's receptivity to Arab-Israeli peacemaking during his mid-February trip to Cairo.

As we have already seen, however, Nasser's hostility to the Turco-Iraqi Pact overshadowed that meeting. Before it even started, Alpha began to fail. Nasser's fury over the Northern Tier made it impossible for Eden to adequately explore Arab-Israeli peacemaking with him. After Eden left Cairo, he flew to Bangkok, where he met up with Dulles. "Nasser," Eden told the secretary of state, "implied [that] Egypt has [an] open mind" about peacemaking, "but said [the] problem was one of timing." This, Eden understood, had been made complicated by "the Iraqi-Turkish Pact, which apparently is consuming his attention."[8] As Eden explained it, Nasser's attitude "hinged on [the] question of leadership in [the] Arab world, which Nasser obviously desired to assume. His opposition to [the] Iraqi-Turkish treaty really stemmed from [the] fact that another Arab nation had taken [the] lead in concluding [a] collective defense arrangement."[9]

Dulles, for his part, was sympathetic to Nasser's ambition. He had always considered a partnership with Egypt as a great strategic prize, and he believed that the continuation of the Arab-Israeli conflict was the greatest impediment to winning it. Dulles told Eden that "we would like to be able to give Nasser support for [the] position of leadership to which he aspired in [the] Arab world but that we could not do this until the Arab-Israel problem was settled."[10] Alpha, in other words, was the ladder that Nasser would ascend in order to reach a position of undisputed Arab leadership.

The Unrecognized Contradiction

Five days after Eden and Dulles discussed the connection between Alpha and the Turco-Iraqi Pact, Israel launched an attack on the Egyptian military headquarters in Gaza, killing close to forty Egyptian soldiers and wounding nearly thirty more. "The Gaza Raid," as the operation became known, was the largest Israeli attack on Egypt since the armistice agreement in 1949. In time, Nasser would come to claim that it was an earthshaking event, one that forced him to reconsider Egypt's alignment in the Cold War. Those claims, as we shall see, were exaggerated and manipulative, but the question remains: why did the Israelis choose to escalate at this moment?

On one level, the Gaza Raid was a simple reprisal attack. Three days before the raid, an Egyptian military unit, probably on an intelligence-gathering mission, had penetrated Israel and murdered a cyclist in the vicinity of Rishon LeZion. The attack was not an isolated incident but part of a pattern of operations—and with the Gaza Raid, the Israelis no doubt meant to notify Nasser that such operations would come at a cost.

But in early 1955 the Israelis also had a second score to settle with Nasser. At the end of January, the Egyptians had hanged Moshe Marzouk and Shmuel Azar, two Egyptian Jews who, as Israeli agents, participated in Operation Susannah, a botched false-flag operation designed to look like the work of communists and the Muslim Brotherhood. In the summer of 1954, Marzouk, Azar, and a number of other agents planted bombs in civilian facilities in Cairo, especially those frequented by British and American expatriates. The goal of this severely ill-conceived operation seems to have been to convince London and Washington that the total evacuation of the British troops from the Canal Zone would lead to uncontrollable chaos in Egypt.

The Gaza Raid and Operation Susannah were not directly connected, but they were both expressions of the same strategic need: gaining leverage over Nasser. If the Gaza Raid was a reprisal operation, in neither size nor intent was it an ordinary one. With the British now evacuating the Canal Zone, the Israelis were searching for a way to force Nasser to respect their vital interests. They were also attempting, in all likelihood, to make him appear weak in the eyes of the Arab world—thus they launched the raid within a week of the announcement of the Turco-Iraqi Pact. The pact had exposed the limits of his political influence; now the Gaza Raid would show up his military impotence.

Whether that was truly the Israelis' thinking, Dulles certainly thought it was. Deeply concerned that Nasser was reeling from a double blow, he informed his staff that it was important to "pursue policies in the area during the next few months that will help build up Nasser and will give us the opportunity to say to him that we are prepared to cooperate with him in strengthening his position, but that it must be accompanied by his cooperation in Alpha."

At the same time, Dulles decided to oppose further expansion of the Baghdad Pact, as the Turco-Iraqi Pact would soon become known. He issued guidance to his staff that "the northern tier should be confined to the northern-tier countries." If Jordan, Lebanon, and Syria were to join the Baghdad Pact, he explained, "it would [only] further isolate and embitter Nasser."[11] The State Department promptly informed the American ambassador in Cairo that it intended "to convince Nasser that we . . . are desirous of extending our support and assistance—political, economic, and military—to Egypt and in general of assisting Egypt to achieve the international standing to which she is entitled to aspire."[12]

Dulles settled the debate over whether to support Egypt or Iraq before it ever started. His decision, however, failed to address a key problem: while Washington was building up Nasser so that he would make peace with Israel, he himself was working overtime to tear Nuri al-Said down. In Dulles's mind, U.S. policy favored Alpha, not Nasser's quest for regional mastery. Dulles is known to history as the consummate Cold Warrior; ironically, thanks to Alpha, he became a key enabler of the Egyptian campaign for neutralism and nonalignment.

American passivity in the face of Nasser's campaign against Iraq and other Western-oriented Arab states created an impression of tacit support, which Nasser cleverly exploited. He whispered to Arab diplomats from Lebanon, Syria, and Jordan—potential adherents to the Baghdad Pact—that the Americans had actually sided with him against the Iraqis, because the Americans believed that a formal defense relationship with the Western powers was unnecessary in order to secure the Middle East.[13] Meanwhile, Egyptian propaganda was relentless in its depiction of the Iraqi leader as a tyrant. Voice of the Arabs described Iraq as an armed camp, with the government violently repressing a popular will to stand together with Egypt against foreign pacts.

Labeling Nuri al-Said a traitor and an ally of Israel and imperialism, Voice of the Arabs called on the people of Iraq to rise up and topple him. In one typical broadcast, a dissident named Adnan al-Rawi addressed his words to Turkish Prime Minister Adnan Menderes, who was visiting Baghdad to sign the pact. Al-Rawi told Menderes, "[T]omorrow, when the gates of the prisons are smashed, when the Iraqi people rise, when the soil is stained with blood, and when the new alliance is torn to pieces—tomorrow, Menderes, you will see how the story ends." Today, al-Rawi continued, embroidering the point, Nuri al-Said will guard the road along which Menderes's motorcade is traveling, will sign the pact, and will throw young men in jail. "Tomorrow," however, "the people will write with their own blood the last chapter." [14]

Not only did the Americans turn a blind eye to Nasser's revolutionary incitement, they encouraged their allies to do the same. In late January, the American embassy in Cairo recommended to Washington that pressuring Egypt to moderate its attacks on Iraq would be counterproductive. In addition, it "would not be helpful," the embassy argued, for the Turks, the British, or the Americans "to take a strong line with Egypt at this juncture. To do so would compound Egyptian embarrassment and possibly distract them from current efforts to save face through some compromise." [15]

The advice of the embassy soon became a fixed policy. As a result, when the Turks went on the counterattack against the Egyptians and their Syrian allies, the American ambassador in Ankara received a worried cable from Washington, expressing concern over "intemperate Turkish criticism of Egypt and Syria," which could be interpreted as an attempt to "incite public opinion" against the two governments. [16] It was important to restrain the Turks, so as not to harm long-term objectives in the Middle East—meaning, presumably, Arab-Israeli peace.

This bias in favor of Egypt only increased when Dulles received word, in March 1955, that the British were intent on adhering directly to the Baghdad Pact. No sooner had he learned this fact than he started to interpret Nasser's hostility to the Northern Tier as an expression of traditional Egyptian distrust of British imperialism. Forgetting entirely that Nasser had railed against the Northern Tier when it was a solely American project, Dulles lamented to his advisors that "it looks as though the UK had grabbed the ball on the Northern-Tier policy and was running away with it."[17] Thereafter, Dulles never wavered from this view. Months later, for example, he explained to Eisenhower that "the trouble" with the Northern Tier "was that the British had taken it over and run it as an instrument of British policy that has drawn upon it a tremendous amount of criticism."[18]

There is much irony in this rewriting of history. Back in January 1955, when Shuckburgh had told his British colleagues that Dulles's intention to push Iraq into the Northern Tier was risky and might fail, he warned, "We must avoid being blamed for its failure." The warning was in vain. Dulles's beliefs ensured both that the Northern Tier would fail *and* that the British would take the blame for it.

The Alpha Ethos

Dulles's anti-imperialism, however, was only one half of the distorting prism through which he viewed the Middle East. The other half was anti-Zionism. Even before he devised the specifics of Plan Alpha, he exhibited what might be called the "Alpha Ethos": the feeling that he had an urgent duty to return balance to the Arab-Israeli policy of the United States by tacking away from Israel.

Many members of the foreign policy elite, including Eisenhower, shared Dulles's belief in the centrality of the Arab-Israeli conflict to American strategy, but Dulles felt even more passionate than most about the subject. He expressed the essence of the Alpha Ethos to the National Security Council in early 1958, two years after Alpha had completely died. Dulles argued that the entrenched positions of the Arabs and the Israelis were far apart and neither party would budge from them. In an ideal world, he stipulated, the United States would side with the Arabs. Such a policy, however, was impossible, because "the state of Israel was in fact the darling of Jewry throughout the world, and world Jewry was a formidable force indeed." He continued:

This Administration had gone further in trying to moderate the policy and position of Israel, and to show greater sympathy for the Arabs, than any previous U.S. Administration. On the other hand, there were certain courses of action which simply could not be followed, from the domestic political point of view. When the state of Israel had been established, both the Department of State and the Department of Defense had been in agreement that the establishment of Israel, in the circumstances, would inevitably lead to the situation in the Near East which now confronts us. Nevertheless, the warnings and advice of the Departments of State and Defense had been ignored.

The best proof of the potency of international Jewry is that the Soviet Union, while constantly hinting to the Arab states that it will agree to help the Arabs to dismember Israel, has never actually come out publicly with such a statement of support. The Soviets rely on hints, and they are playing the game very cautiously despite the great prize which they could win in the Near East if they supported the destruction of Israel. Accordingly, if the USSR doesn't dare to tackle this situation forthrightly, other nations must approach the problem with care too. Among all of our allies, not a single one would support the policy toward Israel which the Arabs are demanding. There is no situation in the world to which this Administration has given more thought than the Arab-Israeli dispute. There are very grave problems to be faced. There is no greater danger to U.S. security. Perhaps, indeed, the USSR will ultimately get control of the Near East; but, in any event, there has been no tendency whatsoever to minimize this danger in the State Department over the last ten years.[19]

For the first two years of the administration, Dulles followed a policy designed, as he explained to Shuckburgh, to "deflate the Jews." With his primary attention focused on the Canal Zone conflict, he could not launch a major effort on the Arab-Israeli front, but he prepared the groundwork by refusing to sell arms to Israel, rebuffing Israeli requests for security guarantees, and diminishing the level of financial assistance to the Jewish state. He designed these steps to increase American leverage so that, when the time came, the United States could offer defense assistance in return for Israeli territorial concessions.[20]

This policy of parsimonious support survived the midterm election in November 1954, when the Democrats, who were more supportive of Israel than the Republicans, managed to gain a majority in both the House and the Senate. Dulles felt, however, that he might not be able to withstand the burgeoning pro-Israel pressures much longer. He remembered all too well how, in the 1948 presidential election, both candidates, President Truman and New York Governor Thomas Dewey, had competed to demonstrate their commitment to Zionism. He assumed that the upcoming presidential campaign of 1956 would similarly force Eisenhower to make concrete commitments to Israel. Dulles, however, wanted to leverage any such commitments to force Israel to make sacrifices for peace.

His belief that the clock was ticking imbued him with an urgency, which he expressed to Eden and Shuckburgh in early 1955 when they came to Washington to deliver the first draft of Alpha. Dulles, Shuckburgh noted, "gave us an enlightening account of the power and influence of the Jews in America" and "said we have just about twelve months to do something in, before another election looms up and makes all action impossible."[21] This feeling of racing against the clock had an obvious impact on Dulles's twin decisions to ignore Egyptian hostility to Iraq and to build up Nasser.

In short, domestic American political considerations deeply influenced Alpha. Gazing out from Washington, Dulles could not see the Arabs clearly, because the supporters of Israel on Capitol Hill were blocking his field of vision.

Shuckburgh and Byroade

The Alpha Ethos also shaped the thinking of two key players in Dulles's circle of Middle East advisors: Evelyn Shuckburgh and Henry Byroade. Both men held views remarkably similar to Dulles's, and held them with a similar intensity. They came by them, however, in very different ways.

As a British diplomat, Shuckburgh focused on the impact of the Arab-Israeli conflict on the British imperial project. The British association with Zionism, he believed, had from the very beginning been a tragic error, both moral and strategic. "Palestine," he wrote, "was the burial ground of our hopes for maintaining the British position in the Middle East. I suppose this was inevitable from the time of the Balfour Declaration." Shuckburgh wrote these words in an autobiographical sketch that he composed in the final years of his life, in the 1990s, but he came to this conclusion very early. As a young man, still in his twenties, while serving in Cairo in one of his first diplomatic positions, he conveyed his growing concern in a letter to his father. "[T]here can be no doubt that the Arab world in general is getting slowly but surely excited about [Zionism]," he wrote. "How can we risk prejudicing our whole position in the Arab world for the sake of Palestine?" In the aftermath of the Munich Agreement, Shuckburgh again wrote to his father, asserting that "the Palestine policy is *infinitely* shame-making compared with the refusal to go to war over Czechoslovakia. In Palestine we, with our own hands, are having to burn and explode villagers out of their villages" in order to suppress a Palestinian revolt against the Zionists.[22]

If British support for Zionism undermined the empire, it also left a deep scar on Shuckburgh personally. In the 1920s, his father held the Palestine portfolio in the British colonial office, and he suffered greatly under the strain. "All through my teens," Shuckburgh remembered, "I was aware that he found this an almost unbearable burden and it brought him to nervous breakdown." To Shuckburgh, the ultimate cause of the problem was obvious and incontrovertible: Jewish intransigence. "After Dachau," the Palestine question "went out of control. The only people from then on who could have brought it to a peaceful conclusion were the Jews themselves. . . . But they would not."[23]

On the American side, Henry Byroade heartily agreed that the key to solving the conflict was convincing the Jews to compromise. "Hank" to his friends, Byroade was a gregarious military officer from Indiana. Graduating from West Point in 1937, he spent World War II in India and China building airfields for the American airlift that flew over the Himalayas, "the Hump," to supply the Chinese nationalist government of Chiang Kai-shek.

When he returned to Washington, Byroade's role in the Hump effort proved useful in organizing the Berlin Airlift in 1948. His military career was brought to an end at a cocktail party when Dean Acheson, the secretary of state, approached the secretary of the army and cut a deal that moved Byroade out of the Pentagon with the intention of asking him to become the assistant secretary of state for the Middle East. At this late point in the Truman administration, the Middle East experts in the State Department were refusing to take the top job—either in protest over Truman's pro-Israel stance, or for fear of being tainted by association with the administration's policy, or both. Acheson sought somebody fresh and free of political baggage. The young brigadier general fit the bill perfectly.

Byroade accepted. But after a quick tour of the Middle East, he also fully absorbed the perspective of the Near East bureau, which regarded Truman's recognition of Israel as one of the greatest strategic blunders in American diplomatic history. When supporters of Israel caught wind of his views, they channeled their concerns to President Truman, who invited Byroade to the White House for a personal vetting. Byroade did not disguise his thinking from Truman. "I went into considerable detail about my concern at the position of the United States in the Arab states, because of our almost all-out support for Israel," he recounted years later in an oral history interview. In the event, Truman mounted no opposition, and Byroade served in his administration for seven months before the election of November 1952.

When the Eisenhower administration took over, Dulles approved of Byroade's views and kept him in place. "I was," Byroade later recounted, "the only Truman appointee left in the State Department, after they had cleaned house, so to speak." And he was "glad to stay," thinking that "we could have a more sensible policy on the Middle East." After all, Eisenhower "knew more about the Middle East problem and its strategic significance and all that, which Truman really hadn't the background, when Israel was created in 1948, to fully appreciate."[24]

Collective Blind Spot

Before long, however, Byroade made several public remarks that disparaged Zionism. A barrage of Jewish criticism rained down on him, forcing Dulles to move him out of Washington. Byroade took up a posting as ambassador to Egypt, where he would play a central role in implementing Eisenhower's Middle East strategy. He arrived in Cairo in February 1955—at the very moment when Dulles was rolling out Alpha, the Turks and Iraqis were signing their pact, and Israel was launching the Gaza Raid.

To another man, the crosscurrents might have seemed bewildering, but Byroade had a very clear idea of the task before him. Like Shuckburgh, he believed strongly that Arab-Israeli peace was within reach—if only the Americans could muster the will to keep the Israelis in check. Byroade and Shuckburgh thus had a north star to guide them through the Middle Eastern night: compelling Israel, first, to moderate the kind of aggressive behavior that it exhibited in operations such as the Gaza Raid and Operation Susannah, and, second, to make painful concessions for peace. Years later Byroade registered no second thoughts about this firm belief. "I felt Israel would be far wiser to make the kind of peace that I still think they could have made in the '50s," he said. "I remember telling [Israeli Prime Minister David] Ben-Gurion, 'If you go ahead and do it, your people are so capable, they'll be running every bank in the Middle East in 50 years. And isn't that better than sitting here behind barbed wire?' He said, 'No.'"[25] Byroade's confidence in this view was unshakable until the day he died.

As for Shuckburgh, during Alpha's planning and launch, he showed no inkling of the full significance of Nasser's regional ambitions—a surprising fact given his prediction of an Egyptian backlash to the Baghdad Pact. Moreover, on February 10, 1955, after meeting with the Egyptian ambassador in London, Shuckburgh wrote in his diary, "The Egyptians are in a state of fury about Nuri's determination to sign a pact with Turkey, and will not be comforted. I had no idea they were quite so jealous of Iraq."[26]

When he arrived in Cairo, Byroade, like Shuckburgh, was shocked to discover the depth of the Egyptian hatred for the Northern Tier. At his first meeting with Nasser, the entire evening was spent talking about nothing else. "I sensed an intense dislike for Nuri Said as a person that I had not previously taken into account," he reported back to Washington candidly.[27] "I am unable at this early stage to understand fully the apparent depth of Egyptian feeling. There is no doubt in my mind that Nasser sincerely feels he was cast aside by the US in favor of Nuri of Iraq."[28]

Byroade's ignorance of inter-Arab politics and his deep conviction that forcing concessions from Israel was the key to winning over Nasser made it easy for him to convince himself that Nasser's conflict with Iraq was ephemeral. Like Caffery before him, he produced reports that helped Dulles remain comfortable in his belief that building up Nasser would entail no significant costs to the United States elsewhere in the region. The desire of Egypt "to resume its Arab world leadership," Byroade argued, was causing it to build a "new club"—that is, the Egyptian-Syrian-Saudi alliance. (In fact, the club had been in existence for ten years, since the foundation of the Arab League.) "We believe that once Egypt considers it has regained the initiative and restored its prestige, it will be more inclined to think and act reasonably. We do not believe that Egypt is particularly enthusiastic about the new club or that she has any illusions regarding its military potency."

Nasser's anti-Iraqi alliance would fall of its own weight, Byroade believed. It would be "counter-productive," therefore, to meet the new organization "head on with public disapproval." A hostile American policy would only provoke an "all-out counter-attack on the US in much of the Arab world and only increase Egyptian-Syrian-Saudi determination to proceed as planned."[29] The State Department endorsed this view, which comported with its own deep-seated inclinations. "We are encouraged," it cabled to Middle East ambassadors, by Byroade's view that the new alliance will "likely wither away."[30] Thus with the State Department's blessing, Byroade was free to focus on his top priority: restraining Israel. On the same night that Nasser talked to him at length regarding his hostility to the Northern Tier, the Israelis launched the Gaza Raid, which Byroade, having only just arrived in Egypt, took as a personal affront. "Damn it," he later told the Israeli ambassador to Washington, Abba Eban. "I told you I'd do what I could do out there, but you didn't give me 24 hours before you come charging across the border."[31]

Had Byroade not been convinced that Nasser's aspiration to destroy the Iraq-centered alliance was destined to wither away, he might have analyzed the Gaza raid differently. He might have recognized that, however painful the raid was to Nasser, it also provided him with valuable benefits. Not least of all, it won him deep sympathy among many Americans, including Byroade himself— a valuable commodity at a moment when Nasser was working to subvert Iraq, an ally of the West. Second, the Israeli attack helped Nasser substantiate his claim to be the shield of the Arabs. Voice of the Arabs immediately seized the opportunity. "Israel," it falsely reported, "launched an attack against Egypt because of [the latter's] well-known opposition to the pact, her frank hostility to Israel, and her jealous support of Arab nationalism."[32] The Gaza Raid, from this perspective, was a propaganda coup for Nasser.

In sum, as American and British officials were just beginning to develop an awareness of the strategic implications of Nasser's opposition to the Northern Tier, they were also reaffirming one of the core assumptions of the honest broker paradigm: that distancing the United States from Israel would win the goodwill of all Arabs, and especially the Egyptians. This reaffirmation prevented them from recognizing the deepest drivers of the Arab and Muslim states, namely their rivalries with each other for power and authority. Impelled by these false assumptions, the Americans and the British had become convinced of the need to build up Nasser and to help him recoup the prestige that he had lost from the twin blows of the Baghdad Pact and the Gaza Raid.

Therein lies the Alpha contradiction: in blind pursuit of an illusory Arab-Israeli peace, the Americans consciously strengthened the regional actor who saw greatest advantage in perpetuating the conflict with Israel and who was also working to undermine the Western position in the Middle East.

CHAPTER 7

Deception

On September 27, 1955, Nasser shocked the world with the announcement that Egypt had concluded an arms deal with Czechoslovakia. The deal, it would soon emerge, was huge. According to credible reports, it included, among many other elements, 170 tanks, 90–100 fighter jets, 48 jet bombers, 20 transport planes, 2 destroyers, 12 torpedo boats, and 6 submarines. Once the Egyptians managed to absorb all of this equipment into their ranks, the military balance with Israel would tip decidedly in Egypt's favor.[1] Prague, everyone knew, did not act independently of Moscow. In one deft move, the Soviets had leapfrogged over America's allies on its southern perimeter and opened up a Middle Eastern front in the Cold War.

To Eisenhower and his advisors, it was obvious that leaders in Moscow intended to undermine the Western security system in the region. But what about Nasser? Did Nasser share the Soviets' goals? The Americans concluded, incorrectly, that he did not. No innocent misperception, their error was the product of a sophisticated Egyptian campaign of deception. Their mistaken judgment was one of Nasser's greatest achievements.

The announcement of the arms deal may have shocked the world, but it did not surprise Eisenhower. He had received ample warning—from, of all people, Nasser himself. Throughout the summer of 1955, the Egyptian leader had periodically kept Ambassador Byroade apprised of his dealings with the Soviet Union. In giving Nasser credit for his transparency, the Americans failed to recognize that he was shaping their perceptions, subtly persuading them that his new relationship with the Soviet Union did not imply any hostility on his part to the West.

To understand just how Nasser managed this feat, we must spool back six months, to the beginning of the Soviet-Egyptian arms negotiations, and examine the gap between how those negotiations actually began and what Nasser told the Americans about them.

The Bandung Myth

Nasser's successful deception has had a lasting impact on Western historiography, which has tended to accept his misinformation as truth. Perhaps the best example of this tendency is the widespread acceptance of what might be called the Bandung Myth— a largely false account of how, in April 1955, at the first Afro-Asian conference of nonaligned nations, Nasser first hit upon the idea of getting the Soviets to arm Egypt. Nasser and his colleagues told a standard story about Bandung—first to Western diplomats and then to journalists. Patrick Seale's *The Struggle for Syria*, first published in 1965, contains a clear and concise version of the rehearsed Egyptian account, based on long interviews with Salah Salim, the Dancing Major, a principal player in that mythic version.[2]

According to Salim, the key event that drove Nasser to search for arms was the Gaza Raid of February 28, 1955. The Israeli attack came at a moment when the Egyptian military was desperately short of equipment and spare parts, which, so the story goes, neither the British nor the Americans were willing to supply. Six weeks later, when Nasser attended the Bandung Conference of African and Asian states, he was still stinging from the raid. As he departed Egypt for Bandung, Indonesia, the arms deficit between him and Israel troubled him greatly. He saw no viable option on the horizon.

When the Egyptians arrived for the conference, a remedy appeared, wholly unexpectedly and from a surprising source—the foreign minister of the People's Republic of China, Zhou Enlai. Zhou suggested to Nasser that the Egyptians should turn to the Soviets for help. The idea of reaching out to Moscow, Salim asks us to believe, had never really occurred to Nasser before this moment. According to Salim, who joined Nasser in the meeting with Zhou, it was he who suggested to Nasser that the Egyptians should ask the Chinese for help in acquiring weapons. "Let us try," he said to Nasser. "We have nothing to lose!" Nasser relented. When he and Salim proceeded to raise the subject, Zhou said, "This matter should be discussed with the Soviets." He then helped connect Cairo to Moscow. Back in Egypt after the conference, the Soviet ambassador in Cairo, Daniel Solod, came to the Egyptians and said, "The message you sent [through Zhou] has reached us and we are ready to come to an understanding."[3]

We can say with confidence that this tale is fanciful, thanks to the pathbreaking work of historian Guy Laron, who has unearthed key Soviet diplomatic dispatches, which allow us to sketch out a rough timeline of the arms negotiations between Moscow and Cairo.[4] In March 1955, a month before Nasser had set out for Bandung, he had already authorized an Egyptian official to begin the negotiations that culminated in the September announcement. In short, Nasser needed no prodding from Salim to talk to Zhou; and Zhou, in turn, did not play a pivotal role in bringing the Soviets to Nasser.

This is not to say that the meeting with Zhou did not take place, or that Zhou did not help facilitate in some way—just that the character of the meeting was very different from what Nasser had us believe. Some details about that meeting appear in a cable that the Soviet ambassador in Cairo sent to Moscow after Nasser briefed him on the Bandung Conference.[5] The cable does not mention Chinese mediation. Nasser did tell Ambassador Solod about his meeting with Zhou, but his account of the conversation with the Chinese statesman focused not on the question of weapons for Egypt but on the difficulty for Nasser of recognizing the Chinese communist government, a step that the Soviet Union was urging him to take. Nasser explained that, "in his heart of hearts he was for recognizing China," but he had to tread carefully, because "the Americans and the British were exerting pressure on the Egyptian government not to have any relations with China." Zhou, Nasser said, understood the constraints on him. "Egypt could not ignore the Anglo-American position for fear that they might stop the evacuation of the British forces from the Canal Zone."[6]

From Solod's report, two points are obvious. First, a conspiratorial tone had already crept into Nasser's relationship with the Soviets. Moscow understood that Nasser was moving Egypt out of the Western security system; it was helping him as he carefully navigated his course. Second, Nasser had to hide his actions from the Americans, because his regime was still highly vulnerable to retribution. The last British soldier would not leave the Canal Zone until mid-1956. If his collusion with the Soviets were to anger the Americans, they had at their disposal many tools for punishing him. As Nasser himself intimated to Solod, Washington and London could halt the withdrawal of the British troops from the Canal Zone. In addition, they might work to build up Iraq and the Baghdad Pact, or to support Israeli border raids—or to drive down the value of Egyptian cotton on the international market. The menu of available punishments was long.

Moderates and Hard-liners

The beauty of the Bandung myth was the illusion of transparency that Nasser created by revealing his burgeoning relationship with the Soviets. His deception was subtle: he concealed his motives and intentions, not his actions. He convinced the Americans that he, personally, was pro-Western but surrounded by more extreme elements. Any effort to undermine him would only bring to power hard-line nationalists who were even more anti-American, more hostile to Israel, and more favorably disposed to the Soviet Union. The Bandung Myth reinforced this argument by making it seem as if Nasser never actively solicited any offers from Moscow. It was Salim, not Nasser, who advocated speaking to Zhou, and it was Zhou who brought the Soviets to the Egyptians. Nasser was a virtual bystander.

The role of Salim in the myth is particularly noteworthy. In reality, Salim was a weak individual—a man so subservient to Nasser that he broke down crying when, at the Sarsank summit, he disappointed his boss. In the myth, however, he is a member of a camp of hard-liners, men ready to topple Nasser if he moves too close to the Americans or appears too deferential to Israel. In short, the myth allowed Nasser to play on the Americans' sense of guilt, because *their* support for Israel was undermining Nasser, leaving him politically exposed, vulnerable to an attack from the political right.

In retrospect, we can hear the Egyptians broadcasting that theme loud and clear in a set of exchanges that took place in Cairo in August 1955 between Ahmed Hussein, the Egyptian ambassador to the United States, and Henry Byroade. Two months earlier, in June, Nasser had informed Washington that Moscow had offered him weapons, and now, the Soviets and Egyptians were putting the final touches on their arms agreement. Hussein, who had a pro-American reputation, told Byroade that he had personally warned Nasser about "the danger of [the] Salim brothers . . . particularly Salah Salim." Nasser, however, had his back to the wall. His fellow officers "were desperate for arms and word was getting out that these new [Soviet] offers had been made. With the army in this mood and with its general lack of confidence in America . . . ,

[Nasser] had to reckon with [the] fact [that] he would be placing his position in jeopardy" if he were to reject Moscow. To do so "would appear nonsensical to [the] average officer who [was] convinced [that the West was] determined [to] keep Egypt weaker than Israel and who saw no danger [in] accepting arms from any source available."

A few days earlier Hussein had provided Byroade related information designed to prove that the Soviets and the Egyptian hard-liners had painted Nasser into a corner. Radio Moscow, Hussein reported, had announced, in an Arabic-language broadcast, that the Soviet Union was on the verge of offering "free military assistance to Egypt." Nasser had managed to keep the full text of the report out of the press, but news of the broadcast "was getting around." The Revolutionary Command Council (RCC), the junta's ruling body, discussed the broadcast in one of its meetings, and the prevailing sentiment was, Hussein said, that "Egypt should not refuse such an offer if it were in fact officially made."[7]

To substantiate his claim that the hard-liners had nearly checkmated Nasser, Hussein passed to Byroade a partial transcript of the Soviet radio broadcast. Washington quickly informed Byroade that a review of Soviet broadcasts, which were closely monitored, revealed no evidence of an offer even remotely resembling the one that Hussein described. Byroade, however, refused to entertain the idea that Nasser was conning him. "[T]here [is] absolutely no doubt [in] my mind," he replied to Washington, "that Hussein and Nasser believe [that the] broadcast was made and that [the] RCC meeting was held on this subject."[8]

The transcript, however, was almost certainly a fabrication. When talking to the Soviet ambassador in Cairo, Nasser presented himself not as a man with his back to the wall but as a leader with a strategic plan. "To begin with," he said, "the proclamation of an independent Egyptian policy was one of the revolution's main aims," but the presence of thousands of British troops in the Canal Zone, just 100 miles from Cairo, made it impossible to break with the West openly on matters of regional defense. Nasser, therefore, had intended to wait, "to implement a neutralist policy only after the complete evacuation of British troops from the Canal Zone." That patient plan, however, became unworkable when the West began to build a regional defense organization without Egypt. "[T]he signing of the Turkish-Iraqi pact in February 1955, and Egypt's fear that the rest of the Arab countries might join in, left the Egyptian government no choice other than to proclaim a neutralist policy ahead of the allotted time and [to] declare that it would not participate in any Western military alliances."[9] Clearly, Nasser's deep-seated opposition to Western domination, his desire to make Egypt the master of the Arab world, and his hostility to the Baghdad Pact had laid the foundation for strategic cooperation with the Soviet Union.

Dangle and Delay

At the precise moment when Nasser was making his move toward Moscow, Dulles, in consultation with Eden, decided in favor of launching Alpha. In mid-March 1955, Dulles instructed Byroade to begin discussions with Nasser. "We are fully cognizant of [the] difficulties in an approach to Nasser on Alpha at this time," he wrote, "but we are inclined to resolve [those] doubts in favor of an approach rather than in favor of further delay."[10] Byroade and his British colleague disagreed. They produced a shared assessment arguing that the Baghdad Pact and the Gaza Raid had conspired to create an atmosphere that was inhospitable to Alpha. "Nasser is sore and suspicious," the ambassadors reported. "It would be both unwise and useless to make [an] official secret approach to [Nasser] at the present time."[11]

Byroade cabled Dulles separately to explain his thinking in greater depth. A move to solve the Arab-Israeli conflict at this moment, he argued, would play into the hands of the hard-liners.

Salah Salim, he reported, was disseminating propaganda claiming that the "real motive" of the Americans for having supported the Baghdad Pact was to force the Arabs to accept Israel and integrate it into a regional defense system. Nasser had "acquiesced" in the propaganda of his hard-liners, but he did not really believe it. However, Byroade warned, if Nasser were to learn "that the US and UK have been working for some time on [a] specific plan for [the] settlement of [the] Arab-Israeli dispute, there is [a] great danger [that] he would conclude" that Salah Salim was correct.[12]

Byroade was being played, to be sure; nevertheless, there was a grain of truth in the line that the Egyptians were feeding him. An American initiative to solve the Palestine question would place Nasser on the horns of a dilemma. On the one hand, if he were to help lead a peace initiative, he would destroy the ideological foundation of his campaign against the Baghdad Pact, which his propaganda was depicting as a Western conspiracy to support Israel. On the other hand, if he rejected the peace process, he would lose the goodwill of the Americans, which he still needed in order to restrain the British. To manage his dilemma, Nasser devised a clever stratagem. Call it dangle and delay. He dangled out the possibility of launching a peace process, but then concocted a series of plausible reasons for delaying any action. The dangle earned him goodwill; it kept the Americans sympathetic and solicitous. The delay bought him the time that he needed to establish his relationship with the Soviets and to attack the Baghdad Pact without fear of Western retribution.

To make it harder for the Americans to see through this maneuver, Nasser led the Americans to conclude that the regime was divided, hard-liners versus moderates, over whether the time was ripe to solve the Arab-Israeli conflict. The moderate faction, supposedly led by Foreign Minister Muhammad Fawzi, was eager to find a solution, but the hard-liners, led by Salah Salim, worked to scuttle their efforts. Nasser, of course, was caught in the middle.

On March 26, five days after Byroade told Dulles that launching Alpha would be "unwise and useless," Fawzi shocked the American ambassador by arguing the exact opposite. In the midst of a routine conversation, he suddenly volunteered that the Egyptians and the Americans should work together to solve the Arab-Israeli conflict. Within the regime, he said, "there were widely varying schools of thought as to when a real effort should be made to solve this problem. He personally was inclined to think that there was no time to lose." Only a few days earlier Byroade had met with Nasser and Salah Salim, who were both in a very different frame of mind. Byroade described the meeting to Fawzi and said, "I hoped I had been able to erase some of the suspicions from Nasser's mind but was certain I had failed as regards Salah Salim."

Fawzi assured Byroade that he, for one, was ready to get down to serious business. As if to prove his point, he began discussing specific terms of a peace deal. No doubt thrilled by what he was hearing, Byroade told Fawzi that he "was certain" that the president and the secretary of state "would wish me to have extremely frank and quite secret talks on this subject here in Egypt."[13] Within a week, Byroade and Fawzi met again, now fully empowered by Eisenhower and Nasser to explore possibilities for peace.

Byroade launched Alpha. He emphasized that time was of the essence. The United States, he explained, had been following a "tough policy of deflating Israel," refusing to sell it arms, rejecting its requests for a security guarantee, and reducing financial assistance to it. This policy could not be pursued indefinitely, especially because the 1956 presidential campaign was looming. "Our view," Byroade stated clearly, "is that we should work out with Egypt a basic plan." Once Cairo and Washington were in agreement, they would then engage the Israelis and the other Arab states. "In a general way," Byroade explained, "what we had in mind was [a] slightly smaller Israel."

Fawzi said he "was in complete agreement" with the basic concept. However, a slight delay was unavoidable. For the next month the Egyptian elite would be busy with the Bandung Conference, which would not end until April 24. After we return from the conference, Fawzi said, "we should try to reach a meeting of the minds." The "iron was now hot," Fawzi said.[14]

But was it? Two days later Nasser came to dinner at Byroade's house and stayed until three in the morning. The personal atmosphere between the two was warm, but, on Alpha, Nasser was "less forthcoming than Fawzi." He doubted whether he could take an initiative "until things had calmed down somewhat in [the] Arab world." He did not, however, close the door entirely on Alpha. Like Fawzi, he suggested the two resume their conversation after the Bandung Conference—a delay of three or four weeks.[15]

Wanting No for an Answer

Byroade was riding high. He was the lead officer on Eisenhower's top priority in the Middle East, an area that was quickly becoming a main arena in the Cold War. He enjoyed the full support of the secretary of state, and the president himself was tracking his work with great interest. What more could an ambassador to Egypt want? Just one thing: an appointment with Nasser. That, however, was too much to ask. When Nasser returned from Bandung, he dodged Byroade for two months, refusing to meet until the second week of June. In the meantime, Nasser's negotiations with the Soviets proceeded apace.

When Nasser finally received Byroade, on June 9, he refused to discuss Alpha. A series of violent incidents between Egypt and Israel had erupted (incidents for which the Americans held the Egyptians at least as responsible as the Israelis). Under the circumstances, Byroade reported, it was impossible to expect "serious talks regarding Alpha."[16] As disappointing as this news was, it paled in comparison with what Byroade reported next: the Soviet Union had made

Nasser an offer of weapons—and Nasser was inclined to accept it. Why? Nasser told Byroade that "he felt personally responsible" for the Egyptians killed in the Gaza Raid.[17] He was in desperate need of weaponry in order to reestablish his tattered credibility with his hard-line officers. "At [the] present moment," Byroade explained, "it [is] clear [that Nasser] would pull down [the] temple on top of [his] regime rather than suffer what he considers humiliation and pressures upon him, particularly from Israel."[18]

Moscow, Nasser claimed, had cleverly presented its arms offer to the Egyptians as a purely commercial transaction. In contrast to Western offers, that is to say, it came with no political strings. Therefore, he said, it would be impossible for the United States to match the Soviet offer.

This assertion was false, and Nasser knew it. On two earlier occasions, Eisenhower had offered to *give* Egypt weaponry—in July and October 1954, after the two major advances in the Anglo-Egyptian negotiations. Nasser had turned down both offers, citing his fear of offending Egyptian public opinion. United States law mandated that, in order to receive military aid, foreign governments must sign an aid agreement. The Egyptians, Nasser claimed, would interpret such a document as a violation of their sovereignty, a tool for placing Egypt once again under the control of Western imperialism.

Nasser was, of course, being deceptive. For the better part of two years, Egyptian propagandists had been demanding that Baghdad sever its independent security relationship with the West, and that it work to build a multilateral Arab security system, within the framework of the Arab League, dedicated to combatting Zionism and imperialism. If Nasser himself were to accept weaponry from the United States, he would have undermined his core message.

The Americans, however, took Nasser's deceptive explanation at face value—for the time being, at least. As we will see in Chapter 9, many months later the State Department would come to the conclusion, over the strenuous objections of Byroade, that Nasser's explanations for rejecting American arms had been entirely insincere. In summer 1955, however, their suspicions had yet to be aroused. When Nasser told Byroade, disingenuously, that Americans would never supply Egypt with arms, Byroade vigorously disputed the contention. Egypt, he was almost certain, was entirely free to purchase arms from the United States (the idea being that a purely commercial transaction would match the terms of the Soviet Union, and would bypass the need for the aid agreement, the factor that Nasser had cited as the stumbling block to cooperation).

The Egyptian leader expressed further skepticism. Out of deference to Israel, he said, the United States would never sell Egypt "significant amounts of equipment."[19] Determined to prove Nasser wrong, Byroade strongly urged him to put the Americans to the test. Nasser relented. Shortly thereafter he produced a list of armaments for purchase, which, on July 2, Byroade forwarded on to Washington with a strong recommendation for approval.[20]

On July 11, Eisenhower reviewed the list, approved it, and said, "[W]e should make a concerted effort to woo Nasser."[21]

But Nasser was beyond wooing. He did not respond to the American offer for another seven weeks; then, in mid-August, he gave Byroade some bad news. Egypt's foreign currency balances, he had just discovered, were low, and the purchase of American weapons would break the bank. Would Washington, therefore, allow him to buy the weapons in Egyptian pounds instead? Byroade told Nasser that the United States, as far as he knew, had never let any other nation pay in local currency. He doubted that Washington would break with this precedent, but he would see what he could do.[22] Before he received a definitive answer to the question, Nasser announced the Soviet-Egyptian arms deal.

On the eve of the announcement, Nasser explained in detail to the Soviet ambassador how he had played the Americans. He had, first of all, rejected their offer to grant Egypt weapons, and then, second, refused to purchase them in dollars. He agreed only to pay in Egyptian currency, he explained to Solod, because he knew "full well that American law allowed acquisition of weapons in dollars only."[23] By putting on an elaborate show of attempting to find a solution, Nasser corroborated his claim that he, personally, was laboring to keep Egypt in the Western camp. And by forcing the Americans, in the end, to give him a no for an answer, he placed the onus for failure, at least partially, on them.

Hiding in Plain Sight

Throughout the summer, while the Egyptian-Soviet and Egyptian-American arms discussions were going on simultaneously, Nasser continued his policy, with respect to Egyptian-Israeli peace negotiations, of dangle and delay. On June 24, Dulles met with Foreign Minister Fawzi in San Francisco, where they were celebrating the tenth anniversary of the United Nations. Having recently revealed to the Americans that he had received a Soviet offer of arms, Nasser no doubt ordered Fawzi to soften them up by resuscitating Alpha. In any case, Fawzi advocated the immediate launch of an initiative to achieve "a definitive settlement" of the Arab-Israeli conflict.[24]

Dulles readily agreed, but Nasser again dragged his feet, and as the weeks wore on, the secretary of state grew increasingly impatient. In his restless search for a way to regain momentum, his mind settled on a major public address, by him, announcing the readiness of Eisenhower to pursue an Arab-Israeli peace agreement. On August 26, Dulles indeed delivered the speech, which pointed to three major problems plaguing the Middle East: refugees, a climate of fear, and the absence of permanent borders between the warring sides. President Eisenhower, he said, stood ready to help solve all three—by, among other steps, providing economic assistance and security guarantees.[25]

Nasser could not afford to anger Dulles by directly opposing this initiative, which the Americans regarded as a highly significant development. So, instead, he scuttled it indirectly. On the night of August 25, the day before Dulles's speech, the United States received intelligence indicating that Nasser was in the midst of launching a massive attack against Israel. Byroade took the unusual step of contacting Egyptian military officers to warn them not to attack. The secretary of state's speech was "an extremely good development for [the] Arab side," he argued. "[W]hat a great pity it would be if Egypt would be drawn into [an] action which might either cancel [the] speech or cause [a] radical change in [the] text."[26]

The officers took Byroade's message, conveyed it to Nasser, then called back later to inform him that the Egyptian leader, heeding the American request, had called off the attack. There was, however, one glitch. Before the order to halt the operation had reached them, some commando units had already set out on their missions—units that, supposedly, had no radios and therefore could not be recalled. In the following days, those commandos penetrated deeper into Israel than ever before, reaching the outskirts of Tel Aviv. By the end of the first day, they had carried out at least three raids; by the end of the first week, more than twenty—killing eleven Israelis and wounding nine.

Meanwhile, Nasser's propaganda machine gloated over the attacks. Ahmad Said, the leading personality on Voice of the Arabs, commemorated the raids with a poem: "O Israel! Repent your aggression and be ready for the day of your destruction. The Arabs of Egypt have found their way to Tel Aviv. [. . .] O Israel! Listen to this very carefully, the end of your life is imminent. The Arabs of Egypt have found their way to Tel Aviv."[27]

Two contradictory pictures of Nasser emerged from these attacks—one among rank-and-file Arabs on the street, and the other among American diplomats and officials in the upper reaches of government. Arabs saw Nasser as the defiant nationalist, a leader who was prepared to challenge Israel and the United States on the very day when the American secretary of state was calling on the Arabs, as they saw it, to bow down and surrender. Meanwhile, American officials saw Nasser as a cooperative partner, a moderate working to calm hotheads who had lost control of a volatile situation.

The American ambassador in Cairo, for one, always saw Nasser as honest, transparent, and pro-Western. The day after Dulles's speech, Byroade met with the Egyptian leader to elicit his response to the secretary of state's proposals. Nasser professed to be "somewhat confused" by the address, parts of which he "did not understand." He asked many questions. After this show of befuddlement, he switched topics entirely to, of all things, Morocco. He explained that Iraqi Prime Minister Nuri al-Said had taken the lead in calling on the Arab states "to attack France" for the war it was waging against the Algerian National Liberation Front. Seeking to one-up the Iraqis, Nasser planned to criticize the United States for arming France against the North Africans. He asked Byroade's permission to state publicly that he had lodged a complaint with the United States about its support for France. "Certainly," the American ambassador said.[28]

Byroade had come to the meeting hoping to hear a favorable review of Dulles's speech. He left disappointed, but only after granting Nasser assistance in broadcasting anti-American propaganda. Nasser had picked his pockets—and not for the last time. The August attacks ensured that the announcement of the Soviet arms deal, one month later, would receive a tumultuous reception. All of this, however, was lost on Byroade. One week before the announcement, Nasser sent an intermediary to notify the ambassador that the arms deal was now an accomplished fact. Nasser conveyed his appreciation for Byroade's sincere efforts to inform him of the dangers of friendship with the Soviet Union. He hoped Byroade understood that he was acting against Israel, not the United States, and that he had no choice. Things had simply gotten to such a grave state that he "could not hold off revolution in [the] Army if he did not accept the Soviet offer."[29]

When Byroade reported this conversation to Washington, he expressed unqualified agreement with Nasser's assessment. If the Egyptian leader had turned down the Soviet offer, Byroade explained, he "probably could not have survived."

Nasser's deception had worked like a charm.

CHAPTER 8

K and Big Brother

Eisenhower was not asking for much—just one more day of golf before returning to Washington. It was a Friday, September 23, 1955, and he was in Denver on the tail end of a vacation. No sooner had he taken to the course at Cherry Hills Country Club than he received word that Foster Dulles was trying to reach him on the phone. Eisenhower went straight back to the clubhouse and picked up the receiver, but there was no one on the other end of the line. In the meantime, Dulles had scurried off to another meeting, leaving word with the operator that he would call back in an hour. Eisenhower returned to the course, hit a few shots, and then came back at the appointed time. When Dulles tried calling again, a technical glitch prevented him from getting through, and Ike headed back out to the course. Before long, however, he found himself trekking back to the clubhouse again. This time he successfully connected with Dulles.

The secretary of state's week had been filled with meetings at the United Nations General Assembly in New York. One purpose in calling now was to update Eisenhower on the Soviet-Egyptian arms deal. Dulles told the president that it was very likely that the Israelis would soon launch a preemptive war, striking before the Egyptian armed forces would have the chance to absorb the new weapons. The only way to prevent such a conflict would be to grant Israel a security guarantee, which, he said, "would throw the

Arabs in the hands of the Soviets." The ideal solution, therefore, would be to stop the deal cold, right now, before it went any further. However, it would be nearly impossible to convince Nasser to turn away from the offer, because, Dulles said, "he feels the Army will overthrow him . . . if he refuses to take it."[1]

The alternative was to try to stop the deal in Moscow. Dulles had gotten nowhere in a discussion in New York with Molotov, the Soviet foreign minister, but he still thought it worthwhile to have the president raise the issue directly with the Soviets. In July, Eisenhower had attended the Geneva Summit of the "Big Four"—Britain, France, the Soviet Union, and the United States—which had generated a temporary thaw in the Cold War. The Soviet decision to start an arms race in the Middle East, however, ran directly counter to the so-called spirit of Geneva. It might help to call the Soviets out on the contradiction, and Dulles volunteered to produce a draft letter for the president. The two made plans to talk the following morning.

Ike returned to his golf game, intent on salvaging at least a few holes before calling it a day. Just as he was beginning to lose himself in the game, however, Dulles rang back—call number four. This time, however, it was a false alarm. Not realizing that Eisenhower and Dulles had finally managed to reach each other, a telephone operator was still trying to connect them. "My disposition deteriorated rapidly," Eisenhower writes in his memoirs.[2] In fact, he was in a towering rage. "The veins stood out on his forehead like whipcords," recalled his golfing companion.[3] That night Ike suffered a massive heart attack and nearly died.

Roosevelt to Cairo

With Eisenhower incapacitated, management of the crisis in the Middle East fell to Dulles, and Dulles alone. One of his first decisions was to approve a trip to Cairo by Kermit "Kim" Roosevelt Jr., a senior CIA official responsible for the Middle East. In World War II, he had been stationed in Cairo while serving in the Office of Strategic Services (OSS), the predecessor of the CIA. During this assignment he befriended some of the leading Arabists in the State Department and became a valued member of a growing network of official experts on the Middle East. The grandson of President Theodore Roosevelt, he inherited not just a taste for adventure, but also a name that opened doors, a valuable asset anywhere but especially in the Middle East, where family ties trump all.

Not yet forty, Roosevelt's star was on the rise. In 1953, Eisenhower had sent him on a secret mission to Iran, where two years earlier the government of Prime Minister Mohammad Mosaddeq had nationalized the British-owned Anglo-Iranian Oil Company. A tense standoff between Britain and Iran ensued. Fearing that Iran was gravitating into the Soviet orbit, Eisenhower sent Roosevelt to fix the problem. And fix it he did—by helping to orchestrate a coup that toppled Mosaddeq.

When Roosevelt landed in Cairo, one of Nasser's aides was waiting for him on the tarmac. The man whisked him straight to Nasser's apartment. With the Egyptians intent on making a deal with the Soviets, and with the Americans eager to stop it, the scene was set for one of the most dramatic encounters of the Cold War. How, then, did Nasser receive Roosevelt? Like a backslapping buddy at a frat party. He poured the liquor, Roosevelt drained it, and the two men bantered amid the raucous laughter of their associates.

Miles Copeland, a CIA agent who accompanied Roosevelt on his mission, has left us with a firsthand report of their meetings. According to Copeland, "Nasser brought out a bottle of Scotch whiskey . . . and just as he did so, the telephone rang: the duty officer downstairs reported that Sir Humphrey Trevelyan, the British Ambassador, urgently wanted an appointment." Trevelyan was anxious to express his government's displeasure over the impending arms deal. He arrived at Nasser's offices a short while later.

While Nasser met with the ambassador downstairs, Roosevelt and Copeland entertained themselves upstairs, their presence entirely unknown to Trevelyan. After the ambassador left, Copeland and Roosevelt laughed with Nasser about what the look would have been on the British ambassador's face if one of the CIA agents had popped his head into the meeting and said, "Excuse me, Gamal, but we're out of soda. Where do you keep the soda?"[4]

The atmosphere between Roosevelt and Nasser was playful and friendly, one might even say *conspiratorial*. Both men thrived in a clandestine world, and for the past three years they had plotted together on sensitive issues, with Roosevelt, when not in Iran, shuttling back and forth between the United States and Egypt. Precisely how and when the relationship began remains a mystery, but by late 1954 Roosevelt and Nasser had grown close. According to Copeland, at one stage Roosevelt stayed in Cairo, undercover, for an extended period, tasked with helping to advance the Suez Canal Zone negotiations. Copeland discloses one very revealing fact: Roosevelt got the job thanks to Nasser, who personally requested his services. The American had a number of qualities that attracted the Egyptian, not least of which was, in Copeland's words, Roosevelt's "closeness to the Dulles brothers."[5]

Direct access to the Washington elite was certainly a priceless asset, but Roosevelt offered one additional advantage that Copeland conspicuously fails to mention: insurance. The CIA was known to have undermined a number of regimes around the world, and Roosevelt had helped to topple Mosaddeq. Nasser kept his friends close, but his enemies closer.

The Lobby

After the signing of the Anglo-Egyptian agreement in October 1954, Roosevelt threw himself into Alpha. The project tapped into a wellspring of passion. Roosevelt was nothing if not the embodiment of the Alpha Ethos—the belief in the strategic necessity of tacking away from Israel. His perspective crystallized early, during his OSS service in Cairo. In 1947, he came back to Egypt to write a book on the growing strategic importance of the Middle East. His arrival coincided with the British withdrawal from Palestine, and Truman's support for Zionism outraged Roosevelt and stirred him to action.

In February 1948, three months before the Israeli declaration of independence, he published an article titled "Partition of Palestine: A Lesson in Pressure Politics." Claiming to be uncovering "well kept secrets," the article traced the history of Zionist pressure on Truman. This was, Roosevelt writes, "an instructive, and disturbing, story." It was instructive because it demonstrated how a small but insistent Jewish minority had succeeded in foisting its narrow priorities on the entire United States government. It was disturbing because the goals of the minority harmed the nation as a whole. "Almost all Americans with diplomatic, educational, missionary, or business experience in the Middle East," Roosevelt explained, "protest fervently that support of political Zionism is directly contrary to our national interests, as well as to common justice." Truman had ignored "the express advice of the War, Navy, and State Departments," and he had, in an effort to win Jewish votes, supported the partition of Palestine in the United Nations.

The policy, Roosevelt argued, was playing directly into the hands of the Soviet Union. In the Middle East, the hour was growing late. If the Americans were to avoid losing the region to the Soviets, they had no choice but to cleanse their foreign policy of any association with Zionism. "The process by which Zionist Jews have been able to promote American support for the partition of Palestine demonstrates the vital need of a foreign policy based on national rather than partisan interests," he wrote. "The present course of world crisis will increasingly force upon Americans the realization that their national interest and those of the proposed Jewish state in Palestine are going to conflict."[6]

Around the time of the article's publication, Roosevelt joined forces with Virginia Gildersleeve, a professor of English and former dean of Barnard College. The two founded the Committee for Justice and Peace in the Holy Land (CJP), with Roosevelt serving as its executive director and motive force. The organization lobbied Washington to rescind the UN partition resolution and leave Palestine under Arab rule. In her memoir, Gildersleeve blamed the committee's failure to achieve its goals on "the Zionist control of the media of communication."[7]

After the founding of Israel, the CJP collapsed due to lack of funds. Roosevelt, who was not independently wealthy, needed a job. In late 1949, he joined the CIA and used his official perch in government to organize and fund a successor organization, the American Friends of the Middle East (AFME), headed by Dorothy Thompson, the famous journalist who did much to turn American public opinion in favor of joining the war in Europe. AFME, to put it bluntly, was a CIA front organization. Its official goal was to promote people-to-people exchanges between the United States and the Middle East, but its true priority was to counter the influence of the Israel lobby in domestic American policy. One aspect of this mission was to explain to Americans the vital necessity of accommodating Nasser's mix of pan-Arab nationalism and Cold War neutralism.[8]

Roosevelt clearly expresses these twin concerns—blunting the lobby and burnishing Nasser—in a letter that he sent to Nasser in late 1954 and that, years later, found its way into an Egyptian book about Hassan Tuhami, Nasser's liaison to the CIA. The letter offers a rare, unfiltered glimpse into the flavor of the relations between Roosevelt and the young Egyptian dictator. Writing from Washington on December 23, 1954, Roosevelt gave himself and Nasser code names: "K" and "Big Brother," respectively.

The subject of the letter is a meeting that "Jim" has proposed. (The reference is to James Eichelberger, the CIA's chief of station in Cairo, who does not receive a code name—a fact suggesting that the practice of disguising identities was a cliquish affectation rather than a true security precaution.) Roosevelt informs Nasser that an Israeli, traveling incognito on a South American passport, will arrive in Cairo. He insists that Nasser *must* receive the visitor, and promises to join the meeting personally in order to ensure that the Israeli representative "pulls no tricks which would enable his government to exploit the meeting for propaganda purposes." Roosevelt is obviously worried lest the Israelis use Nasser's coldness toward the meeting to buttress a claim, in Washington, that Nasser is not a partner for peace. "[Y]ou are in danger of walking into some well laid Israeli traps," Roosevelt writes. "[Y]ou are likely to get yourself into a disadvantageous cold war position vis-a-vis the Israeli with results which will handicap seriously the ability of your friends in the United States to counter Zionist pressures here."

In Roosevelt's portrayal, "the Israeli" (a collective noun) had laid siege to the Eisenhower administration. "As you are aware, these pressures are steadily mounting. The uncertainty of our own political position is such that we are presently most sensitive to them." In a letter such as this, Roosevelt writes, it is difficult to explain "why I am so fully convinced of the necessity for this meeting. . . . It is, I feel, the only way at hand to head off mounting tensions which are certain to endanger your position." Roosevelt's goal is to ensure that Eisenhower will blame the Israelis for any deterioration in Egyptian-Israeli relations. "I am hoping . . . ," Roosevelt writes, "to be able to provide our President with concrete evidence that if tensions continue to increase, it will be due to the Israeli rather than to the Egyptians."[9]

The pro-Israel lobby was the great spoiler, but Roosevelt was turning Nasser into an instrument for foiling the spoiler. Or so he thought.

The Lobby and the Arms Deal

Roosevelt's views on the pro-Israel lobby, in general, were in perfect harmony with those of the Dulles brothers. A few weeks after the announcement of the Soviet-Egyptian arms deal, Secretary of State Dulles called a cabinet-level meeting to assess the problem. He explained to the attendees, who included Vice President Nixon, Treasury Secretary George Humphrey, Defense Secretary Charles Erwin Wilson, and Attorney General Herbert Brownell Jr., that Truman's support for Israel was the reason Nasser had sought arms from the Soviets. "We [are] in the present jam," Dulles said, because Truman "always dealt with the area from a political standpoint and had tried to meet the wishes of the Zionists in this country and that had created a basic antagonism with the Arabs. That was what the Russians were now capitalizing on." It was, he said, "of the utmost importance for the welfare of the United States that we should get away from a political basis and try to develop a national non-partisan policy. Otherwise we would be apt to lose the whole area and possibly Africa, and this would be a major disaster for Western Europe as well as the United States."[10] These words, uttered extemporaneously in 1955, described a strategic perspective identical to the one that informed Roosevelt's tightly argued pamphlet from 1948.

Allen Dulles, the director of the CIA, was not in the meeting, but he was equally vexed by the problem—so much so that he entertained a conspiracy theory that construed the Israelis as the great beneficiaries of the warming relations between Moscow and Cairo. In actual fact, the Israelis regarded the arms deal as an existential threat, a national emergency of the first order. But the director of the CIA, like his brother, had his eyes on the power of the Israel lobby in Congress. The arms deal, he recognized, created the conditions for a coalition in Congress between supporters of Israel and rightwing anticommunists, who would now see Egypt,

the enemy of Israel, as an enemy of the United States in the Cold
War. Was this outcome a mere accident? Perhaps it was actually
the intended result of the arms deal. On September 29, 1955, two
days after Nasser announced the agreement, Allen Dulles met with
Evelyn Shuckburgh, and gave him a taste of his theory. A British
note taker kept a record of the conversation:

> In discussing the Russ-Egyptian arms deal, Mr. Dulles specu-
> lated about the Israeli attitude. He thought that so far their re-
> action had been suspiciously mild, and wondered if they might
> have encouraged, if not actually promoted the deal. Militarily,
> they had nothing to fear for the considerable period it would
> take to train the Egyptians in using any arms they got. In the
> meantime, they would count on easier access to arms from the
> West and a more sympathetic attitude if they [were to adopt a]
> more aggressive policy.[11]

The Israelis, the director of the CIA implied, were slyly empowering the lobby.

While Allen Dulles was sharing this conspiracy theory with the
British, his subordinate, Kermit Roosevelt, was in Cairo working
on the problem from an identical perspective. Roosevelt reported
to his boss that Nasser "remains our best, if not our only, hope
here."[12] Nasser was "absolutely sincere in his belief that acquire-
ment of arms was an absolute necessity, not only for his survival but
that of his country; that in spite of repeated efforts on his part, [the]
U.S. could not or would not give him the kind of deal he needed."[13]

Roosevelt, therefore, approached Nasser in the manner of a
concerned friend—K to Big Brother. He invited Nasser to think
together with him about ways to minimize the political backlash in
the United States.

Copeland reports that during their first meeting with Nasser,
which took place on September 26, the Egyptian "was in a teasing

'I told you so' mood." He was "cheerful" and eager to debate the necessity of taking Soviet arms. "But Roosevelt surprised him. Instead of pressing the Egyptian to back out of the agreement with Moscow . . . , Roosevelt said to Nasser, 'If the deal is as big as we hear it is, it will worry some people but in general it will make you a big hero. Why don't you take advantage of the sudden popularity to do something really statesmanlike?'" What, precisely, did Roosevelt have in mind? Alpha, of course. He urged Nasser to make a peace overture.

Roosevelt was playing a weak hand. A peace initiative would, of course, entirely destroy Nasser's gains. Defiance of the West and Israel was the engine that was rocketing him to the heights of Arab politics. A public call for peace with Israel would cast him back to earth like a stone. For Nasser, however, it made no sense to explain the laws of gravity to the Americans. The Soviet arms were already in the pipeline, and what he most needed from Roosevelt was insurance, lest the Americans were to treat him like Mosaddeq. So he humored Roosevelt, letting him play Big Brother, and bubbled with excitement at the suggestion that he should launch a peace initiative. "Nasser leapt immediately at the suggestion," Copeland recounts. " 'A good idea,' he said. We discussed the idea until midnight."[14]

Nasser was again playing dangle and delay. He didn't just listen to the advice of the CIA agents; he enlisted their active participation by encouraging them to compose the passage of his speech announcing the peace plan. He then sent his most trusted advisors to help the Americans. According to Copeland, "a procession of visitors arrived at our hotel suite to give us their ideas on what should and what should not go into the statement."[15]

When Nasser did announce the deal publicly, on September 27, he labeled it "the Czech arms deal," when in reality it was an agreement with the Soviets. The name stuck: to this day authors refer to it by the name that Nasser gave it. The Soviets themselves were interested in calling it a Czech deal, because, among other reasons, it gave them an excuse to claim that they had not violated "the spirit of Geneva." The fiction allowed Moscow to pretend that it wasn't making a threatening military move into the Middle East.

Nasser somehow planted the idea in Roosevelt's mind that he was adopting the American's suggestion—"the idea being," Copeland brags, "that this wouldn't sound so heretical since the Czechs were also a major source of arms for the Israelis."[16] Copeland is referring to the fact that the Czechs supplied arms to the Israelis at the time of their 1948 War of Independence. Clearly, Roosevelt and Copeland had the Israel lobby in their sights. When Israel's friends in Congress and in the media would screech and howl, the Czech motif would equip the Eisenhower administration with a sprightly defense of its pro-Nasser policy—especially when combined with Nasser's peace overture to Israel. The Czechs had armed Israel in 1948 and Israel never migrated into the Soviet orbit. Why would Egypt?

Spy versus Diplomat

After the drafting of Nasser's statement announcing a conciliatory gesture toward Israel was completed, the Egyptians invited their CIA guests to the house of Ahmed Hussein, the Egyptian ambassador to the United States, who was hosting a dinner in honor of Eric Johnston, Eisenhower's special envoy tasked with brokering tacit cooperation between Israel and its neighbors over the equitable distribution of water from the Jordan River. Nasser and some of his top ministers drove to Hussein's house together with Roosevelt and Copeland. The group arrived an hour late. Everyone at the party was in a festive mood, except for one participant: the American ambassador to Egypt, Henry Byroade, who had no idea that Roosevelt and Copeland were in the country. Byroade, Copeland writes, was "stunned at the sudden sight of Kermit Roosevelt, of all people, walking one hour late into a dinner party with the chief of state of the country and two of his ministers." This cocky performance was no mere oversight; it was a calculated professional blow, deeply destructive to the ambassador's standing as the president's authorized representative in Egypt.

For much of the evening, the ambassador "sat morosely holding a Scotch" while the others laughed and joked. Suddenly, at a very inopportune moment, he exploded. Copeland is at his insouciant best when he tells the story:

Except for Byroade, it was a relaxed and highly convivial evening. Ambassador Johnston launched into one of his stories, a picaresque thing which he delivered in an Irish brogue and which, among other things, had in it a pregnant nun, Moses, Jews, and a bowel movement (and no point); while Ahmed Hussein and I, with great difficulty, were trying to translate it into Arabic, Byroade cleared his throat and interrupted. "Gamal," he said, "there is a matter that I would like to bring to your attention."

The laughing stopped, everyone became silent, and Byroade launched into a tirade against the "Egyptian police state," the Revolutionary Command Council who were "behaving like a lot of juvenile delinquents," and one or two other features of Nasser's regime that had been called to mind by the rough handling, by the Alexandria police, of Byroade's Labor Attaché two days earlier. It was an eloquent performance, with every word and phrase coming out as though it had been written by a skilled playwright. But it was delivered at the wrong time, and to the worst conceivable audience. Nasser suddenly snuffed out his cigarette, rose, and strode out, with his ministers scurrying after him. Roosevelt followed him to the car and made some kind of apology. Byroade sat rigidly at the table, stunned not so much by Nasser's dramatic exit as because the implications (for him) of Roosevelt's and Johnston's presence at the performance

had suddenly dawned on him. Johnston waited until he heard
Nasser's Cadillac drive off, then tapped Byroade on the arm
and said, "Time to go home, Hank." Off they went, Byroade
looking like a somnambulist being led back to bed.[17]

Roosevelt made a beeline to the embassy and fired off a cable to
Washington, describing the events of the evening and stating that
Byroade had outlived his usefulness in Cairo. He "needed a rest."[18]

Copeland met Nasser the next morning. The Egyptian professed to be surprised that the Americans were divided among
themselves. "Oh, Hank's blowing up like that?" he said. "I hope
Kim and Eric didn't make too much of it." When Copeland indicated that Byroade might suffer professionally, Nasser said, "I'll
speak to Kim about it this evening."[19]

Roosevelt's behavior toward Byroade carried more than just a
whiff of bureaucratic rivalry. By undermining the ambassador, he
probably hoped to decapitate the State Department in Cairo, thus
increasing the importance of the CIA channel to Nasser. Despite
this personal friction, Byroade and Roosevelt shared identical views
about the vital necessity of preserving the American connection to
Nasser, even with his so-called neutral position in the Cold War.

Dulles Disagrees

On September 26, Roosevelt informed Allen Dulles of his intention to help Nasser shape the public announcement of the arms
deal.[20] The following morning, the director of the CIA sent back
his approval, and then notified the secretary of state of his actions.[21] Foster Dulles, however, rejected the plan. He immediately
made his views known to Cairo: "We do not believe," he wrote,
"that any statement by Nasser about Egypt's peaceful intent in
making [the] arms pact with [the] Soviet [Union] will serve to mitigate in any substantial degree [the] inevitable public reaction in

[the] US and elsewhere and he should not be encouraged to believe that it would."[22] Nasser was in need of tough love, not sweetness and understanding.

Roosevelt must have been shocked, but Dulles was focused on the bigger picture. Most notable among these was the vital need to maintain the alliance with the British, with whom he was meeting in New York. When Harold Macmillan, who became Britain's foreign secretary when Eden replaced Churchill as prime minister, reminded him of this responsibility, whatever reluctance Dulles may have had to pressure Nasser melted away. Macmillan pointed out that Nasser's deal with the Soviets was "a breach at least of the spirit of the Suez base agreement." Carrots, he said, were proving ineffective with Nasser; perhaps the time had come to turn "to the stick." Dulles showed receptivity to the idea. "We did not all work so hard to get a Suez base agreement," Dulles said, "in order to turn the base over to the Soviets." He also acknowledged that Nasser's gambit would roil the waters at home: "In the United States," he told Macmillan, "we will not be able to put a good face on the matter. It will be regarded as a major defeat."[23]

Dulles instructed a member of his staff to work with Shuckburgh to draft a joint paper on possible measures that could be taken to punish Nasser. His shift into a get-tough mood, however, had no immediate impact on Roosevelt's behavior, because his instructions arrived in Cairo after Nasser had already publicly announced the arms deal. To reinforce his point, Dulles also drafted two stern personal messages to Nasser urging him to back out of the deal and reminding him of his repeated assurances that Egypt would identify with the West. On the basis of those assurances, Dulles said, the United States had provided diplomatic assistance in several areas, most notably the Canal Zone dispute with Britain. It had also offered Egypt arms, supported its economy, and shown a desire to help it settle the Arab-Israeli conflict. The Soviet arms deal, however, "inevitably undermines the basic premise upon which we have worked in the past and sets Egypt upon a course which may well separate her progressively from her natural and long-term friends."[24] The messages stopped just short of an ultimatum: reject the arms deal, or the United States will harm Egypt economically and work against it diplomatically.

Dulles decided to send George Allen, the assistant secretary of state, to deliver the message. Kermit Roosevelt and Eric Johnston were already encamped in Cairo, and George Allen was now on his way. Egypt would soon be awash in high-level American envoys.

Nasser's About-Face

According to Miles Copeland, Nasser hit the roof when he heard about Dulles's decision to dispatch another emissary. It's not hard to see why. Nasser had been closely cooperating with Roosevelt, who gave every impression of speaking for the United States government at the highest levels. Now, suddenly, an envoy with a tough message was en route to Cairo. Adding insult to injury was the way the Americans notified Nasser—over the radio. News of the visit leaked immediately in Washington, so the Egyptians first got word not through normal diplomatic channels but from, Copeland writes, "a news bulletin saying 'Allen to Cairo to present ultimatum to Nasser.' The story was on the Associated Press ticker in Cairo by 6 p.m. local time (11 a.m. Washington time), and by 6:30, when Kim and I were to meet him, Nasser was surrounded by staff officers and was instructing one of them to take 'that silly paragraph' out of his speech and to replace it with something appropriately defiant and anti-American."[25] The "silly paragraph" was, of course, the paragraph conciliatory to Israel that Roosevelt and Copeland had written with the help of a phalanx of Egyptian propagandists.

On this particular point, however, Copeland's account is faulty. Nasser announced the arms deal on the evening of September 27, but Dulles did not even contemplate sending Allen to Cairo until the following morning. The AP bulletin undoubtedly annoyed Nasser, but it could not have influenced the text of his speech announcing the deal. Copeland either misremembered or altered the facts. Why? Perhaps he sought, consciously or unconsciously, to avoid admitting that Nasser was not really taking advice from the CIA. If Nasser had never listened to Roosevelt and Copeland in the first place, then they were not the master manipulators that they imagined themselves to be.

In addition, Copeland's inaccurate account is better at conveying the strong belief that both he and Roosevelt shared—namely, that they had the matter fully under control before the boneheads in Washington started screwing it up. Copeland never hides his condescension toward Dulles. "It cannot be said that John Foster Dulles was a stupid man, but he certainly wasn't brilliant, as he and his boss, President Eisenhower, both thought he was," he writes in one of his memoirs. "And he had a mind that, once made up, couldn't be opened with a crowbar. He gave the phrase 'mind like a steel trap' a whole new meaning."[26]

In Nasser's own account of the Allen mission, we catch a glimpse of Roosevelt conspiring with him to subvert the punitive policy that was developing in Dulles's mind. Nasser provided his account nine months after the fact, on July 26, 1956, in his famous speech announcing the nationalization of the Suez Canal Company. The main theme of that address was the history of Western attempts to thwart him, and he presented the Allen mission as one chapter in that larger tale. He told his audience that he first learned of Allen's impending arrival from wire service reports that were full of dire predictions: "Mr. Allen has a warning for Egypt; Mr. Allen carries a threat to Egypt, a threat to sever this, that and the other." After the news broke, Nasser said, an American official came to see him—a man whom he did not name but who is obviously Roosevelt. "I asked him what [this] insult to Egyptian . . . prestige was about." Nasser continues:

He said: It is a message from Mr. Dulles which is strongly
worded. We are astonished how it came to be sent. We ask you
to have cool nerves. You have always had cool nerves. Accept
this message with cool nerves.

I told him: How can I accept a message which contains a
threat or injury to Egyptian dignity?

He said that no practical outcome would result from this
message and guaranteed this. He said: this message will injure
Egyptian dignity in words only, not in effect.[27]

In Nasser's sketch, we perceive the outline of a familiar figure:
K instructing Big Brother on how to outflank his detractors in
Washington. Roosevelt advised Nasser that a little patience and
forbearance from him would help his friends in the Eisenhower
administration reverse the hard-line policy that was emerging from
Dulles in New York.

If the Allen mission discomfited anyone, it was Roosevelt. For
years, he had been trading heavily on his family name and his access
to the Dulles brothers, presenting himself to Nasser as *the* trusted
conduit to the White House. For the last seventy-two hours he
had been working intensively on a joint strategy with Nasser, who,
in classic dangle-and-delay fashion, had suddenly jettisoned it. The
arrival in Cairo of a super-empowered envoy with a tough message threatened to undermine Roosevelt's personal credibility as
well as his preferred policy. A rupture in Egyptian-American relations would spell the end of Alpha and, with it, Roosevelt's grand
project.

Roosevelt's Tennis Match

On October 1, 1955, a lonely George Allen landed in Cairo, the sole
passenger on a military aircraft. His solitude was soon shattered.
Between a crowd of irate demonstrators and the plane, a clutch of

Egyptian and Arab reporters waited expectantly, every one of them primed to ask: "Are you delivering an ultimatum to Egypt?"

This scene was definitely not the one that Dulles had envisioned when he decided upon sending Allen to Egypt. The envoy was supposed to slip into Cairo unobtrusively, deliver the warning to Nasser, check whether Byroade had truly lost his marbles, and then slip out again. No one in Washington, however, had stopped to ask whether Nasser even had an interest in keeping Allen's visit quiet. He did not. For the Egyptian leader, the Allen mission was the stuff of which great political theater is made. Allen arrived *after* the announcement of the arms deal, when it was too late to make a difference, thus allowing Egyptian propagandists to portray him as the impotent envoy, the representative of a dying imperialism. Allen was a magnificent foil for Nasser as he delivered his core message to the Arab world: I am the first Arab leader who is willing and able to defy the West and Israel in both word and in deed.

Allen was so useful that Nasser was still using him as a prop nine months later, in his nationalization speech. In that address, Nasser painted a picture of the Western powers swaggering through the front door, delivering ultimatums; meanwhile, shadowy men like Roosevelt came in through the back door, begging to cut a deal. Nasser boasted to the crowd that he was as defiant of imperialism and Zionism in private as he was in public. Thus, he said, on the eve of Allen's arrival he issued a stern warning to Roosevelt: "If your representative comes to the office and says something unpleasant, I shall dismiss him. I shall proclaim to the Egyptian people that you wanted to disparage their grandeur and dignity."[28]

This statement, though clearly self-serving, was basically true. Nasser preempted the American ultimatum by issuing one of his own, and it fell to Byroade to deliver it to Allen. The moment Allen's plane touched down in Cairo, Byroade rushed aboard and barked, "If you say anything about an ultimatum, your ass is out of here right now." Before the two reached the newsmen, Hassan

Tuhami, Nasser's conduit to the CIA, made his way to Allen and handed him a note from Roosevelt: "Deny ultimatum, or at least don't mention it, until we can discuss it."[29]

Allen walked out of the plane, with Byroade right behind him, both men smiling for the cameras, friendly American officials on their way to conduct routine business. The two men walked calmly past the cameras, and then raced for the embassy, where Roosevelt, Johnston, Copeland, and Byroade's deputy all nervously awaited their arrival. The six men brainstormed. Johnston captured the consensus in the room when he disparaged the letter from Dulles. "I don't suppose," he said to Allen, "it would do any good to tell you just to tear it up and throw it away?"[30]

In Copeland's vague and impressionistic account of the meeting, Roosevelt was oddly detached. While others about him were fretting over Dulles's new hard-line policy, he supposedly did his best James Bond impression. Roosevelt, Copeland writes, "left the meeting to play tennis."[31] Tennis? Really? He was more personally invested in the relationship with Nasser than anyone, and at the moment the stakes in the game had never been higher. Did Roosevelt truly leave to play tennis?

Of course not. In the nationalization speech, Nasser tells us what Roosevelt really did. He left his colleagues in order to confer with Nasser:

> He then came again and told me . . . that Mr. Allen was wondering whether he would be dismissed when he came to convey his message to me and also whether Mr. Dulles would dismiss him if he went back without conveying his message. What would happen? I told him: I don't know. I only know one thing—if he comes to convey this message to me I will dismiss him.[32]

However sculpted to suit Nasser's propagandistic purposes, this account of the conversation accurately describes Allen's dilemma.

And it presents Roosevelt's general purpose with equal accuracy: he was choreographing the steps of both sides in a last-ditch effort to kill Dulles's hard-line policy in the cradle.

According to Nasser, when Allen finally showed up to meet him, he was as gentle as a lamb. "Then Mr. Allen came and did not open his mouth at all," Nasser told the crowd. "He sat and listened to the Egyptian point of view, and briefly advanced the American viewpoint."[33] Allen actually had two meetings with Nasser, but his reports to Dulles from Cairo corroborate Nasser's description of what transpired. In the first meeting, Nasser emphasized the threat to the Egyptian leader's rule that Israel's military actions had generated. "It is clear," Allen wrote, that Nasser "could not, even if he wished, cancel [the] Czechoslovak deal since he would be overthrown."[34] Allen further emphasized "that [the] absolute determination of [the Egyptian government] and [the] Egyptian people to obtain arms following [the] Gaza attack of February 28 can hardly be conveyed by cable."[35] After the second meeting, Allen told Dulles that issuing the ultimatum to Nasser would imperil the American position in the entire Middle East. Dulles accepted Allen's arguments. He backed off entirely from the idea of putting pressure on Nasser, and his mind focused, once again, on wooing him.

Ten months earlier, K had explained his main goal to Big Brother: to ensure that Eisenhower and Dulles would see any deterioration in the situation as "due to the Israeli rather than to the Egyptians." In that task, at least, Roosevelt had succeeded. He may have failed to disarm Egypt, but he certainly helped Nasser to be disarming.

CHAPTER 9

Blowback

At the end of September 1955, J. B. Van Loon, a Dutch scholar of the Middle East, caught a rare glimpse of the machinery that broadcast Nasser's defiance of the West and Israel to the Arab world. While serving in Iraq as the cultural attaché in the embassy of the Netherlands, Van Loon attended the Conference of Arab University Graduates in Jerusalem (the Old City was Jordanian at that time) as a guest of the Iraqi delegation. Van Loon was one of the very few Westerners at the conference. What he witnessed disturbed him, and he made a point of expressing his concern to the British.

The Egyptian delegation to the conference, Van Loon reported, dwarfed all others in size. The Egyptians used their numbers to dominate the proceedings aggressively, stomping their feet and jeering when speakers from other delegations displeased them. Their behavior, which Van Loon described as "Nazi-like," shocked the Iraqis, nearly half of whom packed up and left immediately.

The unofficial head of the Egyptian delegation was Ahmad Said, the director and chief announcer for Voice of the Arabs. Said hijacked the conference in order to create a media spectacle—a pseudo-spontaneous celebration of Egyptian pan-Arabism. Each of the conference's nine separate committees was "packed with Egyptians," Van Loon explained, so that "Egyptian policy was assured of endorsement." Fierce young men "sat around a tape-recorder, recording their own histrionics" for broadcast on Voice of the Arabs.

Unsuspecting listeners to the program were therefore left with the impression that intellectuals from across the Arab world had erupted in emotional support for Egyptian policies and positions.[1] And what were those? Violent opposition to Israel, a repudiation of the Baghdad Pact, and a total rejection of all major Middle East initiatives by the United States.[2]

Generating stirring radio broadcasts, however, was not the only mission of the Egyptian delegation. Shortly after the conference ended, the British Foreign Office received a cable from John Bagot Glubb, the British commander of the Arab Legion, as the Jordanian military was known at the time. Members of the Egyptian delegation, Glubb reported, had "contacted as many Jordanians as possible of all classes to instill Egyptian propaganda into them." In addition to spreading Nasser's message, they also created a terrorist network. "[A]mong the Egyptian delegates was a number of army officers in plain clothes," Glubb wrote. "These were responsible for organizing terrorist raids from Jordan into Israel under cover of the conference."[3]

Actually, the Egyptians were not so much forming a new terror network as resuscitating an old one—the network of the Palestinian nationalist leader Hajj Amin al-Husseini, the mufti of Jerusalem, who at that time was living in exile in Cairo. In Jerusalem, Nasser's agents contacted members of the mufti's family and his political allies, and together they began planning attacks on Israel. "When the delegation left," Glubb reported, "they informed the Mufti's supporters in Jerusalem that a party of Egyptian officers in plain clothes would shortly return . . . with money and plans for raids. Meanwhile, the Egyptian Military Attaché . . . is in charge of organizing terrorists."[4] Around the time of Glubb's report, the British learned that Nasser's agents, with the aid of Syria, were also organizing attacks on Israel from Lebanon.[5]

Made in the USA

In one of his autobiographies, Miles Copeland makes what he calls an "arresting admission": "While the 'straights' in Washington were increasingly displeased with the anti-American content of Nasser's public utterances and the anti-American propaganda that poured out of Radio Cairo, the Middle East's most far-reaching medium, can you guess who was writing a goodly portion of the material? *We* were." Thirty years after the fact, Copeland was still proud of the help that the CIA had given Nasser in saturating the Arab world with propaganda hostile to the United States and its allies. "[W]e even had Paul Linebarger, perhaps the greatest 'black' propagandist who ever lived, come to coach the Egyptian-American team that turned out the stuff," he writes.[6]

The description of Linebarger is apt. Half-blind, and plagued by health problems his entire life, Linebarger died young, at age fifty-three, but his abbreviated career contained enough achievement for three healthy men. He first entered the arena of international politics as a mere boy growing up in East Asia, the child of an adventurer who worked as an advisor and propagandist for Sun Yat-sen, the Chinese nationalist. The young Linebarger served as his father's secretary—work that initiated him, he later wrote, "into almost every phase of international political warfare, whether covert or overt."[7]

By his late teens, Linebarger was fluent in Chinese and more deeply steeped in Asian politics than seasoned experts more than twice his age. At twenty-three, in 1936, he received a PhD in East Asian studies from Johns Hopkins University. A teaching position at Duke followed. World War II interrupted his academic career, but it also afforded Linebarger an opportunity to return to propaganda, his first love. He rose to the rank of colonel and helped develop the new professional field of psychological operations. After the war, he published *Psychological Warfare*, a classic text in its field.

Placing expertise like Linebarger's at the disposal of a regime like Nasser's came at a cost: blowback. Eisenhower would not come to recognize the full magnitude of the damage done until mid-1958, but the first signs of severe trouble started to register in December 1955 and January 1956, when Jordan experienced a wave of unrest that Nasser had helped to incite by means of his propaganda machine and the subversive network he had built in Jordan.

The immediate goal of the incitement was to thwart the effort, spearheaded by Britain and Turkey, to bring Jordan into the Baghdad Pact. Britain joined the organization in April 1955; Pakistan acceded in September, followed by Iran in October. Jordan, as a close ally of Britain and Iraq, was expected to join next.

Nasser, however, had other ideas. He had been hostile to the grouping since its inception, and as it grew so did his hostility to it, with the result that the Arab world became ever more polarized. With Nasser dedicated to destroying the Baghdad Pact and its members intent on expanding it, the diminutive Jordanian kingdom became a central battleground in the contest for regional mastery.

In the event, Nasser won resoundingly. That he did so is a well-established fact. Just how he did it, however, has never been fully explained. Generally speaking, historians have failed to recognize the strategic connection that Nasser made between the struggle over the Baghdad Pact and the Arab-Israeli conflict, and have instead treated the two conflicts as if they were separate contests taking place in sealed arenas. This misperception reflects, in part, the bias of contemporary American and British officials (including Byroade, Roosevelt, and Shuckburgh). They, too, failed to recognize that the destabilization of Jordan was in fact the *primary* goal of Nasser's border war with Israel.

Nasser Learns a Lesson

Nasser first learned how violence on the Israeli-Jordanian frontier could advance his quest for regional mastery in October 1953, when

the Israeli commando Unit 101, led by Ariel Sharon, descended on
the West Bank village of Qibya, then part of Jordan. Sharon and his
men laid charges and demolished some forty houses, killing nearly
sixty Palestinians, including a great many women and children. As
the shocked survivors picked through the rubble of their lives, a
wave of outrage swept through Jordan. Demonstrators poured into
the streets demanding vengeance on the perpetrators. Their list of
guilty parties, however, included some surprising names. In addition to the Israelis, the protestors also blamed the Jordanian government, the Americans, and the British. An anonymous Jordanian
soldier explained the underlying logic to a British journalist: "We
hate our government," he said, "for not allowing us to take a gun
and go into Israel to shoot Jews. We know that the Government
only acts because it is paid money by Britain and America. The
money Britain pays might just as well be paid to the Jews because it
bribes the Legion not to attack."[8]

The British came in for especially harsh criticism. Glubb was
particularly exposed and vulnerable because the Legion had inexplicably failed to come to the rescue of Qibya. He reported to London
that when driving through West Bank villages in the aftermath of
the attack, he and his fellow British officers were subjected to "curses
and insults." Villages along the armistice line with Israel received vis-
its from "extremist politicians and agitators" who were "preaching
intense hatred of Britain" and "accusing the Arab Legion of treach-
ery" for remaining in its barracks "while Jews attacked civilians." In
London, government ministers were not above voicing similarly
harsh sentiments. After enduring a particularly harsh grilling before
the Cabinet, Glubb warned that Britain risked losing everything in
Jordan. "[W]e cannot continue like this much longer," he wrote.[9]

Glubb's distress was Egypt's opportunity. Capitalizing on the
Israeli attack, Voice of the Arabs showcased Abdullah al-Tal, a ren-
egade Jordanian army officer. Al-Tal had defected to Egypt after
serving as the personal envoy of King Abdullah in secret peace ne-

gotiations with Israel after the 1948 war. According to al-Tal, those negotiations had been part of a grand British conspiracy to partition Palestine between Jordan and Israel—a conspiracy that, by virtue of al-Tal's presence on Voice of the Arabs, valiant Egypt was determined to thwart. In his broadcasts after Qibya, al-Tal called on the Jordanians to "take united action to expel imperialists" and to bring all Arab armies "under a unified command." Glubb and the other British officers should be sent packing. "Where was Glubb . . . ," al-Tal asked, "when the Jews attacked Qibya and continued to attack for eight hours on Jordanian soil?"[10]

Nasser had learned something very valuable: violence on Jordan's border with Israel stirred up profound anti-British sentiment. In October 1953, he was not yet ready to put that information to practical use, being engaged in a charm offensive to enlist American help in ousting the British from Egypt. By late 1955, however, the situation had changed; his priority now was to stop the advance of the Baghdad Pact as it moved to envelop Jordan. For that particular task to succeed, Nasser required the Americans less than he required the Palestinians, who, after the 1948 Arab-Israeli War, had become a very substantial portion of the Jordanian population. What better way to appeal to them than to embroil Jordan and Israel in a bloody border conflict?

The Qibya Vise

Around the time that Nasser announced the Soviet-Egyptian arms deal, the Israelis were gaining a clear picture of the new Egyptian terror network with its various nodes in Lebanon, the Gaza Strip, and, of course, Jordan. On October 3, 1955, Colonel Yehoshafat Harkabi, Israel's chief of military intelligence, explained at a press conference that Egyptian intelligence had taken over a Syrian-sponsored group of terrorists stationed in Irbid, Jordan. It had also established an entirely new hub in the Hebron hills, also then in Jordan, under the direct control of the chief Egyptian diplomatic representative in Amman.[11]

Neither the British nor the Jordanians doubted Harkabi's claims. Everyone understood clearly that Nasser was launching a clandestine border war—everyone, that is, except for the Americans. "We have recently sent to Washington a report by the Jordan Military Attaché in Cairo of the Egyptian organization of terrorist gangs," a British Foreign Office official informed his colleagues in September. "This is to convince the State Department that such activities are going on, which they did not believe."[12]

The lead skeptic in the State Department was Henry Byroade. In November, he met with Nasser to convey the concern of Dulles over mounting reports that Egypt was sponsoring terrorism against Israel. Nasser denied the charges. He explained that the Fedayeen attacks were "spontaneous," implying that the Palestinians were acting on their own. He went on to say, however, that the Egyptian military did possess "an organization for such operations and he supposed knowledge of this might be being used as evidence of Egypt's complicity in present operations."[13]

As Byroade should have known, this admission was damning. The Fedayeen campaign was covert only insofar as Nasser downplayed its existence to Western officials. In Jordan it was an open secret. As Glubb reported to London, Voice of the Arabs was publicly taking credit for the attacks.[14] Indeed, Glubb, who was fluent in Arabic and had spent his entire adult life working on the ground in the Middle East, understood the Egyptian game perfectly. Nasser's goal, he explained, was to play the role of the "heroic leader [of the] whole Arab world," precisely in order to embarrass the Jordanian government by making it look "timid and treacherous" before its own public.[15]

The Soviet arms deal, Glubb stressed, had made Nasser extraordinarily popular on the streets of Jordan, where people now believed that the "Jews . . . will very soon be destroyed." Nasser's portrait, distributed freely by the Egyptian embassy, was ubiquitous, hanging in shops and public places and putting the government on the defensive. Although local authorities monitored Egyptian agents, they refrained from rounding them up for fear of a backlash in the form of "street riots whipped up by Egypt."[16]

Nasser had already won the moral high ground. He had Glubb right where he wanted him: squeezed between the Egyptian-Palestinian terror network and the Israeli military—in the Qibya vise.

Threading the Needle

Using the Qibya vise to hobble the British and destroy the Baghdad Pact was a tricky matter. Nasser's propaganda was inviting Jordanians to break with Britain and join an Egyptian-led coalition against Israel. This call had a direct emotional appeal, but a significant, practical obstacle stood in Nasser's way: the livelihood of the Jordanian military. The Arab Legion was organically tied to the British, who had established it after World War I and even now still paid for its upkeep to the tune of £10 million annually. Egypt, a very poor country, could not possibly replace the British subsidy. How, then, could Nasser persuade King Hussein and his officers to turn against Britain?

Making the challenge even greater was the traditional distrust between Jordanians and Palestinians. The Arab officers in the Legion hailed primarily from the East Bank of the Jordan River, where support for the Hashemite monarchy was strongest. By contrast, Nasser's Fedayeen strategy was based on its obvious appeal to the Palestinians: West Bankers who harbored a deep ambivalence, if not hostility, toward the Hashemite monarchy. If he were to overplay his appeals to them, he might provoke a backlash among East Bankers who had no love for Zionism but who loved their king; they valued the livelihood that a great many Jordanians derived from the Legion.

To thread this needle, Nasser refrained from directly attacking the Jordanian government. This contrasted sharply with his propaganda in Iraq, which routinely reviled the Hashemite monarchy, which was unpopular at home. In Jordan, Nasser never attacked King Hussein personally. Instead he portrayed him and, especially, his army as loyal Arabs who were eager to fight Israel but who were restrained by the British. This approach was perfectly consistent with the advice offered by Paul Linebarger in *Psychological Warfare:* "The sound psychological warfare operator will try to get enemy troops to believing that the enemy is not themselves but somebody else—the King, the Fuehrer, the elite troops, the capitalists. He creates a situation in which he can say, 'We're not fighting *you*.'" [17]

Even before the Soviet arms deal, the Egyptian military attaché had been advancing just such an argument to Arab officers in the Jordanian military, inviting them to break free of Britain's shackles and join together with Egypt in its war against Israel. By late October, Egyptian propagandists had given their policy a Jordanian face, circulating, for example, a broadsheet supposedly written by a group of Jordanian "Free Officers." Britain had created Israel to keep the Arabs divided and weak, the sheet charged, and it was now using the Baghdad Pact as a new version of the same policy.

Even as Nasser's propaganda invited the Jordanian army to join him against the imperialists and Zionists, his terror network was intensifying its attacks launched from Jordanian soil. Both actions fostered a strong sense of Arab solidarity and hostility to Britain and Israel, but they still could not answer the key question facing East Bankers: if they were to throw out the British, who would pay for the army, the source of their livelihood?

Nasser soon came up with an answer. In early November an exciting rumor spread through the ranks of the Arab Legion: *the Saudis* would pay with their oil money. On November 9, Glubb reported to London that the Egyptians and the Saudis were "offering

King Hussein a blank cheque for any amount of Communist arms, equipment and money, apparently with Russian authority for doing so."[18]

The offer to replace the British subsidy stripped the Jordanian government of its strongest argument for joining the Baghdad Pact—namely that the kingdom had an undeniable need for free military training and equipment. King Hussein was boxed in.

The Struggle for Jordan

If the young Jordanian monarch was in a very tight spot, Glubb was in absolute peril. Nasser was stealing the military—*his* military, the one he had built up over the course of decades—out from under him. He raised the alarm in a long memorandum to London, but also took pains to attack the Alpha Ethos, which still dominated in both Washington and London.

"[T]he Middle East is no longer divided into the two camps of Arabs and Jews," he wrote, "although unfortunately the Western Powers still seem to be thinking largely on those lines." He continued: "There is very nearly as much bitterness and hatred between [the] two Arab groups [the Egyptians and the Iraqis] as there is between the Arabs and the Jews." By implication, Glubb was suggesting that the Arab-Israeli conflict was a subset of the struggle for mastery between the two regional blocs.

The majority of Arabs, Glubb stipulated, did regard the Soviet-Egyptian arms deal "as an exceedingly astute move to outwit the Western Powers"; they also believed "that the whole object of Egypt . . . is to strengthen herself against Israel with a view to . . . driving the Jews into the sea." But Glubb, personally, rejected that view. For the Egyptians, he wrote, "the Palestine question is merely a political platform by means of which they aspire to achieve the leadership in the Arab world."[19]

Glubb's analysis led to two profound conclusions. First, Egypt was headed, almost inevitably, toward an alignment with the Soviet bloc and with revolutionary forces in the Arab world. Second, the only way to block further Egyptian advances in Jordan was to convince King Hussein to join the Baghdad Pact—by offering him a massive increase in the annual subsidy. Like it or not, Glubb argued, Britain was in a bidding war with Egypt and the Soviet Union for the loyalty of the Arab officers in the Legion.

While Glubb was drafting a memo that aspired to dismantle the Alpha perspective, Eden was drafting a speech to advance it. With Eisenhower still recuperating from his heart attack, Eden saw an opportunity to seize the role as lead peacemaker. He turned to Shuckburgh to draft his speech. To be effective, Shuckburgh told him, the address must call for painful concessions from Israel. With this goal in mind, Shuckburgh inserted a line identifying the 1947 United Nations resolution on Palestine as a basis for a solution to the conflict—a loaded reference signaling an intention to force Israel to retreat from large swaths of territory that it had seized when the Arabs attacked Israel and lost.[20] Infused as ever with the Alpha Ethos, Shuckburgh still considered Nasser a strategic partner and still believed that the best way to anchor him in the Western camp was by helping him pressure Israel.

Shuckburgh's thinking, however, was out of touch with the current of opinion among Britain's other allies in the Middle East. They read Nasser precisely as Glubb did—as a severe threat. The Turks were especially alarmed. In early November, President Celal Bayar traveled to Amman and urged King Hussein to join the Baghdad Pact. Several days later, the king signaled that he was willing to entertain an offer, his assent coming just in time for the inaugural meeting of the pact's ministerial council in Baghdad. At that November 20–21 meeting, the Turks joined with the Iraqis to impress upon Harold Macmillan, the British foreign minister, the urgency of bringing Jordan into the pact. Macmillan was easily convinced, and his report to Eden communicated the requisite sense of urgency. If the British failed to act quickly and decisively, Macmillan warned, Jordan "will drift out of our control." [21]

With Eden's wholehearted agreement, Macmillan immediately notified Dulles. Britain, he wrote, "must go all out in support of the pact," and he urged the United States to join it as well.[22] Meanwhile, the British government began preparing an offer that would, among other things, substantially increase the annual subsidy to the Arab Legion and assist it in forming a fighter squadron. Two weeks later, on December 6, Sir Gerald Templer, chief of the Imperial General Staff, flew to Jordan to present the offer to the Jordanian government.

Nasser, however, was a step ahead. For weeks, the British and the Turks had telegraphed their intentions, giving the Egyptian leader an opportunity to organize a counterstrategy. His first move was to drive a wedge between Britain and the United States—a task he accomplished through the familiar ploy of dangle and delay. On November 9, Nasser expressed a renewed interest in Alpha. He told Byroade that he was "ready to discuss Palestine on a confidential basis . . . if nothing new happened, meaning if neither the US nor any other Arab States should join [the Baghdad Pact]." [23]

Over the next month, Nasser and Fawzi, his foreign minister, continued to express eagerness to initiate a peace process. The ploy achieved its desired effect. On December 6, some two weeks after Macmillan had urged him to support the effort to bring Jordan into the pact, Dulles responded with a request to postpone the effort. "[W]e need to keep in mind our present plans to make another try through Egypt towards an Arab-Israel settlement," he explained. Since Nasser had expressed to Byroade a readiness to explore this possibility, the priority "should be another major effort to secure Egypt's cooperation" in Alpha. "An immediate move to expand the Baghdad Pact would probably deny us Nasser's cooperation."

Dulles's advice came too late to have any effect. On the day he sent the letter to Macmillan, Sir Gerald Templer was already en route to Jordan on his mission of persuasion. Nasser, however, was ready. Through masterful use of his propaganda machine and the subversive network he had built in Jordan over the previous six months, he turned the Templer mission into a diplomatic fiasco for Britain.

With the goal, no doubt, of shaping Palestinian perceptions of the impending British offer, Nasser dispatched General Abdel Hakim Amr, the Egyptian chief of staff, to Amman during the week before Templer's arrival. Amr's trip, in the course of which he toured Jordanian positions along the Israeli frontier, was presented by Egyptian radio as a step toward Arab unity. Jordan's "amalgamation in the Arab bloc," it was reported, was advancing "on a direct course."[24] Nasser's propagandists thus created the (false) impression among Palestinians that Jordan was on the verge of joining the Egyptian-led coalition against Israel. Moreover, to hear Egyptian radio tell the story, Templer was coming to Jordan in order to scuttle the benefits of Amr's visit—to drive a wedge between Jordan and the combined Arab command dedicated to liberating Palestine.

When Templer finally arrived, he discovered firsthand the effectiveness of Nasser's message. Although the young and inexperienced King Hussein gave Templer strong support, he had failed to assemble a domestic coalition capable of withstanding the Nasserist onslaught, which had instilled in Jordanian politicians a healthy fear of crossing the Egyptian strongman. Said al-Mufti, Hussein's prime minister, refused to commit the government to joining the pact. Templer complained bitterly of al-Mufti's "spinelessness," calling him "a jelly," "a broken reed," and a politician who displayed "all the typical obstinacy of a weak man." Al-Mufti's character, however, was hardly the point: the real problem lay in the irredentist climate that Nasser had generated in Jordan. Templer himself recognized as much when he identified one of the main reasons for his failure as "fear of alienating Egypt."[25]

That fear manifested itself most consequentially when four Palestinian ministers in the al-Mufti government adamantly opposed the British offer, conditioning their acceptance of it on, of all things, Nasser's approval. Templer negotiated with the government for a week; the four Palestinians resigned in protest, making their reasons known to the public; Templer left; and the government fell. When King Hussein appointed a new government headed by Hazza Majali, a strong supporter of the Baghdad Pact, the country exploded in riots.

During the negotiations, Templer had assumed that the four Palestinians were simply responding to public opinion. Little did he realize that a high-ranking Egyptian official had shadowed him and thwarted his mission by, among other measures, suborning the four ministers. That Egyptian official was Colonel Anwar al-Sadat, the future president of Egypt. He went undetected because he had come undercover, ostensibly in his capacity as the secretary general of the Islamic Congress, an Egyptian-sponsored international religious organization. In his memoirs, Sadat acknowledges his true mission, but is short on details. "It is no exaggeration to say," he writes, "that I played an important part in the frustration of the Baghdad Pact."[26]

The British and Jordanian authorities would arrive at the same conclusion, but they managed to retrace Sadat's movements only after he had left the country. "Sadat was the evil genius of the four Palestinian members of Said al-Mufti's Government [who brought down] the government," an official from the British embassy informed London. Dining with three of the ministers the day before the government fell, Sadat gave them a large bribe "to defect from

the [Jordanian] Cabinet and thus terminate the negotiations . . .
abruptly and disruptively." Sadat's visit, the official concluded, was
"one of the direct causes of the breakdown of the negotiations with
the Jordan Government, of the collapse of that Government and
the cause of the disturbances."[27]

While Sadat was working to hobble Jordan's government from
above, a team of Egyptian and Saudi agents was surreptitiously
organizing riots from below. The Saudis spread money liberally
to opposition groups, while the Egyptians activated the political network that had been built under the cover of the Fedayeen
campaign—a network that included Baathist schoolteachers, communists, hired thugs, and opposition politicians, all of whom played
a role in bringing people into the streets.[28]

Suppressing the riots was hard on the morale of the Legion.
"It was heartbreaking work for the troops," Glubb wrote in his
memoir, *A Soldier with the Arabs*. "They were abused, periodically
stoned, and called Jews and traitors."[29]

With the rejection of the Baghdad Pact, Nasser won a great
victory—just how great, would soon become clear. In the second
week of January 1956, Jordan experienced another major riot; on
March 1, King Hussein unceremoniously expelled Glubb and the
other British officers in the legion. Nasser's propaganda and subversion had sought to place the young monarch before a stark choice:
either go down with the British, or make Jordan subservient to
Egypt. In the end, Hussein managed to create a third option. He jettisoned the British officers and struck out on an independent course.

In Washington, the events in little Jordan were almost an af-
terthought, but the ouster of Glubb had profound implications,
signaling as it did the demise of the existing Middle Eastern order.
If Nasser could compel Jordan, the quintessential client state, to
send Britain packing, then what couldn't he do? The scene was set
for a major clash between Nasser and his enemies, now led by Anthony Eden.

Shame and Regret

In his memoir, *Uneasy Lies the Head*, King Hussein acknowledges the power of Nasser's broadcasts and complains that "ordinary Jordanians" were "unaware that they were duped by the Egyptians."[30] *Duped* is a strong word, but fully justifiable. After all, Nasser succeeded by promising the Palestinians that ousting the British, *his* priority, was an immediate and necessary step toward achieving *their* priority, the destruction of Israel—a disingenuous argument and a promise on which he never delivered.

Nevertheless, it is easy to understand why the Palestinians believed him. Viewed from the streets of Jordan in 1955, Nasser appeared a paragon of integrity, whose words and deeds meshed perfectly.

The same was not true of Nasser as viewed from Washington. Unlike the Palestinians, the Americans were perfectly situated to grasp Nasser's contradictory faces: on the one hand the friend of America, on the other hand the scourge of both Israel and the West. The Americans, however, chose to ignore what their eyes were telling them. In ordinary life, the most successful con men often evade detection because their victims are so entranced by the fantasy on which the con is based that they fail to realize they have been fleeced. So, too, in political life. The promise of Nasser was so beguiling to Kim Roosevelt, Miles Copeland, and Henry Byroade that the scales never fell from their eyes.

Not all Americans, however, were permanently duped. One who eventually awoke to reality was Cordwainer Smith, a science fiction writer who also served as a consultant to the CIA. Credited with inventing the sympathetic cyborg, Smith was a gifted storyteller—a talent the CIA put to good use, sending him as a propaganda consultant to many countries, including Egypt.

One of Smith's novels, *Quest of the Three Worlds*, offers coded penance for having helped Nasser. The story traces the efforts of the protagonist, a man named O'Neill, to obtain intergalactic support for toppling the dictator of his home planet, an army officer named Wedder who had himself successfully conspired to dethrone the planet's former king. O'Neill had backed that earlier revolt, but realized he'd been duped when Wedder emerged as a ruthless tyrant.[31]

With playful names and descriptions, Smith discloses his allegory of the U.S.-Egyptian relationship under Nasser. O'Neill's home planet, "the land of the twelve Niles," is Mizzer, a play on "Misr," the Arabic word for Egypt. The deposed king is Kuraf— "Faruk" spelled backward. The name of Wedder's chief accomplice, Gibna, is an anagram of "Nagib." Nasser pocketed American support and then pursued an anti-Western agenda; Wedder, having won over O'Neill, sets about "reforming" the culture of his planet "so violently that whatever had been slovenly now became atrocious." For his part, O'Neill becomes a tortured soul, "thirsting for justice and yet hoping in his innermost thoughts that 'justice' is not just another word for revenge."[32]

Nasser had beaten Cordwainer Smith at his own game, and it rankled. This was not, however, the first time that a superior propagandist had bested him. Cordwainer Smith was a pseudonym, one of several used by Paul Linebarger. In his youth, when he worked for his father and Sun Yat-sen, the Chinese communists had defeated him badly, leaving an indelible memory. "There is no better way to learn the propaganda job," Linebarger would write, "than to be whipped thoroughly by somebody else's propaganda."[33]

But at least Linebarger knew when he had been whipped. That is more than could be said of his colleagues.

CHAPTER 10

Three-Dimensional Chess

Today both we and the Americans really gave up hope of Nasser and began to look around for means of destroying him." So wrote Evelyn Shuckburgh in his diary on March 8, 1956.[1] In his own diary, three weeks later, Eisenhower was lamenting "the growing ambition of Nasser, the sense of power he has gained out of his associations with the Soviets, his belief that he can emerge as a true leader of the entire Arab world—and because of these beliefs, his rejection of every proposition advanced as a measure of conciliation between the Arabs and Israel."[2]

This understanding of Nasser was new. For the previous three years, Eisenhower had assumed that the Egyptian leader, like a man locked in a deadly fencing match, was thrusting and parrying in direct response to the Jewish adversary poised opposite him. Suddenly, and rather mysteriously, the president had come to the realization that Nasser's attention was actually riveted on his Arab rivals, and that he was challenging Israel militarily in order to facilitate his domination of those rivals politically. This was no bilateral contest; it was a game of three-dimensional chess.

In the fencing match, Ike had seen himself as a mediator. Nasser, Eisenhower believed, was eager to bring the bout to a close; therefore, the job of the Americans was to produce a package of incentives, including concessions from Israel, that would provide the Egyptian leader a safe and honorable exit. In the game of three-

dimensional chess, Nasser had no interest in ending the conflict—
to the contrary, he sought to prolong it, because the border war
was a key instrument of his foreign policy; therefore, the job of the
United States had to change. Eden and Eisenhower had thus arrived at an identical understanding of Nasser and of his attitude toward Israel. How did they get there?

Ike's Tutorial

Eden's route is easiest to explain. The riots in Jordan, followed by
the ouster of Glubb, convinced London that Nasser, working hand
in glove with the Soviets, aspired to dominate the Arab world. On
March 5, just days after King Hussein expelled the British officers from the Arab Legion, Eden sent an urgent letter to Eisenhower, claiming that Cairo was closer to Moscow than previously
suspected, and that both were intent on destroying the Baghdad
Pact. "[W]e can no longer safely wait on Nasser," he wrote, because "a policy of appeasement will bring nothing in Egypt."[3] Ten
days later, he buttressed his argument with secret intelligence, forwarding to Eisenhower reports from an agent, code-named Lucky
Break, who was located in Nasser's inner circle. Lucky Break's reports detailed an Egyptian plan to foment pan-Arab revolutions
that, among other things, would topple the Hashemite regimes in
Iraq and Jordan.[4]

What did Eden mean by "no longer . . . wait[ing] on Nasser"?
On the evening of March 5, he reviewed a staff paper outlining options for a tougher policy. But evidently not tough enough: upset
by what he read, Eden phoned the hotel where Anthony Nutting,
the document's author, was hosting an official reception. Eden
had the hotel staff drag Nutting to the phone; on an open line,
he shouted, "But what's all this nonsense about isolating Nasser or
'neutralizing' him, as you call it? I want him murdered, can't you
understand? I want him removed, and if you and the Foreign Of-

fice don't agree, then you'd better come to the Cabinet and explain why."[5] One week later, Eden told Shuckburgh "that Nasser must be got rid of. 'It is either him or us, don't forget that.'"[6]

Eden's hard-line mood placed Shuckburgh under unbearable stress. Between March and June 1956, his diary entries howled with agony as he frantically searched for a new job, any job. On June 20, liberation came in the form of a teaching position at a military institution—a step down for a diplomat who was in line for a major ambassadorship. Leaving the Foreign Office, he performed a postmortem on his work. "Today I left the FO for (I hope) at least a year and a half and perhaps I shall never work in it again. . . . Obviously my policy and efforts to save relations with Egypt have been all wrong. . . . Meanwhile I wonder if my other ideas are wrong too."[7]

In Eisenhower's case, the factor that changed his thinking and made him realize that his policy had been misguided was unique and surprising. In the opening months of 1956, he received a private tutorial on Nasserism from an unimpeachable source: Nasser himself. The Egyptian leader was frank in explaining key elements of his regional strategy to Robert B. Anderson, the president's personal envoy. A Texas businessman, former deputy secretary of defense, and an individual whom Eisenhower trusted deeply, Anderson shuttled back and forth secretly between Israel and Egypt from January to March 1956. His mission was to ascertain whether it was possible to corral Nasser into peace negotiations with the Israelis. In the end, he concluded that the task was impossible. In the process, however, he gained fresh insight into the thinking of the young Egyptian leader.

In their first conversation, Nasser told Anderson that "the Israeli problem was a combination of issues," of which the bilateral conflict between Egypt and Israel was the least important. The key problem, he explained, was the Baghdad Pact, which he called "a political ideology designed to isolate Egypt." The expansionist nature of the pact had forced Nasser to launch a counterattack in the form "of a propaganda campaign against Turkey" and, in addition, "against Great Britain, the United States, and colonialism." With regret, he explained that this campaign had created hard feelings "in the Arab countries and particularly in Egypt against the Western powers," emotions that "would now make more difficult a settlement with Israel."[8]

Nasser was describing the Arab-Israeli conflict as a subset of the struggle among the regional blocs (just as Glubb had done in his long memo two months earlier). At this early stage, however, Anderson had yet to grasp the profound implications of the point. Even as Nasser identified the struggle against Iraq and Turkey as the main priority, and implied that his anti-Zionism was a component of that struggle, he also expressed a willingness to explore the possibility of a deal with Israel. Heartened by this cooperative attitude, Anderson sent an upbeat report back to Eisenhower.

Over the subsequent weeks, however, Nasser's attitude gradually hardened until it killed Anderson's initial optimism. At their final meeting, in early March, Nasser adopted a combative demeanor. Peacemaking with Israel, he told Anderson, was a purely American responsibility. "You continue to talk of the problems with Israel as if they were my problems which I have to settle," he said. "They are, in fact, your problems, and you must settle them."[9]

What explains this newfound candor? One likely part of the answer is Nasser's spectacular success in Jordan. His meeting with Anderson took place only five days after King Hussein had expelled Glubb. Flush with success, Nasser perhaps told himself that Egyptian neutralism was now the only game in town; if the United States wanted anything done in the Arab world, it had no choice but to work through him. Another part of the answer is probably the steady advance of the British withdrawal from the Canal Zone, due to be completed in June. As long as the British troops were ensconced along the canal, Nasser had a gun pointed at his head—a circumstance that gave him no choice but to cultivate the Americans, his most reliable insurance against British pugnacity. As the British guns disappeared, so did the need to kowtow to America.

As Anderson reported home on March 6, the Egyptian leader "made clear . . . that he does not want to sponsor any settlement of a controversial issue under either his personal leadership or the leadership of Egypt. This he fears would endanger his prestige in the Arab world." [10] These two simple lines did more than anything to destroy the image of Nasser as a leader locked in a bilateral contest with Israel. A week later, Anderson returned home and personally briefed the president. "Nasser proved to be a complete stumbling block," Eisenhower wrote in his diary. "He is apparently seeking to be acknowledged as the political leader of the Arab world." The desire for dominance in Arab politics forced him to take into consideration public opinion in all of the Arab countries when contemplating proposals for Arab-Israeli peace. "The result," the president wrote, "is that he finally concludes he should take no action whatsoever—rather he should just make speeches, all of which breathe defiance of Israel." [11]

The discovery of three-dimensional chess opened new avenues for strategic thought. One of them led in the direction of Israel. Suddenly, the Jewish state seemed a potential strategic partner. "In fact," Eisenhower mused, "I know of no reason why we should not make . . . a treaty with Israel." [12] At this stage, the idea represented little more than thinking out loud. But a seed had been planted, and over the next two years it would only grow.

From Alpha to Omega

As the failure of the Anderson mission became apparent, Eisenhower outlined for Dulles the contours of a new policy toward Egypt. The bureaucracies fleshed out the policy, code-named

Omega, and Eisenhower officially approved it on March 28, 1956. It took a harder line, though not as hard as Anthony Eden would have liked: it sought behavior change, not regime change. The goal of the new policy was to make "Colonel Nasser realize that he cannot cooperate as he is doing with the Soviet Union and at the same time enjoy most-favored-nation treatment from the United States."

Thus, Omega called for quietly cutting back on assistance to Egypt while simultaneously extending aid to countries in the Middle East that were standing up to Nasser. The idea was to change Nasser's calculus without provoking a direct confrontation. As a key Omega memorandum described the approach, "[W]e would want for the time being to avoid any open break which would throw Nasser irrevocably into a Soviet satellite status, and we would want to leave Nasser a bridge back to good relations with the West, if he so desires." [13]

The necessity of strengthening Nasser's rivals forced Eisenhower to think seriously, for the first time, about inter-Arab politics. "It would begin to appear," Eisenhower wrote in his diary on March 13, "that our efforts should be directed toward separating the Saudi Arabians from the Egyptians and concentrating . . . in making the former see that their best interests lie with us, not with the Egyptians and with the Russians." [14] Two weeks later, after the inauguration of Omega, Eisenhower's thoughts were still focused on Saudi Arabia. "I suggested to the State Department," he wrote on March 28, "that we begin to build up some other individual as a prospective leader of the Arab world—in the thought that mutually antagonistic personal ambitions might disrupt the aggressive plans that Nasser is evidently developing. My own choice of such a rival is King Saud." [15]

Whereas Eisenhower had seen the United States as a mediator between Arab and Jew, he was now beginning to see it as a power balancing rival Arab coalitions.

Byroade versus State

The new strategy displeased some of the career bureaucrats, Kermit Roosevelt and Henry Byroade among them. The two men did not express their opposition in the same manner. From the very limited evidence we possess of Roosevelt's thinking, it appears that he tried to soften Omega from behind the scenes, mainly by promoting efforts to reengage Nasser.[16] By contrast, Byroade mounted a one-man insurgency. After receiving a directive about the new policy from Washington, he sent back a long critique—respectful but uncompromising.

Omega, Byroade argued, failed to grapple with basic Middle East realities. It falsely assumed that Nasser himself was the problem. This attitude, he wrote, ignored the key fact: "Nasser is the product of an area and an era, and has become as much a symbol of nationalistic forces as he is a leader of these forces." American efforts to weaken his influence would backfire, and end by enhancing his status as a symbol of defiance. The problems of the United States in the region derived from its association with Zionism and imperialism; if America would only tack away from Israel and the European powers, it would find Nasser much more congenial. "Prior to establishment of Israel we were popular in [the] area by simply following a policy of open friendship and understanding," Byroade explained. "This will still work today."[17]

Dulles addressed Byroade's criticisms in a note briefer than a haiku: "I have read [cable] 2087 with interest."[18] The brush-off failed to deter Byroade, who continued to fight a running battle against the new policy even as he dutifully carried out his Omega-based instructions. By late June, having never missed an opportunity to express his disagreement, he had exhausted the secretary of state's patience. Dulles wrote to express his conviction that "after more than 4 years of identification with the nerve-straining problems of the Near East, a change of environment and change

of pace would be in your long-term interest."[19] He offered a new
ambassadorship—in South Africa. Nevertheless, Byroade remained
in Cairo until September, thus serving as in-house dissenter even
as the Suez Crisis erupted.

In July, Under Secretary of State Herbert Hoover Jr. sent Byroade a very detailed refutation of his criticisms of Omega. The
paper resulted, evidently, from a painstaking review of the history
of relations with Nasser—and it reached a startling conclusion: the
young Egyptian leader had successfully conned the United States.

For more than three years, Hoover informed Byroade, the Eisenhower administration had based its "policy in large part on cooperation with Egypt often at considerable cost, both domestic
and foreign." In doing so, it had relied upon "repeated assurances"
from Nasser that Egypt intended to help the West grapple with the
Cold War and the Arab-Israeli conflict. On the basis of his assurances, the United States had pressured the British on issues critical to Nasser's political success, such as, especially, the Canal Zone
dispute. It had also strengthened Nasser by providing development
aid in addition to diplomatic support. But the promised reciprocity,
by way of help in the Cold War and in solving the Arab-Israeli conflict, had never materialized. Like a mirage in the desert, Nasser's
cooperation glittered and beckoned from a distance but vanished
upon approach.[20]

Particularly startling was Hoover's reappraisal of the American offer of military assistance. A reconstruction of events, he explained, indicated that Nasser had always intended to conduct an
arms deal with the Soviet Union. His request to receive exceptional
financial terms for purchasing American weapons, therefore, had
been a ruse; its goal was to permit him to claim, after the fact, that
the Americans had rebuffed him. As we've seen in Chapter 6, recently discovered Soviet documents vindicate Hoover's reappraisal.

Byroade was unmoved. In response, he labeled Hoover's paper
"misleading," having failed to take into account the advent of a

more solicitous Soviet policy toward Egypt. Nasser had never run after the Soviets; they had run after him, and boxed him in, making it impossible for him to deliver on his original commitments to the United States. Washington, Byroade suggested, should lift a page from the Soviet book and tailor its policies to appeal to Arab nationalism. "Neutralism exists over a large portion of this part of the world," he explained. "If we fail to develop [a] means of fruitful cooperation with this large body of people and continue to consider them as being either in the enemy camp or as 'fellow travelers' I fear that [we will appear as] the unreasonable member of the East-West struggle."[21]

The statement was an oblique allusion to the recent controversy that Dulles had stirred up by defining neutralism as "an immoral and shortsighted conception."[22] Indeed, the argument between Byroade and Hoover had profound implications for American relations with the entire developing world. More to the point, it had immediate relevance to what was about to become the most momentous of issues: the controversy over the Aswan High Dam.

Congress Balks

The dam to be built across the Nile River at Aswan was Nasser's flagship development project. Still in the planning stages, it was expected to bring under cultivation hundreds of thousands of acres of arid land and to generate millions of watts of electricity. In its effort to woo Nasser in the aftermath of the Soviet arms deal, the Eisenhower administration had teamed up with the British and the World Bank to help finance the dam. The consortium submitted a funding proposal to Nasser in December 1955, which he rejected. In February, he had presented a counteroffer that would have required the United States to take much more responsibility for the entire project, and the Americans had yet to respond. In accordance with Omega, they were stalling.

Byroade strongly disapproved, arguing that these delaying tactics would inevitably backfire. They would result, he predicted, in a repeat of the fiasco of the Soviet arms deal (as he understood it). Just as Moscow had stepped up with weapons in the past, it was now in the process of coming forward with a proposal to fund the dam. Here again, Byroade argued, the Egyptians had a "compelling need" for foreign aid; they resented the "appearance of Western indifference"; and they were struck by the "Soviet eagerness to help."[23] Why, Byroade was asking, did Washington want history to repeat itself?

Eisenhower and Dulles read the history differently. As they saw it, Nasser was simply playing the United States off against the Soviet Union. Their unease only increased when they considered the escalation in his policies of defiance, which now included supporting anti-French rebels in Algeria; backing anti-British forces in East Africa; prosecuting an endless border war with Israel; conducting subversive activities in Iraq, Jordan, and Lebanon; and steadily increasing economic, military, and diplomatic cooperation with East Bloc countries. In May, Nasser recognized Communist China, a move that Washington regarded as a slap in the face—and one that Nasser had earlier said was too risky to undertake at that time.

Not surprisingly, then, Eisenhower and Dulles now faced a bipartisan congressional coalition strongly in favor of isolating Egypt. This coalition included, in addition to pro-Israel elements, Cold War hard-liners and politicians from southern, cotton-growing states who viewed the Egyptian cotton industry as an unwanted competitor. Throughout June, a movement against funding the Aswan High Dam gathered steam in Congress.

Contemplating his next steps, Dulles was largely on his own. On June 7, Eisenhower suffered an attack of ileitis, an inflammation of the small intestine, which required emergency surgery and lengthy recuperation. During the ensuing weeks, Dulles took charge of foreign policy. Eisenhower returned to work on July 15, the very moment when the issue of the dam was coming to a head. Though the president was fully aware of the major developments and approved all of Dulles's most consequential decisions, he did not play the leading role.

On Tuesday, July 17, Senator William Knowland, the ranking Republican on the Senate Appropriations Committee, warned Dulles that Congress was poised to insert in the next foreign aid bill an explicit prohibition against the use of American money for the Aswan High Dam. His committee, he said, would decide the issue on Friday, the twentieth—just three days away. Replying, Dulles conveyed his feeling that the committee "won't feel it necessary" to take action, "because we have just about made up our minds to tell the Egyptians we will not [fund the dam]."[24]

In fact, Dulles had already made up his mind—and Nasser, as he himself would later explain to Byroade, knew it.[25] Recognizing that the Americans had been stringing him along and had no intention of following through on the funding, the Egyptian leader had devised a plan that, among other things, would portray the decision as an act of vengeful imperialism. Springing that plan would prove to be his masterstroke.

The Jujitsu Master

The first step was to force Dulles's hand. Apparently reversing course, Nasser withdrew his February counterproposal and accepted the original terms that the United States and its partners had offered him the previous December. Having thus stripped Dulles of the ability to argue that Egypt was being unreasonable, he then had Ahmed Hussein, the Egyptian ambassador, make an appointment to see Dulles in order to receive an unambiguous, yes-or-no answer.

With Congress moving in on Dulles from one direction and Nasser pressing from the other, the secretary of state's freedom of maneuver disappeared. He discussed his predicament with his brother Allen, the CIA director, by phone on July 19, just twenty minutes before Hussein was due to arrive at his office. Hussein, Foster Dulles said, had already sent a warning in advance: if the United States refused to fund the dam, then the Egyptians "will go ahead with the Soviets." Dulles's hands, however, were already tied. If he failed to withdraw the offer today, he said, "Congress will chop it off tomorrow." He preferred to do the chopping himself.[26]

When Hussein showed up a few minutes later, Dulles offered him an explanation that was at once frank and disingenuous. On the frank side, he freely admitted that Congress intended to block all funding for the Aswan High Dam, and he blamed Nasser's co-operation with the Soviets for this development. To be sure, Dulles said, there were highly interested parties (such as those seeking to prevent an increase in "Egyptian cotton production in competi-tion with American cotton growers") who were lobbying against the dam, but the crux of the problem was the basic opposition of "the rank and file of the American people and the Congress," op-position that flowed "from a feeling that the Egyptian Government was working closely with those hostile to us who sought to injure us wherever they could."[27]

Dulles was being more calculating when he proceeded to claim that, even with outside help, the project itself was a bigger bur-den than the Egyptian economy could handle. Building the dam, he said, would impose severe austerity on Egyptians, instilling in them resentment of the United States. A statement that the State Department circulated after the meeting dwelled further on this theme, suggesting that Egypt's financial circumstances had deteri-orated since December, when the consortium had made its original offer, and that the United States now doubted "the ability of Egypt to devote adequate resources to assure the project's success."[28] In short, Egypt was a credit risk that no responsible lender would touch.

None of these latter factors had any bearing on Dulles's actual decision, and he would later receive harsh criticism, especially from Nasser himself, for having drawn attention to them. Why, then, did he bother? In his call with his brother, he'd explained that he was laying the predicate for a propaganda campaign targeting Eastern Europe. By making out the dam to be an enormous expense, the United States could then claim that the Soviet Union had assumed an unwieldy burden. As Dulles told his brother, the message to the captive nations of Eastern Europe would be, "You don't get bread because you are being squeezed to build a dam."

A clever tactic, but one that played directly into Nasser's hands. Learning of Dulles's decision, the Egyptian leader countered with the single greatest move of his career: nationalization of the Suez Canal. The announcement speech he gave on July 26 in Alexandria recounted the history of relations between Egypt and the West. Long and rambling, it was also rousing, peppered with examples of how, time and again, the Egyptians had unmasked the rank hypocrisy of the West. After speaking for hours, Nasser delivered an unforgettable crescendo: "At this moment as I talk to you some of your Egyptian brethren are proceeding to administer the canal company and to run its affairs," he said. "They are taking over the canal company at this very moment—the Egyptian canal company, not the foreign canal company."[29]

Nasser stunned his audience. It is impossible to exaggerate the power of the emotions that the canal takeover stirred in ordinary Egyptians. If Europeans claimed that the company was a private concern, Egyptians saw it as an instrument of imperial exploitation—"a state within a state," Nasser called it in his speech—plundering a national asset for the benefit of France and Britain. Every inch of the canal resided in Egypt, yet ships paid their transit dues to an office in Paris, and only a fraction of the money made its way to Egyptian coffers. The company, Nasser stated, collected $100 million annually, of which the Egyptians received only $3 million. In this allegedly "private" corporation, the British and French governments were the major shareholders.[30]

Dulles had claimed that the Egyptian economy was not strong enough to support the dam. The Egyptian economy, Nasser countered, would be plenty strong if only the Westerners would stop plundering it; in fact, the money to be collected by Egypt in transit fees would suffice to fund the Aswan Dam. "[T]oday," Nasser thundered, "when we build the High Dam, we are also building the dam of dignity, freedom and grandeur. We are eliminating the dams of humiliation, and servility."[31]

By striking a blow at a British and French asset, Nasser thus brilliantly transformed the disagreement with Dulles over the dam into a contest between Arab nationalism and European imperialism. Dulles had planned an elaborate jujitsu move on both Nasser and the Soviet Union, only to become tripped up by a master of the art.

The Power of the Pen

No American official predicted the nationalization itself, but Henry Byroade did loudly and repeatedly warn that failure to fund the dam would boomerang. The assumptions that produced this prediction may have been misguided, but the prediction itself was accurate; combined with the obvious miscalculation of the secretary of state, the result worked to enhance Byroade's reputation. It also helped fuel a theme that, for the past sixty years, has run through many accounts of Middle East diplomacy: namely, that Dulles "lost" Nasser. Losing the trust of his superiors, Byroade won the contest for the American historical memory.

He did so with significant help from Kermit Roosevelt. In the 1950s the two men eagerly conveyed their views directly to influential contemporaries and made themselves generously available to authors who in the 1960s, '70s, and '80s would pen in-depth accounts of Eisenhower's Middle East diplomacy. Their number included Donald Neff and Kennett Love, whose respective volumes, *Warriors at Suez* and *Suez: The Twice-Fought War,* would become two of the most influential books written before the official archives opened.[32]

The greatest impact came in the 1980s when the diplomatic correspondence became available to historians. In terms of pure quantity, the vast majority of American documents between July 1952 and March 1956 support the Byroade-Roosevelt perspective. The American embassy in Cairo alone generated thousands of dispatches, including dozens upon dozens of accounts of personal conversations with Nasser. Virtually all of these take it as axiomatic that the Egyptian leader was honest, forthright, and deeply desirous of an alliance with the West. It was only after March 1956 that a new view of Nasser crept into the discussion, but even then it was not a view emanating from Cairo, where Byroade was continuing to press Nasser's case.

"History will be kind to me," Winston Churchill once quipped, "for I shall write it." In the matter of Egyptian-American relations, Dulles, who died in office, never took up the pen in his own defense. It was, rather, the team of Byroade and Roosevelt who told Dulles's story for him—on the basis of information that derived, ultimately, from Nasser. If history has been unkind to Dulles on the matter of the Aswan High Dam, it is because Nasser wrote it.

Dulles's Blunder?

Was the decision to cancel the offer of funding for the dam truly a blunder? If Dulles had not "offended" Nasser, would he have refrained from nationalizing the canal? Such is the frequent contention of historians. At times, even Eisenhower, wily politician that he was, fed oxygen to this analysis by dropping hints that, had he not been ill and less than fully in charge at the time, he would have handled the matter with greater aplomb.[33]

Such arguments ignore the fact that Congress was moving to cut the funding no matter what; one way or another, Nasser was going to receive no for an answer. Given that fact, to suggest that Dulles somehow provoked the nationalization is to believe that the clumsy manner in which he delivered the message—his statements to Ambassador Hussein, the ill-crafted press release—made all the difference. On its face, this reasoning is flimsy, and all the more so when one considers Byroade's first meeting with Nasser just days after the nationalization. In the course of their conversation, the ambassador gleaned that the nationalization "was not as hurried as we have thought." Nasser explained that he had told Hussein, in advance of the meeting with Dulles, of his intention to nationalize the canal "if [the] West backed out of [the] offer."[34] In other words, Nasser had cast Dulles in the role of arrogant imperialist even before the meeting in Washington.

Indeed, the Dulles-lost-Nasser thesis ignores the utterly irresistible appeal to Nasser of the nationalization scheme. In his July 26 speech, he would point to the essence of the matter: "This money is ours, and this Canal belongs to Egypt."[35] The nationalization speech, which Nasser delivered on the fourth anniversary of the Free Officers' revolution, was the Egyptian equivalent of a declaration of independence. To this day, Egyptians who were alive at the time remember exactly where they were when they heard the news. It was Nasser's greatest moment, an act of defiance in a class all its own, and one that secured for him a special place of pride in his nation's history.

Justice, glory, gold, and vengeance were motivators powerful enough; Nasser hardly needed a snub from Dulles to spur him to action. If one needs to specify a single "triggering" moment for the nationalization, that moment was June 13, 1956. On that day, the last British soldiers evacuated the Suez Canal Zone, and the Union

Jack was lowered for the final time. No trumpets sounded and no cannons boomed, but Egypt, after seventy-four years, was free at last of foreign occupiers. With the British troops gone forever, the Suez Canal Company dangled like a plum ripe for the picking.

Why did Nasser nationalize the canal in July 1956? Because he could.

CHAPTER 11

The End of Empire

On July 31, 1956, five days after Nasser nationalized the Suez Canal, Eden transmitted a few simple messages to Eisenhower. War was "necessary and inevitable," he said, and he was determined "to drive Nasser out of Egypt." He invited the United States to join the fight.[1] No sooner had Eisenhower received the message than he called his top aides to the White House to discuss it. "What would be the result of the type of war that Eden envisioned?" he asked Allen Dulles. The question was as much a statement of exasperation as a request for information. "[T]he whole Arab world would unite in opposition," the director of the CIA responded.

"[T]he whole *Moslem* world," Eisenhower corrected him.[2] Nasser, he continued, "embodies the emotional demands of the people of the area for independence"; he stands for "slapping the white man down." War, therefore, could "array the world from Dakar to the Philippine Islands against us."[3]

This depiction of Nasser as a symbol of Muslim aspirations bore a surface similarity to Ambassador Byroade's thinking, but the resemblance was misleading. Eisenhower remained committed to the Omega strategy, which called for reducing Nasser's power through indirect actions. He had firmly and permanently rejected Byroade's contention that Nasser was eager to establish a stable partnership with the West. What troubled the president about Eden's proposed war was not that it would eliminate Nasser, but that it would drive the countries emerging from European colonialism into the arms of the Soviet Union.

With this fear foremost in his mind, Eisenhower dispatched Foster Dulles to London with orders to stop the march to war. In doing so, he wagered that aligning the United States with the sentiments of "the whole Arab world" would serve the West better than a policy of supporting traditional allies and punishing enemies. As Dulles flew to London, he carried a letter from Eisenhower to Eden and Guy Mollet, the French prime minister, urging them to convene "a meeting of interested states" as soon as possible.[4]

Eden and Mollet clamored for war; Eisenhower demanded a conference.

Jaw Jaw, not War War

The president had hit on the idea of a conference four days earlier, on July 27, when he first heard first reports from London indicating that the British were determined to go to war. Dulles, at that moment, was traveling in South America and unavailable for consultation. Alarmed by the mood in the British government, Eisenhower immediately dashed off a note to Eden. "We are of the earnest opinion," he wrote, "that the maximum number of maritime nations affected by the Nasser action should be consulted quickly in the hope of obtaining an agreed basis of understanding."[5] The ambiguous note was quintessential Eisenhower. On the one hand, he sounded supportive, as if he were in favor of racing to assemble a broad anti-Nasser coalition. On the other hand, he was slowing Eden down, forcing him to swim through molasses. Consultations with the other maritime nations would take weeks, months perhaps. The more governments Eden would consult, the harder it would be to forge a consensus in favor of war.

Eden chafed at the restraint. His first encounter with Dulles, when the latter arrived in London, was stilted. Eden insisted, Dulles wrote in a memorandum on the discussion, "that prompt forcible action was necessary." If Nasser kept control of the canal, "it would mean disaster for British interests in the whole Middle East." Dulles responded by saying that the American public "was not ready to back a military venture by Britain and France which . . . could be plausibly portrayed as motivated by imperialist and colonialist ambitions."[6] It was a blunt statement. Dulles tried to soften the blow with language that was less candid. The United States and Britain, he said, were in total agreement about ultimate aims; their disagreement was simply over tactics and timing. Dulles then issued a promise that Eden would never let him forget. He vowed that America was determined "to make Nasser disgorge what he was attempting to swallow."[7]

Disgorge—the word was music to British ears. On the basis of its promise of a coercive policy, Eden dropped his opposition to Eisenhower's proposed conference. Dulles's immediate mission was accomplished, but as he flew home, he was hardly celebrating. The gap between the American and British positions was, he knew, much greater than his rhetoric had admitted. Eden was determined to strike at Nasser, to destroy him if possible—not just to retake the canal, but also to reassert British authority throughout the entire Middle East. To Eisenhower and Dulles, however, British authority had already suffered an irreversible loss in value. Nasser had turned out to be a great disappointment, to be sure, but smart money was still on an alliance with moderate nationalism, not with dying empires.

Without a credible threat of war, however, how could the West force Nasser to disgorge anything? Less than three weeks later, Dulles was back in London grappling unsuccessfully with that crucial question. In the interim, the British had convened what is now known as the first London conference. Lasting a week starting on August 18, it brought together twenty-four powers with a strong interest in the free flow of shipping through the Suez Canal.

Though formally chaired by the British foreign secretary, Selwyn Lloyd, the conference was Eisenhower's in every respect. It transformed the conflict, as Eisenhower had envisioned, from a two-sided dispute between Egypt and European imperialism into a multilateral discussion with more than twenty participants. Nasser, for his part, boycotted the proceedings, denouncing them as an imperialist affront to Egyptian sovereignty. Be that as it may, the conference complicated the work of Nasser's propagandists. They were itching to tell a simple morality tale about the struggle of heroic Egypt against the nefarious colonialists, but Eisenhower was equally determined to complicate their job. Despite strenuous British objections, the Americans insisted, for example, on Moscow's participation.

From Eisenhower's point of view, the greatest benefit of the conference was the potential that it created for a face-saving compromise. The primary Western interest in the canal, Eisenhower reasoned, was oil. Two-thirds of the oil burned in Europe flowed through the Suez Canal. What Britain and France needed most, therefore, was a solid guarantee that the canal would continue to function as an unimpeded international waterway. Nasser should never be in a position, whether in concert with the Soviets or on his own, to deprive the Europeans of their energy supply.

As for the interests of Egypt, Eisenhower assumed that Nasser had his eyes firmly fixed on profits and, above all, prestige. If the lion's share of the money from the canal dues could remain in Egyptian hands, and if Nasser could point to tangible signs of direct Egyptian control over the canal, then maybe he would compromise with Britain and France. Convincing him to cut a deal would be an exceedingly difficult challenge. Perhaps it was impossible. Even if the effort failed, however, the mere pursuit of it would buy time and string out the crisis, making it ever harder for the British and French to launch a war.

As Eisenhower's conference idea developed, it turned into a

two-step process. The first step was to convince the attendees to authorize the replacement of the Suez Canal Company with an international body, one that would assist the Egyptians in managing the operations of the canal on behalf of the interested maritime powers. The second step, the really hard part, was to convince Nasser to accept the body, which would soon become known as the Suez Board.

The conference opened with a keynote address from Dulles, who surveyed the legal history of the canal, which had first opened in 1869. Pointing to the 1888 Convention of Constantinople, the treaty that had governed operations for the last seven decades, Dulles asked whether the plan for a Suez Board violated Egyptian sovereignty. He rejected the very thought. "Egyptian sovereignty," he stated, "is and always has been qualified by the Treaty of 1888 which makes of the Canal an international—not an Egyptian— waterway."[8] Both in his speech and his backroom negotiations, Dulles was at his finest, and, in the end, eighteen out of twenty-four delegates voted in favor of creating the Suez Board.

To all appearances, Dulles had won a major victory. In fact, things were not going well. He had come to the conference with a secret plan—to cut a backroom deal with Moscow. "I feel," he had originally written to Eisenhower, "that the Soviets would be open to making some kind of an arrangement with us and perhaps join to impose it upon Egypt if on the one hand it were couched in a way which would not gravely prejudice the Soviet Union with the Arab world and if on the other hand we would more or less make it a two-party affair with some downgrading of the British and the French."[9] As it turned out, the Soviet leadership harbored no reciprocal impulse to downgrade its Egyptian ally. Moscow was among the six powers who voted against the Suez Board, and without Soviet support, the possibility of convincing Nasser to compromise diminished precipitously. Dulles's secret plan was dead in the water.

The British, however, were blissfully unaware that Dulles had placed them and the French on the downgrade list. Heartened by the vote in favor of the Suez Board, they proposed to Dulles that he should now lead the delegation that would fly to Cairo to present the decisions of the conference to Nasser. The last thing that Dulles wanted, however, was to yoke American policy to the maximalist demands of his allies. To preserve American freedom of maneuver, he declined the British proposal. In his stead Robert Menzies, the Australian premier, volunteered to lead the delegation. Nasser received Menzies hospitably but refused to place the canal under any form of international oversight. "[W]ith a broad and cheerful smile," Menzies writes in his memoirs, "President Nasser took our proposals apart, tore them up, and metaphorically consigned them to the wastepaper basket."[10]

The Australian premier departed Cairo with feelings of great bitterness—not toward Nasser, but toward Eisenhower. And Menzies had very good reason for being annoyed with the American president. As the delegation was setting to work in Cairo, Eisenhower appeared at a press conference in Washington and, in answer to a question, said that he was "very hopeful" that Egypt would accept Menzies's offer. If it didn't, however, then the search for a peaceful solution would continue.[11] The Egyptian press celebrated Eisenhower's statement as preemptive surrender by the West—as proof that Nasser would suffer no adverse consequences if he were to reject the Suez Board. Menzies felt betrayed. Returning home by way of Washington, he lodged a direct protest with the president, complaining that Ike's statement had given Nasser the sense that "he could probably get more favourable terms if he rejected" the Suez Board. Eisenhower listened to Menzies sympathetically, defending the statement with the flimsy excuse that it was an unfortunate necessity of "democratic processes."[12]

Dulles Organizes a Union

Eden responded to Menzies's failure by preparing to place the Suez question before the United Nations Security Council. He knew, of course, that the UN would never support a coercive policy. The Soviets would inevitably use their veto to protect Egypt. In domestic British politics, however, seeking redress at the UN was a prerequisite for the use of force. Eisenhower and Dulles therefore regarded Eden's move as a step in the wrong direction, and they feared that the debate in the Security Council would force them to air in public some of their fundamental differences with the British and French. The priority in Washington, therefore, was to dissuade Eden from taking action at the UN. To do so, however, required offering Eden an alternative course of action. But what?

In early September, Dulles escaped to Main Duck Island, his remote, personal retreat on Lake Ontario, where he was entirely cut off from the outside world. Over a long weekend, he brainstormed, scribbling ideas on a yellow legal pad, crossing them out, scribbling more. He emerged from his seclusion with a blueprint for a new organization: a union of maritime countries. The union would negotiate with Nasser collectively, on the model of labor leaders haggling with a large industrial corporation. According to Dulles's interpretation of the 1888 convention, the canal users had every legal right to co-manage shipping through the waterway. By this theory, if Nasser interfered with the union, he would be in breach of his international obligations, and the union could, in effect, strike.

The entire initiative was a lawyer's ruse. As a practical plan, it had two obvious deficiencies. First, the union would have no ability to enforce its will. How would it prevent scabs from working with Nasser? Second, suppose the Egyptians were to block the passage of unionized ships. Would the United States Navy then blast its way through the canal? Obviously not. Dulles's new idea failed to address the fundamental problem that dogged the negotiations from day one. If the West refused to use force, how could it convince Nasser to compromise?

When Dulles returned from his seclusion, he briefed the president on the product of his brainstorming. Eisenhower, Dulles wrote in a memorandum on their meeting, "was not sure" that the idea would work.[13] "I said I was not sure either but that I felt we had to keep the initiative and to keep probing along various lines, particularly since there was no chance of getting the British and the French not to use force unless they had some alternatives that seemed to have in them some strength of purpose and some initiative."[14] Despite his doubts, Eisenhower approved the concept.

And so, surprisingly, did Eden—but not because he actually believed it would work. On the contrary, he was certain it would fail. However, he calculated that its inevitable collapse would demonstrate to the Americans, once and for all, that coercion was the only way to make Nasser "disgorge" the canal. Selwyn Lloyd, the foreign secretary, summarized the thinking in London to Roger Makins, his ambassador in Washington, on September 6. "The great tactical advantage of Mr. Dulles's proposal," he explained, "is that, if the Americans were to participate in the actual setting up of an international body . . . , they would have committed themselves much further towards a policy of compelling the Egyptian Government by some means or other to accept international control."[15]

Dulles Guts a Union

Eden conditioned his support for Dulles's scheme, which soon became known as the Suez Canal Users' Association (SCUA), on an American commitment to a more coercive policy. To force Dulles's hand, Makins informed the secretary of state that Eden was due to address Parliament on September 12. Parliament, he argued, fully expected Eden to present his plan of action at the United Nations.

If the prime minister were to spring British participation in SCUA on Parliament, then the organization must be a robust one. It must be empowered, like the old Suez Canal Company, to collect canal dues and provide pilots for ships. Moreover, if Egypt were to interfere with SCUA, then the United States must agree that the organization's members would be justified in taking the necessary steps to enforce their rights. Interference with SCUA, that is to say, must be a justification for coercive measures, including war. "Anything short of that," Makins explained to Dulles, "would not be regarded as an indication that we meant business."[16]

Makins shared with Eisenhower and Dulles a draft of Eden's proposed statement in Parliament and, remarkably, Eisenhower and Dulles approved it. The Americans, finally, had decided to get tough with Nasser. Or had they?

When Eden actually delivered his statement, he encountered stiff opposition from the Labor Party, which immediately denounced SCUA as a transparent effort to lay a pretext for war. Labor MPs reacted with ferocity when Eden warned that if Nasser blocked the canal, then SCUA members would "be free to take such further steps as seem to be required, either through the UN or by other means, for the assertion of their rights." The phrase "other means" sparked outrage. "You are talking about war!" one detractor yelled.[17] An angry debate erupted, and it continued throughout the entire next day.

The parliamentary debate now overlapped with a press conference that Dulles had scheduled for September 13. This turn of events offered the secretary of state an opportunity to undermine Eden precisely as Eisenhower had undermined Menzies in Cairo. Nasser played a supporting role in the effort. The Egyptian leader, of course, saw the announcement of SCUA as a sinister development—and, as he had time and again over the previous three years, he turned to Washington for help. Just moments before Dulles appeared at his press conference, the Egyptian ambassador, Ahmed Hussein, rushed to the State Department to deliver a short but urgent communication from Nasser. "The scheme which Prime Minister Eden wants to impose is an open and flagrant aggression on Egypt's sovereignty and its implementation means war," the message stated. "If the United States desires war it may support the scheme, but if its desire is to work for a peaceful solution the scheme has to be abandoned."[18]

Dulles's press conference had been the subject of meticulous coordination with the British Foreign Office. According to the agreed script, Dulles was to read a statement, vetted by London, announcing American support for SCUA; meanwhile, in Paris, the French foreign minister would organize a parallel press conference in which he would read an identical statement. This spectacle of tripartite solidarity would, Eden planned, shore up his position against his Labor party critics.

But Nasser's appeal—or, more precisely, Dulles's response to it—destroyed Eden's plan. Before leaving the State Department, Hussein whispered to the waiting reporters that Eden's announcement in Parliament about SCUA "means war."[19] An otherwise routine press conference suddenly became a dramatic event. After Dulles read his statement, reporters pounced with a single burning question in mind: was the United States going to coerce Nasser, or restrain Britain and France? Dulles bent over backward to dispel the notion that SCUA might lead to war. "We do not intend to shoot our way through" the canal, he explained during the question-and-answer period. "It may be we have the right to do it, but we don't intend to do it as far as the US is concerned." If Nasser were to obstruct American ships, he explained, they would simply go around the Cape of Good Hope.

In effect, Dulles was rewriting Eden's statement on SCUA. "I do not recall just exactly what Sir Anthony Eden said" about use of force, he said disingenuously. "I did not get the impression that there was any undertaking or pledge given by him to shoot their way through the canal."[20] Via ticker tape, Dulles's words arrived almost instantaneously in London, where the parliamentary debate was still continuing. Tony Benn, a rising star in the Labor Party, rose to speak: "Mr. Dulles now has a statement on the tape in which he says that he will not use force to go through with the users' association. This debate, therefore, changes its course as it proceeds."[21]

The Labor opposition demanded that the prime minister follow Dulles's example and renounce war as a legitimate means of solving the canal dispute. Eden managed to end the debate without acceding to the demand, but he emerged politically weakened from the ordeal. Years later, his anger at Dulles still burned. "It would be hard to imagine," he wrote in his memoirs, "a statement more likely to cause the maximum allied disunity and disarray." It was, in addition, "an advertisement to Nasser that he could reject the project with impunity."[22]

SCUA was now exposed as a worthless fiction, but the farce still had one more act remaining. On September 19, the British convened the second London conference, the goal of which was to establish SCUA formally. The expectations of the British and French were already extremely low, but Dulles still managed to astound them—this time by refusing to compel American shipping companies to pay their canal dues to SCUA. If American companies were free to flout the authority the association, what was to make Nasser respect it? For the second time, Dulles had gutted his own creation.

Collusion

At a press conference on October 2, Dulles made public the fact that the Eisenhower administration was downgrading its British and French allies. The United States, he said, was not obligated by the NATO alliance to support Britain and France outside of Europe. Washington "cannot be expected to identify itself 100 per cent either with the colonial powers or the powers uniquely concerned with the problem of getting independence as rapidly and as fully as possible." While the Americans and their European allies stood as one in the North Atlantic arena, "any areas encroaching in some form or manner on the problem of so-called colonialism, [will] find the United States playing an independent role." [23]

Faced with this downgrade, Eden saw only two stark choices: defeat at the hands of Nasser, or war. The Americans, however, were still convinced that they were defining a third option. Their realistic alternative to war, in their minds, was not limited to SCUA; they were also proposing a host of other measures, based on the Omega strategy, to diminish Nasser's power—measures that included covert action. Eisenhower's favorite idea, in this context, was still to detach Saudi Arabia from Egypt and to build it up as an alternative center of power. But Omega also called for driving a wedge between Cairo and its other ally, Damascus, where the government was shaky and vulnerable. A well-orchestrated coup in Syria would bring to power a new clique that would align with Turkey and Iraq and thereby tip the regional balance of power against Nasser.

In Eisenhower's view, war would be counterproductive. It would simply play to Nasser's strength, allowing him to pose as the leader of all Arab nationalists. "Nasser thrives on drama," the president had written to Eden in August. "If we let some of the drama go out of the situation and concentrate upon the task of deflating him through slower but sure processes . . . , I believe the desired results can more probably be obtained." [24]

On its face, Eisenhower's indirect approach seemed shrewd and sophisticated, but when viewed from London it had two glaring defects. First, it failed to address the canal question itself—the key issue in British domestic politics. Second, it offered the British no immediate hope of shoring up their position in Jordan, where, post-Glubb, they were hanging on by a thread. Simply put, Eisenhower's preferred strategy did nothing to reassert *British* authority in the Middle East.

In Eden's view, Nasser had established a dangerous precedent of defying Britain with impunity. If he were not seen to pay a price for such behavior, then British basing rights in Jordan and Iraq would evaporate; soon thereafter, other actors would move to plunder British oil interests in the Persian Gulf. "I cannot accept the present US thinking that the two problems of settling the canal issue and deflating Nasser can be separated either as to timing or method," the British foreign secretary, Selwyn Lloyd, wrote to his ambassador in Washington on September 8. "Please convey to Mr. Dulles my grave anxiety at the present state of our consultation and seek to impress upon him the absolute necessity for effective action urgently. Any further dawdling will be fatal."[25]

This urgency drove Eden toward war—yet still he wavered. Three months earlier, when the shock of the nationalization was fresh, invading Egypt might have been politically feasible, but Eisenhower's efforts in the meantime to string out the crisis had done their work. With the canal now running smoothly under Egyptian control, the claim that Nasser threatened international shipping rang hollow. Meanwhile, the domestic opposition in Britain to war had increased. For Eden to pull the trigger, he needed a fresh emergency.

With the help of the Israelis, the French soon concocted one. Over the previous year, France and Israel had developed a burgeoning military alliance. While Nasser was organizing the Fedayeen campaign against Israel, he was also providing arms to the anti-French rebels in Algeria, thus pushing Paris and Jerusalem closer by the day. Even before the nationalization of the canal, the French began delivering heavy weapons to Israel. After the nationalization, a robust intelligence-sharing operation sprang up. Before long, the two sides were surreptitiously discussing the possibility of a joint war on Egypt, with the intent of toppling Nasser.

Israeli Prime Minister David Ben-Gurion welcomed the discussion, but he set British participation in the war as a precondition for Israeli involvement. He was deeply wary of Eden. With some forty years of experience in negotiating with the British, he feared a trap. If Israel were to proceed alone with France, Eden might be tempted to make a play for Arab goodwill by branding Israel as an aggressor in the United Nations. Britain still maintained large military forces in the region. If Eden were given international license to punish Israel, the result could be devastating.

The distrust was reciprocal, and the gulf of suspicion that separated London from Jerusalem posed a major challenge to French Prime Minister Guy Mollet, and his foreign minister, Christian Pineau, both of whom were very sympathetic to Zionism. How, they asked, could they broker an alliance between Ben-Gurion and Eden? They answered their question with a scheme, stranger than fiction, which they previewed to Eden. Suppose, they said, the Israelis were to attack Egypt first. In that case, the British would be free to intervene militarily, together with the French, in order to protect shipping through the Suez Canal. Paris and London would issue an ultimatum demanding that the belligerents withdraw to a position of ten miles on either side of the canal, or face severe consequences. The Israelis, by prior arrangement, would comply. Nasser, however, would inevitably reject the ultimatum, because it would leave Israeli forces inside Egypt while simultaneously compelling Egyptian forces to withdraw from their own sovereign territory. An Anglo-French force would then intervene to punish Egypt for noncompliance. It would take over the canal and, in the process, topple Nasser.

The scenario enticed Eden, but not Ben-Gurion—at least not at first. The idea that Israel alone should catalyze the war activated his deep-seated distrust of the British government. If Eden was double-dealing, or if his commitment were to waver after the war began, then Israel would find itself alone on the battlefield, isolated and branded as an aggressor. Only a plan that called for simultaneous action by all parties could reassure Ben-Gurion. In an effort to bring Ben-Gurion around, the French invited him to a secret rendezvous with Selwyn Lloyd on October 22, in Sèvres, a suburb of Paris. Lloyd and Ben-Gurion circled each other like snarling dogs, and the meeting ended inconclusively.

Nevertheless, Ben-Gurion's position softened. At Sèvres he was joined by, among others, Moshe Dayan, the chief of staff of the Israel Defense Forces. In discussion with the British and French, Ben-Gurion gave Dayan some leeway: he permitted the general to float, as a "private" suggestion, the possibility that Israel might attack first. In that case, Dayan explained to his interlocutors, Israel would be forced to reduce the risk to itself by making the initial attack a border raid rather than a full-scale assault.[26] While Dayan's proposal heartened the French, it irritated Lloyd, who said that Britain could not justify an invasion of Egypt on the basis of a mere border skirmish. Lloyd demanded, instead, that the Israelis launch what he called "a real act of war."[27]

The talks broke down, and Lloyd returned home. The French, however, refused to give up. Pineau trailed behind Lloyd to Britain, where he met up with Eden the next day. Before leaving Paris, he received from Dayan a modified proposal that further strengthened his hand. Dayan suggested that the Israelis would, at the outbreak of the war, strike deep into Sinai, so deep that the British and French could plausibly depict their move as a threat to shipping in the canal. In terms of size, their operation would still be small in scale, but it would come closer to Lloyd's demand for an act of war.[28]

Eden approved the modified scenario on October 23, and to complete the transaction with the Israelis, who were still waiting in Sèvres, he dispatched an emissary, Patrick Dean, to France. Dean was an odd choice, because he was a career diplomat, not a minister. By sending a comparatively low-level official, Eden perhaps intended to insulate the government from the charge of collusion with Israel. Or perhaps he simply believed that the final discussion was a pro forma affair.

In fact, however, the negotiation was not over. Ben-Gurion, wily and experienced, had allowed Dayan to float the proposal without endorsing it himself. In return for his personal approval, he demanded one last concession: France, Britain, and Israel, he told Dean and the French, must ratify their plan with a written protocol. Dean apparently didn't think twice about the request—it being a normal diplomatic practice to set agreements to writing. Three identical copies of the war plan were drawn up, and Ben-Gurion, Pineau, and Dean personally signed each one. Ben-Gurion carefully folded up his copy and put it in his breast pocket.[29]

When Dean returned to England and dutifully presented the agreement to the prime minister, it made Eden blanch. The protocol was ironclad evidence of his collusion with Israel. Eden destroyed his copy and ordered Dean to retrieve and eliminate the other two as well. When Dean returned to Paris, however, he received no help from the French, who, unmoved by Eden's plight, insisted on keeping their copy. As for the Israelis, they were already in the air, flying home.[30]

Indeed, Ben-Gurion was flying high. On the plane his spirits soared. He amused himself on the trip by consulting ancient historical sources, searching for the Hebrew place-names for the points in Sinai that he planned to annex to Israel. The signed agreement, all the while, remained in his breast pocket, snug to his chest.

War

The first week of November was a busy one for Eisenhower. The campaign prior to the election on November 6, which he won in a landslide over Adlai Stevenson, would have been enough to keep anyone busy. But then there was the crisis in Hungary. Over the previous week, a spontaneous anti-Soviet movement had spread across the country, and a new government, under Prime Minister Imre Nagy, responded to it by declaring Hungary neutral in the Cold War. When Nagy appealed to the United Nations to help defend Hungary's independence, Moscow ordered a violent crackdown. By November 4, Soviet tanks had rolled through Budapest and toppled Nagy.

It was against this tumultuous background that the Suez war broke out, starting with the Israeli raid into the Sinai on October 29. Like clockwork, the British and French issued their ultimatum, giving the Israelis and Egyptians twelve hours to comply or face the consequences. When the Egyptians, as expected, rejected the ultimatum and the deadline passed, the British and French began to bombard positions in the Canal Zone. They did not, however, land forces until November 5.

Eisenhower understood from the outset that the French and Israelis were in cahoots, because American intelligence had picked up telltale signs, such as increased military communications between Israel and France, in the days preceding the Israeli attack. Eisenhower suspected Eden as a co-conspirator, but the evidence, at first, was inconclusive. When the British and French issued their ultimatum, however, it was obvious to the president that the three powers had colluded.

Eisenhower now faced the key question of the crisis in its most fateful form: should he support his allies or Nasser? He chose Nasser. More formally, he decided to proceed in accordance with existing American plans about the best way to stabilize an Arab-Israeli war. Those plans looked to the Tripartite Declaration, a statement of policy signed in May 1950 by France, Britain, and the United States. The declaration guaranteed the status quo by promising that the signatories would come to the aid of *any* party who was a victim of aggression. In this case, the party in question was Egypt.

The collusion of the British and the French made it impossible to act in concert with them. Nevertheless, Eisenhower decided, without the slightest hesitation, that the Tripartite Declaration's guarantee of the status quo remained operative. Now, however, the United States would turn the principles of the declaration against not just Israel but the British and French as well. "[W]e must honor our pledge" to assist any victim of aggression, he immediately told his aides, and, therefore, "we cannot be bound by our traditional alliances."

In order to garner international legitimacy for American action, he explained to his staff, "the UN might be the most valuable course to follow"—a reference to the General Assembly, where a pro-Egyptian majority could easily be mustered.[31] At staggering speed and with no debate, Eisenhower chose the United Nations over America's Cold War allies. Why?

There can be no doubt, as many authors have noted, that he felt a deep sense of betrayal, but his policy was far more than just the product of emotion. From the beginning of the crisis, a key assumption had steadily guided his thinking: that a war over the canal was the worst option, because it would drive the Arab world, if not the entire developing world, into the arms of the Soviets.

Shortly after sharing his thinking with his staff, he addressed the nation with a speech that reflected his fear of alienating what would soon be known as the Third World. In a prime time statement broadcast on television and radio on the night of October 31, he firmly rejected both the Israeli invasion and the Anglo-French intervention. "We believe these actions to have been taken in error," he said, because "we do not accept the use of force as a wise or proper instrument for the settlement of international disputes." The behavior of the three powers, he continued, can "scarcely be reconciled with the principles and purposes of the United Nations to which we have all subscribed." The British and French, he said, were using their veto authority to block any effort in the Security Council. He therefore intended to lay the issue before the General

Assembly. "I am ever more deeply convinced," he said, "that the processes of the United Nations represent the soundest hope for peace in the world."[32]

The morning after the television address he assembled the National Security Council. Foster Dulles set the tone. "For many years now," he told his colleagues, "the United States has been walking a tightrope between the effort to maintain our old and valued relations with our British and French allies on the one hand, and on the other, trying to assure ourselves of the friendship and understanding of the newly independent countries who have escaped from colonialism." The Europeans, he stated, were finished. "Recent events," he said, "are close to marking the death knell for Great Britain and France." The key, therefore, was to recognize that "if the United States supports the French and British on the colonial issue," it will go down with them.[33]

Thanks to the television address the night before, everyone in the room understood that the president was not holding the meeting in order to receive advice. Eisenhower was simply informing the top officers in the government of the details of the policy that he had already announced. Nevertheless, there was one participant in the meeting who dissented from the line that Eisenhower had established: Harold Stassen, the former governor of Minnesota, who was serving as Eisenhower's senior aide on disarmament issues. Years later Stassen became known as "the perennial candidate," a nickname earned from mounting nine unsuccessful bids to win the Republican nomination for president. This penchant for lost causes, though not yet part of Stassen's résumé, was certainly on display in the meeting.

The Europeans' methods were questionable, Stassen argued, but their goals were not. Egypt had aligned with the Soviet Union, the enemy of the United States. The American interest, therefore, was to prop up the Europeans and weaken Nasser. The right thing, in these circumstances, was "to save a friend from disaster, even though that friend had brought the disaster on himself."[34] Dulles responded with obvious irritation. "What the British and French had done," he thundered, "was nothing but the straight old-fashioned variety of colonialism." Maybe so, Stassen said, but "the future of Great Britain and of France was the most important consideration for the United States."[35]

Unequivocal support for Britain and France, however, was not Stassen's recommendation. Instead, he called for a more nuanced position: a cease-fire in place. The United States could stand up for principle by halting the attack against Egypt, but it would also refrain from delivering a humiliating defeat to its allies.

This proposal would hardly merit a footnote if it were not for the fact that, years later, Eisenhower (as we will see in Chapter 13) would come to see Stassen's general approach as the wisest course of action. As history actually unfolded, however, Dulles dismissed the suggestion out of hand, and Eisenhower strongly and unambiguously supported him. The president's mind was focused on the Soviet threat. Anti-imperialism was a fact of life in the Middle East, and if the United States tried to swim against the current, the Soviet Union would simply channel popular emotions against the West. Dulles, the president said, "was dead right in his view that if we did not do something to indicate some vigor in the way of asserting our leadership, the Soviets would take over the leadership from us."[36] The British and French were declining powers. "How could we possibly support Britain and France," Eisenhower asked, "if in doing so we lose the whole Arab world?"[37]

There was that phrase again. To prove to the Arabs that the preeminent Western power was not imperialist and, thereby, to stymie the Soviet Union, the president issued orders to inform the public that "we are going to suspend arms shipments to the whole Near Eastern region while the UN is considering the crisis." Washington, he reassured his colleagues, would continue "to assist Britain in order that she might meet her NATO requirements." However, if the British were to divert NATO supplies to other purposes, he warned, "we would have to consider such an action to represent another case of 'perfidious Albion.'" [38]

The order soon took on the force of international law. Later that afternoon, Dulles traveled to New York, and, acting personally as the representative of the United States in an emergency session of the United Nations General Assembly, he shepherded an American-sponsored resolution to a successful vote of sixty-five to four. It called for an immediate cease-fire, a withdrawal by the Israelis behind armistice lines, and a halt to the movement of arms and military goods into the area.

This resolution by itself would have been largely consistent with the approach that Stassen had advocated, were it not for the fact that Eisenhower's refusal to provide the British with supplies soon took on the form of an extreme economic sanction. The moment Nasser came under attack, he sank ships in the Suez Canal, blocking oil tankers en route to Europe from the Persian Gulf. At the same time, Egypt's allies in Syria sabotaged a pipeline carrying British-bound oil from Iraq to the Mediterranean coast. With a one-two punch, Nasser cut off the entire oil supply of Britain. When London turned to Washington for North American oil, Eisenhower refused, saying to his aides on October 30, "those who began this operation should be left to work out their own oil problems—to boil in their own oil, so to speak." [39]

When the financial markets caught wind of the blocked oil supply, the value of the British pound plummeted and a run on sterling reserves ensued. With his currency in free fall, Eden became ever more vulnerable to pressure from Eisenhower. Stabilizing the markets required the cooperation of the United States, which the Americans refused to give until the British accepted a complete, immediate, and unconditional withdrawal from Egypt.

To Kill Nasser?

The crisis in Eastern Europe had the effect of intensifying Eisenhower's and Dulles's frustration with the British and the French. As they saw it, Soviet repression in Hungary offered the West a prime opportunity to capture the moral high ground in international politics—an opportunity that the gunboat diplomacy in Egypt was destroying. Dulles complained to Eisenhower that, just as the Soviet Union was clamping down on dissent, "the British and French are going to be doing the same thing."[40]

Of course, Moscow also recognized the propaganda opportunity. On November 5, the Soviets proposed to Eisenhower a joint Soviet-American military action against the aggressors in the Middle East. Ike rejected the proposal out of hand—but that was precisely the response that the Soviets expected, according to the memoirs of Nikita Khrushchev, who at the time was the leader of the Central Committee of the Communist Party. When Khrushchev first came up with the idea of proposing a joint action with the Americans, he ran it past Vyacheslav Molotov, the former foreign minister. "Eisenhower will never agree to join forces with us against England, France, and Israel," Molotov replied. "Of course, he won't, but by putting him in the position of having to refuse, we'll expose the hypocrisy of his public statement condemning the attack against Egypt," Khrushchev explained. "We'll make him put his money where his mouth is. If he were really against the aggression, then he'd accept the Soviet Union's proposal."[41]

While working to discredit the moral authority of the United States, the Soviets also moved to make the United States appear as the militarily weaker party—by issuing direct, brutal threats to Eden, Mollet, and Ben-Gurion. To all three prime ministers Premier Nikolai Bulganin sent messages with similar wording, which raised the specter of nuclear annihilation. The letter to Eden, for example, asked how the British would feel if they were subjected to bombardment of the kind that Britain had unleashed on Egypt. "In what situation would Britain find herself," he asked, "if she were attacked by stronger states, possessing all types of modern destructive weapons, and such countries could . . . refrain from sending naval or air forces to the shores of Britain and use other means— for instance, rocket weapons."[42]

Eisenhower never believed that Bulganin was truly on the verge of rocketing London. He recognized the threat for what it was—grandstanding before the Third World. Nevertheless, he still feared Soviet intervention in some form. Having already managed the Anglo-Egyptian negotiations of 1953–54, he did not assume that an Anglo-French occupation of the Canal Zone would automatically humble Nasser. The Egyptian leader might react by launching a guerrilla war, then turn to the Soviets for assistance. In response, Moscow might send in "volunteers," Soviet commandos operating under cover. Egypt, in that case, would become a second Algeria—a protracted anticolonialist war that would further tarnish the image of the West among newly independent peoples. To prevent this scenario, it was imperative to stop the Anglo-French forces in their tracks and frog-march them out of Egypt.

Despite their opposition to the Anglo-French operation and their sense of betrayal, Eisenhower and his colleagues never had any doubt that, when all was said and done, the British were still their allies. This realization injected into their thinking an odd, contradictory quality. Even as they took every step short of war to stop the Anglo-French invasion, they furtively cheered for its success.

The contradictory emotions were particularly evident in the first week of November as the Americans watched the snail's pace of the ground operation in the Canal Zone. The British and French did not land troops until nearly a week after they had issued their ultimatum, in the name of international shipping, to Egypt and Israel, and American officials were shocked at the delay. Shortly after the war, Walter Bedell Smith, who had recently left the Eisenhower administration, expressed his frustrations to an Israeli official in Washington who relayed them to Ben-Gurion in Jerusalem. Bedell Smith, the Israeli prime minister wrote in his diary, believed that the British "should have conquered the entire Canal in five days. Then there would have been no Nasser, no Soviet threat and the world would have sighed with relief."[43]

Bedell Smith's statements were not just those of an ordinary civilian. In the midst of the crisis, Robert Amory Jr., the deputy director of the CIA, expressed an identical view. On November 3, he contacted Chester Cooper, a CIA official stationed in London, to say, "Tell your [British] friends either to comply with the goddamn cease-fire or go ahead with the goddamn invasion. Either way, we'll back them up. But tell them to do one or the other fast. What we can't stand is their goddamn hesitation waltz while Hungary is burning."[44]

Eisenhower himself clearly shared Amory's feelings. Four days later, in a meeting of the National Security Council, he "severely criticized the conduct of the British and French military operations against Egypt, pointing out that there was no excuse for the long delay in the landing of British and French troops in the Suez Canal area once they had made the decision to do so."[45] Years later, in an oral history interview, Eisenhower's view remained unchanged. "Had they done it quickly," he said, "we would have accepted it."[46]

To British ears, such attitudes were incomprehensible. If the Americans truly believed that toppling Nasser would be beneficial, then why were they objecting to it? To Eisenhower, the master of "the hidden hand," there was no contradiction between recognizing that Nasser's destruction was desirable, and calculating that the costs of actually destroying him were prohibitive. The British and French were wrong to have attacked Egypt. Once they chose war, however, they opened for themselves a narrow window of opportunity, which they then failed to exploit.

To Goldeneye

By November 6, 1956, the specter of economic ruin forced Eden to beg Eisenhower for leniency. Even though the Anglo-French forces had not yet taken over the whole canal, he decided in favor of a cease-fire in place, and immediately telephoned the president to convey the good news. Eisenhower was certainly pleased; to Eden's dismay, however, he was not prepared to relieve the economic pressure until the British and French announced an immediate and unconditional withdrawal.

In Eden's preferred scenario, Eisenhower would have condemned the invasion rhetorically while still using it to pressure Nasser to make concessions—in the spirit of the Stassen recommendations. The president would also encourage the secretary general of the United Nations, Dag Hammarskjöld, to fold the Anglo-French troops into a multinational peacekeeping force (soon to be known as UNEF, the United Nations Emergency Force) that he was assembling. But Eisenhower would hear nothing of it. In genial but unyielding language, he made clear that UNEF's purpose was to oust the Anglo-French force, not to absorb it. Eisenhower even rehearsed for Eden the precise lines that the prime minister should say to the UN secretary general: "Mr. Hammarskjöld, we trust you. When we see you coming in with enough troops to take over, we go out."

"May I think that one over?" Eden asked.

"[C]all me anytime you please."

"If I survive here tonight I will call you tomorrow," Eden answered, referring to the battle that awaited him in Parliament.[47]

Eden did survive and did call. Mounting a last-ditch effort to soften Eisenhower's position, he suggested that he, together with Mollet, immediately come to Washington for a summit meeting. Without hesitation, Eisenhower wholeheartedly agreed. "[A]fter all," he said, "it is like a family spat."[48]

The president's senior staff, however, strongly opposed the summit. After he hung up the phone with Eden, Eisenhower immediately called Herbert Hoover Jr., the deputy secretary of state, and briefed him on the impending arrival of the prime ministers. Hoover in turn called Foster Dulles, who was recuperating in the hospital after emergency abdominal surgery. The secretary of state, it would appear, instructed Hoover to convey to the president personally his strong recommendation to rescind the invitation to Eden and Mollet. Before leaving for the White House, Hoover apparently called over to the president's chief of staff, Sherman Adams, to alert him of Dulles's opinion. Without waiting for Hoover to arrive, Adams engaged Eisenhower on the subject, and the president wobbled. He immediately called Eden back—not to rescind the invitation, but simply to toughen up his basic message. He warned Eden not to come to Washington with any misconceptions: the American position would not soften. "[W]e are committed to Hammarskjold's plan" for an immediate and unconditional withdrawal of the Anglo-French expeditionary force, Eisenhower explained.[49]

This stern message, however, did not mollify the staff. Just as the president was hanging up with Eden, Hoover entered the Oval Office and relayed Dulles's recommendation to rescind the invitation to Eden and Mollet. It was vitally important, Hoover said, "not to give the impression that we are teaming with the British and French." While this discussion was already under way, another senior official, Secretary of the Treasury George Humphrey, entered the room and added his voice to the chorus. Faced with united opposition, Eisenhower relented, but not without expressing feelings of regret. "He had really looked forward to talking with Eden, and was quite disappointed," Colonel Andrew Goodpaster, the president's military aide, wrote in a memorandum of conversation.[50]

Eisenhower called Eden—their third talk in less than two hours. This time, the president postponed the invitation indefinitely, claiming that, in the wake of the election, his schedule was simply too chaotic to receive visitors.

This bout of indecision was not typical. Having run World War II in Europe, Eisenhower was accustomed to making highly consequential decisions at a moment's notice. The mixed feelings that he demonstrated that morning were indicative of profound misgivings about undermining allies—misgivings that would never leave him. In later life, he would conclude that, on that fateful morning, he had been too hard on his friends and too kind to his adversaries.

Indeed, the tough American policy destroyed Eden, whose health had never fully recovered from his abdominal surgery in 1953. By mid-November, the American ambassador in London, Winthrop Aldrich, reported that Eden's health had deteriorated to such an extent that, despite the ongoing crisis, he would soon be taking a rest, and would probably not survive in office. Aldrich received this sensitive information from none other than Chancellor of the Exchequer Harold Macmillan, the man who would soon replace Eden as prime minister. On November 19, Eden indeed announced his impending departure for Jamaica, where he recuperated for three weeks. On December 14, he returned to London, apparently still harboring some hope of remaining in power. Within a month, however, he stepped down and retired from politics, his career destroyed.

In the meantime, the British government, bowing to the demands of Eisenhower, announced the unconditional withdrawal of its troops from Egypt. The British Empire had come to its definitive end—first with a bang, then a whimper.

It is perhaps fitting that Eden's three weeks in Jamaica were spent at Goldeneye, the beachfront estate of Ian Fleming, the creator of James Bond. Fleming's books helped British readers, who were raised on the self-confident imperialism of Rudyard Kipling, to cope with the grinding decline of empire and the meteoric ascendancy of the United States. In the Bond myth, Britain no longer rules the world alone; it now works in concert with America. Although the British are obviously the junior members of the partnership, their panache, personified by Bond, gives the West its special edge. The Americans, of course, fully recognize Bond's talent and, therefore, always support him.

When Eden returned home from Goldeneye, the first thing he did was to claim that America was coming around to see the wisdom of his actions. "Now I am sure from my mailbag and otherwise that what we have done is right," Eden said after he touched down in London. "There is a growing understanding [of this] in Canada and . . ." At this point, he raised his voice for emphasis and looked directly into the lights of the cameras. "And also in the United States."[51]

After three weeks at Goldeneye, Eden could hear the footsteps of Felix Leiter, James Bond's supportive American counterpart, as the CIA agent ran to the rescue. Even as the doomed prime minister spoke, however, events were telling a very different story: the United States was allowing Britain to go down in flames. Yet again, Ike's policies were teaching Eden that Felix Leiter represented only one of America's several personalities. In real life, unlike in fiction, it was impossible to know whether Felix, that old faithful friend, would actually turn up.

CHAPTER 12

Ike's Second Bet

Eisenhower had repeatedly warned Eden not to attack Egypt. Typical was this message from late July 1956: "I have given you my personal conviction, as well as that of my associates, as to the unwisdom even of contemplating the use of military force at this moment." Given the clarity of such warnings, what was Eden thinking? What made him believe he could get away with it?

Of course, he had no illusions about American opposition, but he never imagined that Eisenhower would impose crippling economic sanctions. He banked, in the first instance, on Eisenhower's well-known tendency to avoid direct confrontation. Macmillan, for one, had worked closely with Eisenhower during the war, and he promised Eden a torpid American opposition. "I know Ike," Macmillan confidently asserted. "He will lie *doggo*."[1] Eden also assumed that domestic American politics would tie Eisenhower's hands. It was undoubtedly by conscious design that the French, British, and Israelis took military action just one week before the American elections. Popular support for Israel in America, they no doubt calculated, would restrain Eisenhower, as would his own personal concern for allied solidarity. However angry and betrayed he might *feel*, he would *do* nothing.

Like so many others before him, Eden had mistaken Eisenhower's affable exterior for lack of spine. Behind the agreeable mask, Eisenhower was pure steel. What is more, he was shrewd—so shrewd that even his close advisors often failed to read him correctly. For example, shortly before his television address, Eisenhower made a show of telling his staff that he was not playing the political angles at all. There was simply no connection between his Suez policy and his presidential campaign strategy. The president said, according to the note taker at the meeting, that "he does not care in the slightest whether he is re-elected. . . . He added that he did not really think the American people would throw him out in the midst of a situation like this, but if they did, so be it."[2] This high-minded sentiment deeply impressed Foster Dulles, who, in a telephone conversation with Vice President Nixon, praised the president for his determination "to do what is right regardless of the election" and his refusal to "sacrifice foreign policy for political expediency."[3]

Nixon did not argue with Dulles, but he obviously knew better. Eisenhower, he would later observe, was "a far more complex and devious man than most people realized, and in the best sense of those words."[4] Nixon's envy is palpable. Brooding and shy, Nixon came across as shifty even when he was sincere. Eisenhower, by contrast, appeared guileless even when scheming. Years after the crisis, Nixon confessed to a friend that there was an obvious domestic imperative for opposing the allies. Eisenhower, he explained, was running on a peace platform. He had won in 1952 on the claim that he would end the war in Korea and he was promising in the 1956 campaign to extend the peace for four more years. Seen in this light, the most significant line of Eisenhower's television address was this simple pledge: "[T]here will be no United States involvement in these present hostilities."[5]

When calculating the odds that Eisenhower would destroy him, Eden failed to realize that he was dealing with a shrewd candidate—and one, moreover, who was juggling two campaigns simultaneously. Domestically, Eisenhower was running against Adlai Stevenson, while abroad he was competing against the Soviet Union.

This dual-campaign approach clearly shaped the speech that the president gave on November 1 in Philadelphia, where he developed the idea that core American values and Third World anti-imperialism flowed from the same sources. The president professed "a special concern for the fate and fortune of those 700 million people—in 18 nations—who have won full independence since World War II." Thanks to its anti-imperial heritage, the United States understood and sympathized with their aspirations. "We, too," he said, "were born at a time when the tide of tyranny, running high, threatened to sweep the earth. We prevailed. And they shall prevail."[6]

Two days later, Nixon, in a campaign speech, made this anti-British message explicit. He hailed the General Assembly resolution as nothing less than a second American Revolution. "In the past," he proclaimed, "the nations of Asia and Africa have always felt we would, when the pressure was on, side with the policies of the British and French Governments in relation to the once colonial areas." But a new era had now dawned. "For the first time in history we have shown independence of Anglo-French policies towards Asia and Africa which seemed to us to reflect the colonial tradition. That declaration of independence has had an electrifying effect throughout the world."[7]

Eisenhower versus Ben-Gurion

The surprising collapse of the Anglo-French position left the Israelis, just as Ben-Gurion had feared, alone on the battlefield.

In the weeks prior to the invasion, Ben-Gurion had been dreaming big, very big—not just about toppling Nasser and forcing Egypt to make peace, but even about remaking the political map of the Middle East. Though he allowed his imagination to soar, he never lost sight of his core interests, which were in the Sinai, where he hoped to maintain a permanent Israeli presence. The focus of his aspirations was the mouth of the Red Sea, guarded by Sharm el-Sheikh and the island of Tiran, both of which he hoped to wrest from Egypt. Nasser had used his control of these points to close the Straits of Tiran to Israeli shipping, thereby shutting off commerce between the Jewish state and East Asia.

Scouring historical sources, Ben-Gurion discovered evidence that, in ancient times, Tiran fell under a Jewish dominion, which in the Hebrew of the day was named "Yotvat." On November 6, he sent a message to the troops of Sinai, saying that Yotvat, known as Tiran, which until 1,400 years ago was an independent Hebrew state, would again become part of the Third Commonwealth of Israel. The following day, in a speech in the Knesset, he proclaimed an intention to restructure relations with Egypt. He declared the armistice agreement of 1949 null and void and demanded a peace treaty as well as the opening of the Suez Canal to Israeli shipping. He also expressed a clear intention to annex some part, if not all, of the conquered territory.[8]

The word *Yotvat* was unfamiliar to Israelis. To Eisenhower it was repellent. The moment he learned that Ben-Gurion had staked a claim to the Sinai, he fired off a stern letter reminding the prime minister that the United Nations General Assembly had ordered the Israeli forces to vacate Egypt immediately and unconditionally. Refusal to comply, he warned, "could not but bring about the condemnation of Israel as a violator of the principles as well as the directives of the United Nations." What is worse, Israeli intransigence might "impair the friendly cooperation between our two countries."[9]

Eisenhower's letter was not the only mail that Ben-Gurion received. Soviet premier Bulganin also sent him a threatening letter calling on the "criminal" Israeli government to respect the will of the United Nations.[10] Its failure to do so, he said, was calling the very existence of Israel into question.

It is a bracing experience for a leader of a small country to be

at odds with both superpowers simultaneously. Ben-Gurion back-
pedaled. He immediately wrote a conciliatory letter to Eisenhower,
welcoming the impending arrival of United Nations forces. "We
never planned to annex the Sinai Desert," he fibbed. The dishon-
esty was less important than the compliance it signaled. The following sentence was the most important of the letter: "In view of
the United Nations Resolutions regarding the withdrawal of foreign troops from Egypt and the creation of an international force,
we will, upon conclusion of satisfactory arrangements with the
United Nations in connection with this international force enter-
ing the Suez Canal area, willingly withdraw our forces." [11]

The sentence sounded a partial retreat, not surrender. Ben-
Gurion promised to withdraw, but he conditioned the evacuation
on "satisfactory arrangements" with the United Nations Emergency Force (UNEF). Ben-Gurion, like Eden, was determined to
extract tangible gains from Nasser before capitulating. Eisenhower,
however, was equally determined to force unconditional compliance
with UN resolutions. An epic test of wills was under way, the worst
crisis ever in American-Israeli relations. It would last four months.

When the negotiations began, the Americans took the position that they would be happy to discuss Israeli grievances against
Egypt, but only after Israel complied with United Nations resolutions. On December 30, for instance, Dulles told Golda Meir, the
Israeli foreign minister, "that the United States was not in a position to come to agreements with Israel over matters being dealt
with by the United Nations Secretary General." [12] Dag Hammarskjöld, for his part, took a similar position: Israel must withdraw
first, and negotiate later.

Using these tactics, Eisenhower successfully compelled the Israelis to partially evacuate the Sinai, and he whittled down their
long list of other demands. But in late January 1957, Ben-Gurion
dug in his heels. In a speech before the Knesset, he demanded international guarantees on two major issues: the opening the Straits

of Tiran to shipping, and preventing the Egyptian army from returning to Gaza, which it had used as a springboard for Fedayeen attacks.

In response, Eisenhower began threatening to sponsor a sanctions resolution in the General Assembly. Sanctioning Israel, however, was a thorny political problem. In early February, Dulles complained bitterly to a colleague about the "terrific control the Jews had over the news media and the barrage which the Jews have built up on Congressmen." He described the opposition to sanctions in Congress as "overwhelming." The idea of a bill rejecting sanctions on Israel was being bandied about on Capitol Hill and, Dulles said, it would certainly pass both the House and the Senate unanimously. If the administration were to move on its threat, it was in very serious danger of having Congress strip it of any authority to punish Israel. He stressed that he did not want "the Israelis to know we were weak on this."[13] He preferred, if possible, to bluff—to slow the sanctions resolution as long as possible while pressuring the Israelis.

At the same time, he also gave ground. He compromised on the hitherto firm principle that the United States could not make deals with Israel on the outstanding issues between it and Hammarskjöld. On February 11, Dulles passed to the Israelis a memorandum that contained two concessions: a guarantee to support Israel in the affirmation of its right to freedom of shipping through the Straits of Tiran; and American support for the indefinite stationing of the UNEF in Sharm el-Sheikh and Gaza, where it would serve as a buffer between the Israelis and the Egyptians.

Much to the consternation of Dulles, Ben-Gurion rejected the offer. Neither of Dulles's concessions represented an ironclad guarantee. Neither, moreover, represented a concession from Nasser. The assurance on the straits was in the form of a unilateral American statement of good intentions. While Dulles was presenting the presence of UNEF as a benefit to Israel, the reality was much more ambiguous. UNEF had purposely been fashioned, by UN resolution and by Hammarskjöld's policy, as an instrument for removing the Anglo-French and Israeli invaders. In February 1957, Hammarskjöld agreed with the Americans on expanding its mission so that it would serve for an extended period as a buffer between Egypt and Israel. But he made sure to condition its presence on Egyptian agreement. In short, UNEF explicitly served at the pleasure of Nasser. Ben-Gurion preferred, instead, a force that had the authority to prevent Nasser from closing the Straits of Tiran, remilitarizing the Sinai, and reoccupying Gaza.

On February 16, Dulles conferred with Eisenhower. With an ugly fight with Congress looming, the next steps required very close coordination with the president. Dulles summarized their conversation in a memo for the record. "I expressed the view," he wrote, "that we had gone just as far as was possible to try to make it easy and acceptable to the Israelis to withdraw and I felt that to go further would almost surely jeopardize the entire Western influence in the Middle East and make it almost certain that virtually all of the Middle East countries would feel that United States policy toward the area was in the last analysis controlled by the Jewish influence in the United States and that accordingly the only hope of the Arab countries was in association with the Soviet Union."[14]

The fear of undermining moderate Arab leaders continued to haunt Eisenhower and Dulles. On January 5, the president appeared before Congress to announce what became known as the Eisenhower Doctrine. He requested authority and resources to strengthen allied states in the region. Though cast overtly as resistance to Soviet encroachment on the Middle East, the initiative aimed to fill the vacuum left by the collapse of British prestige and to stiffen the resolve of Arab governments against the growing wave of Nasserist pan-Arabism. The single most important partner, in Eisenhower's mind, was Saudi Arabia. On January 30, the king was invited to Washington for a state visit.[15] While the administration was building a new regional architecture, the last thing it wanted was to present a target for radical Arab nationalism by being seen to support Israel.

Sanctioning Israel?

On February 20, Eisenhower made another prime-time radio and television broadcast. It contained the toughest message that an American president ever sent to Israel.

Ben-Gurion, Eisenhower explained, had personally assured him that he would willingly withdraw Israeli forces. But he had failed to keep his promise. The United Nations and the United States had made repeated efforts to convince him, but he was insisting on firm guarantees as a precondition for withdrawing. "This," Eisenhower said, "raises a basic question of principle. Should a nation which attacks and occupies foreign territory in the face of United Nations disapproval be allowed to impose conditions on its own withdrawal?" It would be wrong, Eisenhower affirmed, "to lend the influence of the United States to the proposition that a nation which invades another should be permitted to exact conditions for withdrawal." To allow Israel to achieve its goals "would be a blow to the authority and influence of the United Nations in the world and to the hopes which humanity placed in the United Nations as the means of achieving peace with justice." What is more, it would jeopardize Middle Eastern peace, bringing "incalculable ills" to Israel, the United States, and its allies. "I believe," he stated, "that—in the interests of peace—the United Nations has no choice but to exert pressure upon Israel to comply with the withdrawal resolutions."[16]

The implication was obvious. Eisenhower was prepared to fight Congress over the need to impose sanctions. If Israel failed to withdraw, therefore, it would find itself locked in bitter conflict with a president who had just won four more years in a landslide reelection. That prospect was deeply unattractive to Ben-Gurion. Although Congress had taken a public position of support for Israel, behind the scenes Israel was receiving signals from top senators that they did not relish the prospect of a fight to the death with the White House.

Shortly after Eisenhower addressed the nation, he played another card against Ben-Gurion: he convinced the French to pressure the Israeli leader. The Mollet government was eager to repair relations with Washington and it also felt the economic need to open the Suez Canal. Nasser, cleverly, had refused to clear the waterway until the Israelis withdrew, thus creating an oil shortage in Europe. If Ben-Gurion were to lose the support of France, his primary supplier of arms, Israel would be truly isolated.

Ben-Gurion began to waver. Not all Israelis, however, were as intimidated by the American power play. Moshe Dayan, for one, argued that Israel could withstand sanctions for six months. Surrender was always an option. Why was Ben-Gurion in a hurry to fall to his knees?[17] But Ben-Gurion had a more sophisticated understanding. In the event of another conflict with Egypt, he argued, Israel would find itself in need of American goodwill. If the Sinai campaign proved anything, it was that victory on the battlefield, by itself, was not enough to shift the balance of power in Israel's favor. Turning military gains into political advantage required the support of the United States. He overruled Dayan and decided to accept the American guarantees, such as they were. He haggled over a few minor details of the February 11 memorandum and then gave the order to withdraw.

Eisenhower's Realism

In the diplomacy of the Suez Crisis, one figure played a surprisingly minor role—Gamal Abdel Nasser. To be sure, he perpetually stood center stage, but he rarely delivered major lines. At every turn, Eisenhower interposed himself between the Egyptian leader and the other major actors. When the enemies of Egypt threatened, Eisenhower restrained them; when they attacked, he rushed to block; and when they sought to dig in, he uprooted them. Eisenhower's policy allowed Nasser to turn military defeat into the kind of political victory that was denied to the British and the Israelis. Nasser had simultaneously defied Britain, France, and Israel—the three major antagonists of Arab nationalism—and won. His reputation in the Middle East skyrocketed to mythic heights.

Benefiting Egypt, however, was never the goal of Eisenhower's policy. On the contrary, throughout the crisis, the president had remained consistently hostile to Nasser. Typical of his attitude was a note he sent in December 1956 to Dulles. The British and French, he wrote, "know that we regard Nasser as an evil influence. I think also we have made it abundantly clear that while we share in general the British and French opinions of Nasser, we insisted that they chose a bad time and incident on which to launch corrective measures."[18]

American historians tend to give Eisenhower extremely high marks for this judiciousness. Especially when compared with Eden and Mollet, Eisenhower appeared wise, steady, and statesmanlike. Above all, he exhibited moral fiber. He protected a small power against imperialism. He championed the authority of the United Nations. And he stared down Israel's supporters in Congress in the midst of an election. By elevating international law over the parochial interests of the United States, he set the standard, in the eyes of many, for the kind of principled foreign policy that has otherwise been sorely lacking in the Middle East.

British accounts, by contrast, are more attuned to Eisenhower's contradictions. Eden's memoirs started the trend by strongly suggesting that Eisenhower and Dulles were hypocrites. "We could not help contrasting," he wrote, "the American attitude now with our own attitude at the time of the Guatemala campaign."[19] The statement was an oblique reference to the part the CIA played in toppling Guatemala's Arbenz government in 1954. As the American plot swirled around him, Arbenz turned to the Security Council for help. The British, according to Eden, looked the other way at the United Nations in order not to hamper the United States.

The Arbenz episode is hardly an isolated case. The overthrow of Mosaddeq in Iran also proves that Eisenhower did not shrink from ordering regime change when it suited him. By citing this fact, however, Eden inadvertently blunts his own accusation of hypocrisy, because it only serves to remind us that Eisenhower was a steely-eyed realist. Consistency for consistency's sake had no place in his thinking. The only sensible test of policy was whether it achieved the desired goals.

In the case of Suez, Eisenhower's goal was to stabilize the Middle East and prevent the Soviet Union from making further inroads. Under the cover of gauzy rhetoric, Eisenhower placed his second bet: that supporting traditional allies was less beneficial to the West than a policy aligning the United States with "the whole Arab world." The concept is unusual. Steely-eyed realists like Eisenhower tend to bet on tangible entities: organized political movements, states, and individual leaders. They work with what actually exists rather than what might be. Above all, they support friends and punish enemies. The French, British, and Israelis repeatedly urged Eisenhower to adopt this conventional conception, but he steadfastly refused. He was unshakably convinced that a bet on his traditional friends would undermine the Western position in the Cold War.

It would take another eighteen months, but he would come to regret this conviction.

CHAPTER 13

Regret

W hen Eisenhower went to bed on July 13, 1958, Iraq was an ally—"the country," he wrote in his memoirs, "that we were counting on heavily as a bulwark of stability and progress in the region."[1] When he awoke the following morning, the bulwark was gone.

Under cover of darkness, two Iraqi army officers, Brigadier Abdel Karim Qasim and Colonel Salim Arif, launched a coup that eliminated the Hashemite monarchy. Detachments under their command quickly took control of the palace, the ministry of defense, and the broadcasting authority. At the palace, rebel soldiers corralled the royal family and its attendants into the garden, and then mowed them down with submachine guns. Afterward, the killers released the body of Crown Prince Abdel Ilah into a crowd, which had gathered near the palace. Someone tied the corpse to the back of a vehicle and then proceeded to drag it through the streets of Baghdad. A mob trailed behind. Men with knives and clippers emerged and cut off Abdel Ilah's hands, feet, and genitalia.

The macabre parade came to a halt at the ministry of defense, where the crowd hung the carcass from a balcony, like a side of beef in a butcher's shop. A young man with a knife climbed a lamp-post standing in reach of the dangling corpse; he stabbed it repeatedly in the back, and then sliced flesh from its buttocks. While he busied himself with carving, men on the street took a long white stick and inserted it up into what remained of the man, who just hours before had been the most powerful figure in Iraq.

Eisenhower did not know all of these details, but he knew enough to realize that the monarchy was finished. He recognized, further, that the coup counted as a triumph for Nasser. In Baghdad, Waldemar Gallman, the American ambassador, translated the broadcasts of the new regime and streamed the transcripts to Washington. Qasim and Arif identified themselves as "Free Officers," cast in the Nasser mold, and proclaiming the rise of an Arab nationalist republic in emulation of the Egyptian regime. Meanwhile in Cairo, Voice of the Arabs, which had saturated Iraq with seditious propaganda for years, was now howling with joy, dancing on the corpses of the royal family.

The blow to the United States was enormous—a strategic victory for Nasser. For the last year and a half, the United States had been working in vain to isolate Egypt, and the coup in Baghdad marked the definitive failure of the effort. In actual fact, Nasser had outsmarted the Americans at every turn. In the process, he racked up a long series of victories, the greatest of which was the formation of the United Arab Republic (UAR), the political union of Egypt and Syria. Founded six months earlier, in February, the UAR sent a jolt of electricity through the Arab world. In the view of his followers, Nasser was erasing the borders drawn by the imperialists. He was announcing the dawn of a new era of unity and power. Across the Arab world, his admirers watched the events in Baghdad with rapt attention. "Would Iraq merge with the UAR?" they asked. "Would Nasser create an Arab superstate?" "Would a pan-Arab flood wash away the pro-Western governments of Lebanon and Jordan?"

In Washington, Eisenhower asked himself the same questions. At 10:50 in the morning on July 14 he convened a meeting of the National Security Council (NSC) to formulate the American answer. The session focused on an urgent request from the Lebanese president, Camille Chamoun, who was battling an insurgency supported by the UAR. Fearing that he was next in line on Nasser's hit list, Chamoun demanded that Eisenhower send in the U.S. Marines to save him. In Jordan, King Hussein had the same fear—and he appealed to the British to intervene on his behalf. From Riyadh, the Saudi king had already sent two messages to Washington saying that if the British and Americans failed to act, they were finished as great powers in the Middle East.

Eisenhower did not wait to hear the views of his advisors. "[W]e must act," he announced, "or get out of the Middle East entirely." Foster Dulles took an identical position, but Vice President Nixon introduced a note of caution. The proposed intervention, he said, would have "an adverse reaction around the world," in sharp contrast to the "favorable reaction at Suez."[2] The director of the CIA agreed. A military operation, Allen Dulles predicted, would open a sharp divide between the West and the developing world. "Most of Asia will be against us, including India." People "will say we are simply doing what we stopped the British and the French from doing at the time of the Suez crisis."[3]

Remarkably, Eisenhower shrugged off these concerns. "In Lebanon," he wrote in his memoirs, "the question was whether it would be better to incur the deep resentment of nearly all of the Arab world (and some of the rest of the Free World) and in doing so to risk general war with the Soviet Union or to do something worse—which was to do nothing."[4]

This, of course, had been Anthony Eden's argument—to the letter—for his war against Egypt in 1956. At that time, however, Eisenhower had dismissed the reasoning as preposterous—precisely because preventing an Arab nationalist backlash and avoiding war with the Soviet Union were unquestionable imperatives. But that was then and this was now. Somehow, avoiding offense to Arab nationalism had ceased to be a strategic priority. Somehow, risking war with the Soviet Union was no longer unthinkable. Somehow, thoughts that had been preposterous in 1956 had now become prudent. What had changed?

Fallen Pillars

Eisenhower's paradigm shift was certainly a response to the collapse of his Middle East strategy—but that collapse was not something that happened suddenly, in a single day, on July 14, 1958; it was, rather, a slow process that lasted some eighteen months. The Iraqi revolution was but the last in a series of four blows, each of which toppled a separate pillar of Eisenhower's regional strategy.

The first pillar to fall was the Eisenhower Doctrine. On January 5, 1957, the president announced, in effect, that the United States was succeeding Britain as the dominant power in the Middle East. He asked Congress to authorize $200 million for the United States to provide economic and military assistance to countries that requested aid against "overt armed aggression from any nation controlled by International Communism."[5] This odd phrase, the heart and soul of the Eisenhower Doctrine, was an oblique reference to Egypt. The new policy still focused on containing the Soviet Union, and therefore still spoke the traditional language of containment, but it also sought to line up Arab regimes against Nasser.

Until now, Eisenhower and Dulles had shied away from directly organizing the Middle East, fearing that the Arabs would read such an attempt as a new form of Western imperialism. While several factors led the administration to violate this precept, one deserves special note. The Americans convinced themselves that by standing up for the rights of Egypt in the Suez Crisis, they had shed the stigma of association with Zionism and imperialism. A self-respecting Arab nationalist, Washington told itself, could now hold his head high as he walked arm in arm with America.

This was a dangerous conceit—and a quintessentially American one. The Suez Crisis did not transform Arab perceptions of America in any lasting way, but it did turn Nasser into a hero of epic proportions. Seen through Arab eyes, Nasser had vanquished the combined forces of imperialism and Zionism. He was now a giant, ten feet tall, towering over that feckless midget, the West.

In reality, of course, it was Eisenhower who drove the Europeans and the Israelis from Egypt. In the eyes of those who received their news from Voice of the Arabs, however, Marshal Bulganin's nuclear saber-rattling was the decisive factor. "Soviet threats against the UK made an equal or greater impression on the Arab public," said a National Intelligence Estimate in 1957. After the crisis, the Soviets continued to support Egypt, whereas "the US held back." This on-again, off-again attitude left Nasser's supporters "confused and disillusioned."[6]

It was therefore child's play for Nasser's propaganda machine to paint the Eisenhower Doctrine as a plot to keep the Arabs down—just the latest steel-toed boot of Western imperialism. In March, Eisenhower appointed James Richards, a former congressman from South Carolina, as his special assistant responsible for drumming up support in the Middle East for the Doctrine. Richards left immediately for a tour of the region and quickly learned that even key Arab allies—Iraq, Jordan and Saudi Arabia—had no interest in associating with the new initiative. They understood all too well that endorsing it meant volunteering for the role of traitor in Nasser's propaganda broadcasts.

Nasser, the giant who rose from the Suez Crisis, crushed Eisenhower's doctrine like a cigarette under his shoe.

The Rise of the United Arab Republic

It was only slightly harder for Nasser to destroy the second pillar of American strategy in the Middle East—namely, the effort to peel away Damascus from Cairo. Eisenhower first attempted to orchestrate a coup in Syria in the fall of 1956, but that plan fell apart against the backdrop of the Suez war. By the summer of 1957, Howard "Rocky" Stone, the CIA station chief in Damascus and a veteran of the Mosaddeq coup in Iran, was hard at work preparing a second attempt. But Abdel Hamid Sarraj, the head of Syrian counterintelligence, quickly penetrated Stone's operation. Young, ruthless, and cunning, Sarraj rolled up the American network with ease. The Syrian government expelled Stone from the country and broadcast detailed reports of the plot, complete with firsthand testimony from army officers whom Stone had recruited.

But this embarrassment did nothing to deter Eisenhower, who, concerned by the increasing warmth between Damascus and Moscow, renewed his efforts. In his third plan for regime change, the CIA began stirring up disturbances along Syria's borders. The goal, it seems, was to manufacture a pretext for coming to the aid of Syria's neighbors in accordance with the intervention clause of the Eisenhower Doctrine. After accusing the Syrian government of threatening its neighbors, the United States dispatched the Sixth Fleet to the Eastern Mediterranean, and deployed aircraft to the base in Adana, Turkey. The Turks, meanwhile, massed troops on their border with Syria. Eisenhower then wrote to King Saud and expressed his fear of the "danger that Syria will become a Soviet Communist satellite." Promising American support, he appealed to the king on the basis of religion. "In view of the special position of Your Majesty as Keeper of the Holy Places of Islam, I trust that you will exert your great influence to the end that the atheistic creed of Communism will not become entrenched at a key position in the Moslem world."[7]

But the king, historian Salim Yaqub writes, "had little interest in Eisenhower's jihad."[8] The Iraqi government was equally standoffish. With neither Riyadh nor Baghdad willing to join a regime-change coalition, Eisenhower had no choice but to back down. On September 10, Dulles stated publicly that intervention was unlikely.

Smelling an American retreat, Nasser and his Soviet patrons rushed to pose as the saviors of Syrian independence. Soviet premier Nikita Khrushchev publicly accused the United States of planning, together with Israel and Turkey, to attack Syria. In a direct threat to the Turks, he warned, "If the rifles fire, the rockets will start flying."[9] About a week later, Nasser landed 1,500 Egyptian troops in Latakia, on the Syrian coast near Turkey. A few days later, Andrei Gromyko, the Soviet foreign minister, expressed the readiness of the Soviet Union "to take part with its forces in suppressing aggression and punishing the violators of peace."[10]

In a manner reminiscent of the Suez Crisis, Nasser and the Soviets succeeded in creating the impression that, with a mere flexing of their muscles, they sent the imperialists scurrying for cover. This Potemkin display of force set the scene for one of the most dramatic developments in modern Arab history: the merger of Syria and Egypt.

In Damascus, the air was thick with talk of unification with Egypt. Syrian politicians streamed to Cairo to kiss the ring of the Egyptian leader. Among them was Salah al-Din Bitar, the Syrian foreign minister and a prominent representative of Baathism, a radical pan-Arab doctrine that called for wiping out all of the borders in the Arab world. The Baath Party was the strongest ally of Nasser in Syria (not to mention Jordan), and Bitar began to lobby Nasser publicly to unify the two countries.

The proposal put Nasser on the spot. Traditionally, Egypt had stood for solidarity against the West and Israel. Instead of trying to erase Syria's borders, it had championed the principle of Syrian independence—from imperialism, yes, but also from the Hashemite states, Iraq and Jordan. Nasser's Baathist allies, however, dreamed of integral unity; Nasser, they believed, was the leader who could turn the dream into a reality. Consequently, if the Egyptian leader were to refuse Bitar's offer, he would damage his reputation as the very embodiment of Arab nationalism. Rather than reject the idea, therefore, Nasser set conditions that would ensure him total domination of the project. If the Syrian political parties would disband, he stipulated, and if the military would remove itself from politics, then he would agree to amalgamate the two countries. In the second half of January, Bitar accepted Nasser's terms, and events then moved with great speed. On February 1, the UAR was officially born. Two countries had become one, with Nasser towering over both.

In reality, the long-term prospects for the union were abysmal. Economically and politically, the two countries were fundamentally incompatible, and Damascus was a cauldron of intrigue. Moreover, neither Nasser nor his Syrian allies had prepared their respective countries for the difficulties to come. However, as nationalist theater, the union was exhilarating. Once again, Nasser had performed the impossible. In four short years he had ousted the British from the Canal Zone, shepherded Egypt into the Soviet orbit, nationalized the Suez Canal, defeated Britain, France, and Israel in war—all that, and now this: integral Arab unity, the dream of a significant segment of the generation that was on the rise in the Arab world.

To the governments of neighboring countries, however, the UAR was their blackest nightmare. Its rise deepened the perception that Nasser's victory over the imperialists at Suez meant that Iraq and Jordan, which were creations of British imperialism, were now living on borrowed time. Nasser's Voice of the Arabs hammered the message home daily. Of course, when it came to the task of subversion, Nasser had more in his toolkit than just radio propaganda. Now that he enjoyed a base of operations in Syria, in the heart of the Fertile Crescent, he could more easily extend his arm directly into the domestic politics of both Hashemite states, to say nothing of Lebanon. He thus strengthened what he had already established over the last two years, namely, a loose coalition of anti–status quo forces. Any group with a grievance against its government—Sunnis and Druze in Lebanon, Palestinians in Jordan, Baathists and ambitious army officers in Iraq—could turn to Cairo with a reasonable expectation of receiving material support under the banner of "Arab unity."

By the time the Americans were aware of the threat, it was already too late. In Syria, especially, the momentum behind the merger was unstoppable. Two weeks before the key meeting between Bitar and Nasser, the American ambassador to Syria, James Moose, reported to Washington that, though the dangers of union were considerable, opposition was futile. In Syria, the idea of unity with Egypt was "so politically irresistible" that almost everyone in Damascus felt obliged "to jump on [the] band wagon and whip up [the] horses." Even politicians who hated Nasser felt compelled to praise him. The United States would simply be "wasting its prestige" if it tried to block such a popular plan.[11]

During the Suez Crisis, Eisenhower served up a victory to Egypt on a platter. It had never occurred to the president, however, that he was also helping Nasser to devour Syria.

Saudi Arabia

Nor did he realize that he was simultaneously destroying the third pillar of his strategy, his effort to transform Saudi Arabia into a regional counterbalance to Egypt. Eisenhower's original conception, which he had developed in March 1956, included the fanciful notion of turning the Saudi king into a charismatic, personal rival to Nasser. Over time, however, the president adapted to reality and focused on the more sensible aim of simply detaching Riyadh from Cairo. As Nasser grew into a figure of mythological power, however, even this modest goal proved impossible to achieve. Shortly after the rise of the UAR, Nasser managed to neutralize Saudi Arabia with nothing more than a dramatic speech mixed with a pinch of intrigue.

He delivered the speech in early March 1957 from a Damascus balcony. Speaking before streets packed with Syrian admirers, Nasser revealed that he had foiled a conspiracy to destroy the UAR. But he gave few specifics, preferring instead to whet the appetite of the crowd so that the suspense might build. At a press conference after the speech, it fell to Abdel Hamid Sarraj, who was at the center of events, to walk reporters through the intricate details of the plot. The head of Syrian counterintelligence explained that an agent of King Saud had recruited him to assassinate Nasser. The conspiracy called for Sarraj to place a bomb on Nasser's plane, and then to break up the UAR by carrying out a coup in Damascus. To support his accusations, Sarraj produced corroborating documents, including photostats of checks drawn on an official Saudi account.[12]

Having ensnared Rocky Stone and now King Saud, Sarraj demonstrated his rare talent for entrapment—and Nasser appreciated the skill greatly. Before long, Sarraj would become his viceroy in Damascus. Meanwhile in Saudi Arabia, Sarraj's sting provided King Saud's rivals in the royal family with an opportunity to sideline him. On March 22, they launched a velvet putsch, forcing the king to delegate his major day-to-day responsibilities to his brother, Crown Prince Feisal. According to an official CIA analysis, the shake-up was a major blow to American regional interests. Feisal, the report explained, possessed a strong pro-Nasser streak, and he would likely move closer to Egypt. "Regardless of Feisal's actual intentions in regard to the UAR," the report stated, "his coming to power will be construed throughout the area as a repudiation of Saud's open anti-Nasser, pro-West policy, and as a victory for Nasserism."[13]

Two weeks later, at a meeting in the White House, Allen Dulles confirmed the worst. Feisal, the CIA director told Eisenhower, had just "broadcast a statement in which he proclaimed a policy of 'positive neutrality' for Saudi Arabia. . . . He had likewise requested the

United States to cease to fly the U.S. flag at the Dhahran air base."
Both moves were concessions to Nasser: "positive neutrality" was
the stance of the Non-Aligned Movement championed by Egypt,
and Voice of the Arabs had for some time been attacking the Saudis
for allowing the Americans use of the airfield in Dhahran.[14]

With only minimal exertion on his part, Nasser had toppled another pillar.

The Fall of the Iraqi Monarchy

When King Hussein of Jordan first learned that Nasser and Bitar
were contemplating a merger between Egypt and Syria, he feared
that the resulting union would have a magnetic attraction to the
Palestinians of the West Bank. Hussein contacted the Saudi and
Iraqi kings and proposed that they create a rival federation. He argued that the UAR, due to its ties with Moscow, was vulnerable
to the accusation of being a tool of foreign influence. By contrast,
the federation of monarchies could present itself as a truly independent Arab bloc.[15] The Saudis were unresponsive, but the Iraqis
agreed to participate.

On February 14, 1958, two weeks after the founding of the
UAR, the Iraqi and Jordanian kings announced the formation of
the Arab Union, a federal structure that preserved executive authority for each monarch in his own land. The American embassy
in Amman reported that "sizeable frustrated elements" in Jordan
are inclined to reject the federation as a "mere gimmick" designed
to block "real" unity—represented by Syria and Egypt.[16] Nevertheless, the Arab Union managed to capture the imagination of Foster
Dulles, and it became the fourth pillar of the American strategy of
isolating Nasser.

Dulles dreamed of turning the Iraqi-Jordanian federation into a
power bloc capable of coming to the defense of Chamoun in Lebanon, who was now the target of an insurgency supported by the

UAR. Then on May 20, he instructed the ambassadors in Amman
and Baghdad to express his frustration to the Jordanians and Iraqis,
who were moving too slowly to transform the Arab Union, which
was so far a paper merger, into something truly vibrant. Their foot
dragging, Dulles complained, was giving Nasser material "to convince public opinion" that the Arab Union was a "sham," and that
the leaders of the UAR were the only true adherents to the principle
of Arab unity. If Jordan and Iraq failed to fulfill their commitment
"their political position in the area will be seriously damaged."[17]

Their position, in fact, would soon be destroyed. On July 11,
three days before the Iraqi Revolution, King Hussein discovered
a conspiracy among officers in his military to assassinate him and
align Jordan with Nasser. In the view of the U.S. military attaché,
Sarraj—and, by extension, Nasser—had planned the operation.[18]
Three days later, the Iraqi revolutionaries stormed onto the scene.
Their timing, so close to the foiled plot in Jordan, makes one wonder whether Nasser had a hand in their coup, too, but no evidence
of Egyptian involvement has ever emerged. Whatever the case, the
revolution worked to the obvious advantage of Nasser by destroying the Arab Union, the Baghdad Pact, and his most significant
Arab rival. It also toppled the final pillar of the American strategy.

After the slaughter of the Iraqi royal family was complete, there
remained only one man who was capable of mounting a restoration
of the old regime—Prime Minister Nuri al-Said. He managed to
hide for twenty-four hours, but was then captured and killed. An
angry mob intercepted his body on the way to the morgue and
mutilated it. Day two of the revolution ended, therefore, just like
day one: with the lacerated remains of a once-powerful man hanging from a balcony of the ministry of defense. As Qasim and Arif
butchered the monarchy and its key supporters, they brought an
era in modern Arab history to an abrupt end. At the same time,
they eviscerated the paradigm that had shaped the thinking of Eisenhower and Dulles for the past five years.

Eden's Revenge

The Foster Dulles who participated in the NSC meeting at which Eisenhower gave the order to intervene in Lebanon was not the same man who had broken with his European allies during the Suez Crisis. He looked the same, to be sure, and his voice had not changed. He had identical mannerisms, and there was no mistaking the forceful, self-assured demeanor. The man was the same in every respect except one: his thought. Dulles's brain in 1958 was identical to Anthony Eden's brain in 1956.

"[M]ost of Asia will be against us," Dulles said.[19] There would also be "a very bad reaction through most of the Arab countries—a cutting off of the pipeline, stoppage of transit through the Suez, and hostile activity throughout the area." Be that as it may, "the losses from doing nothing would be worse than the losses from action—and . . . consequently we should send our troops into Lebanon."

Just as during the Suez Crisis, Dulles now feared a collapse of the American global position. But he had reversed himself entirely on the conditions that might bring about such a collapse. In 1956, he and Eisenhower had argued that failure to respect Third World opinion—especially Arab nationalist opinion—was the road to disaster. Now, however, if America were to allow global public opinion to tie its hands, it would deliver itself to certain ruin. "If we do not respond to the call from Chamoun," Dulles said, "we will suffer the decline and indeed the elimination of our influence—from Indonesia to Morocco." The Soviets, he predicted, would subvert the countries of the northern tier: "Iran would gradually go down; Turkey would probably stand firm but with increasing anxieties." Meanwhile, Nasser would hollow out his neighborhood: "In Africa Nasser is already making gains in Sudan; Libya is in the balance; and Tunis and Morocco are already unfriendly."

Dulles also reversed his assessment of the Soviet threat. In

1956, avoiding a superpower clash was a paramount concern. Now, however, he was itching to take on the Soviets, even if it meant war. Moscow, he explained, did not possess enough long-range missiles and bombers to defeat the United States in the Middle East. But it was busy building up its stock of strategic weaponry, so the military balance might change in the near future. The United States, therefore, should act forcefully while it still had an edge. "If we do not accept the risk now," Dulles said, "[the Soviets] will probably decide that we will never accept risk and will push harder than ever, and border countries will submit to them."[20]

Eisenhower's thinking was moving in parallel with Dulles's. "[T]he most strategic move," he said, "would be to attack Cairo . . . , but of course this cannot be done." Nevertheless, it was important to make a forceful move, and to do so quickly. "[T]o lose this area by inaction," the president warned, "would be far worse than the loss in China, because of the strategic position and resources of the Middle East."[21]

That Eisenhower was abandoning the principles that had guided him during the Suez Crisis was not lost on informed observers. Later that afternoon, the president met with Sam Rayburn, the venerable Speaker of the House. When the president briefed the Texas congressman, together with other leading figures from Capitol Hill, on his decision to intervene in Lebanon, Rayburn raised a number of concerns. He noted, Eisenhower later wrote, "the favorable effect of our Suez policies in 1956 and felt that intervention in Lebanon would be followed by an opposite reaction." In response, the president argued that there were "basic differences" between the two cases: the British and French had launched a war; the Americans were coming to the defense of a people "upon the request of their government."[22] But this legalistic distinction hardly answered Rayburn's concern that the danger of a popular, Arab nationalist backlash—precisely the fear that had driven Eisenhower to oppose the British, French, and Israelis in 1956. And just like Eisenhower in the Suez Crisis, Rayburn also feared the Soviet reaction and the general unpredictability of war. "[I]f we go in and intervene and our operation does not succeed," he asked, "what do we do then[?]"[23]

Eisenhower responded with the flinty realism of a seasoned military commander. He readily admitted that the operation would be very unpopular, and that the venture was risky. In fact, it was so dangerous that it reminded him of the weightiest moment of his life: the D-Day invasion of Europe. "Despite the disparity in the size of the two operations," Eisenhower wrote in his memoirs, "the possible consequences in each case, if things went wrong, were chilling."[24] He told Rayburn that there were no good options. Regardless of whether the United States acted or did nothing, he said, "the consequences will be bad." What mattered most was demonstrating strength. "[I]t was better," he said, "if we took a strong position rather than a Munich-type position."[25]

Throughout the Suez Crisis, Anthony Eden had made an identical argument.

Millstones Crumble

On the same day, Eisenhower also called Prime Minister Harold Macmillan and initiated the discussions that would result in the division of labor between the United States and the United Kingdom. The American Marines would land in Lebanon; the British would intervene in Jordan with the assistance of the U.S. military. This close cooperation marked another revolution in Eisenhower's approach. Heretofore he had studiously avoided any association with Britain in the Middle East for fear that it would appear to Arab audiences as American collusion with imperialism. Even the close diplomatic coordination on Plan Alpha had taken place in secret.

And the British millstone was not the only one to crumble.

Within weeks, it emerged that Eisenhower's traditional aversion to partnership with Israel had also dissipated. After the Lebanon and Jordan operations were under way, the Soviet Union demanded that Ben-Gurion close Israeli airspace to the British and the Americans, who were overflying the country to supply the British troops in Jordan. On August 2, Ben-Gurion complied with the Soviet demand—presumably to prove to the United States that Israel would not be taken for granted. The decision, however, served only to exasperate the Americans. Dulles hauled in Abba Eban, the Israeli ambassador in Washington, and treated him to a tongue-lashing. The secretary of state said that both he and the president were shocked to learn that "Israel was preparing to acquiesce to the Soviet request that the flights be stopped." They expected better of the Israelis. "We had believed that Israel fully agreed with the . . . purpose . . . of showing the Soviets and Nasser there was a point beyond which they could not go." It was vitally important not to give "the USSR a sense of power in the Middle East by such subservient actions as Israel seemed prepared to take."[26]

Ben-Gurion relented. Being paddled like a naughty schoolboy by Headmaster Dulles was no doubt a bitter experience, but the irony must have been a deliciously sweet compensation. The same Dulles who had censured Israel in 1956 for assisting a British military intervention designed to weaken Nasser was now admonishing Israel for refusing to support another British military intervention designed to weaken Nasser.

Ike Converts—but to What?

Historians have long recognized that Eisenhower's perspective on the Middle East changed in 1958. With a few notable exceptions, however, they have mischaracterized the evolution. According to the reigning misconception, Eisenhower recognized the futility of trying to contain Egypt and he returned, in effect, to the policy of

1955, the heyday of Byroadism—to the policy, that is, that sought a strategic accommodation with Nasser. Thus the historian Fawaz Gerges writes, "[T]he most important outcome of the Lebanese crisis was that it brought about a rapprochement between the United States and Egypt. Before the Lebanese crisis was over, Eisenhower and Dulles had recognized the futility of trying to oppose Nasser's brand of Arab nationalism." In support of this claim, Gerges quotes Eisenhower as saying, " '[W]e are about to get thrown out of the area, [so] we might as well believe in Arab nationalism.'"[27]

It was on July 25, 1958, that Eisenhower made this statement—just eleven days after ordering the Marines to Lebanon. Did he really convert to Nasserism less than two weeks after saying that the most desirable strategic play would be to bomb Cairo? The question answers itself.

Of course Eisenhower recognized that the containment of Nasser had failed. The only Arab actors now willing to work against Egypt were King Hussein of Jordan and President Chamoun of Lebanon—embattled leaders of diminutive and internally divided countries. They hardly constituted a solid foundation for a regional strategy, so a policy of taking on Nasser directly was now impossible. Eisenhower was bowing to reality, yes, but the documents do not support the assertion that he therefore sought a strategic understanding with Egypt. In fact, at the July 25 meeting, the one at which Eisenhower made the quip about converting to Arab nationalism, he flatly rejected the idea of a rapprochement with Nasser. And that's not all. That meeting marked the beginning of NSC process devoted to formulating a new strategy. Throughout the entire deliberation, which lasted four months, Eisenhower consistently and clearly argued against embracing Nasser.

It was the Arabists in the State Department and the CIA, not the president, who claimed that the UAR was now the only horse to ride. They summarized their case in a briefing paper prepared for the July 25 discussion. "We must face up to the fact," the paper argued, "that Arab nationalism is the dominant force in the Arab world, and that it has assumed a radical form symbolized by Nasser." The United States would pay a grave price if it failed to reach an understanding with him. "Inasmuch as Nasser is the symbol of radical Arab nationalism, unless and until we are able to work with him we cannot really avoid the onus of appearing to oppose the dominant force in the Arab world."[28]

This was Byroadism, raised from the dead, and Eisenhower, just as he had done in March 1956, quickly rammed a stake through its heart. He did so by skewering its basic assumption: the idea that Nasser embodied the aspirations of all Arabs. "[N]ationalism in the area was of course radical but was it necessarily pan-Arab?" he asked rhetorically. He thought it possible "for a Near Eastern country to be nationalistic but not pan-Arab," and he pointed to the regime in Iraq as an example. It was certainly nationalistic, in the sense that it sought to chart a course independent from the West, yet it was not rushing to join the UAR, as some had expected. Gordon Gray, the national security advisor, informed the president that the experts on the Middle East disagreed with him. They believed that "Arab nationalism today was both radical and pan-Arab."[29]

But the president had the stronger argument. Eisenhower, who had spent very little time in the Middle East, was actually schooling the experts on the most elementary division in Arab politics. The Arabic language has two separate words for "nationalism": *qawmiyya* and *wataniyya*. The former describes ethnic nationalism, the love that one feels for the Arab people as a whole, and it aspires to their unity. In its most extreme form, *qawmiyya* calls for wiping out the boundaries that separate, say, Iraq from its sister Arab countries. Nasserism drew its power from *qawmiyya*. By contrast, *wataniyya* refers to the love that one feels for one's homeland— patriotism. Iraqi *wataniyya*, for example, seeks to strengthen the power of Iraq. Without using the Arabic terms—indeed, without even knowing them—Eisenhower was arguing that *qawmiyya* and *wataniyya* were in a permanent state of tension. What is more, he was ordering his staff to develop a strategy to exploit that tension so as to circumscribe Nasser's power.

Thus when Eisenhower called for the United States to convert to Arab nationalism he was referring to *wataniyya*. The final text of the strategy transcribed the president's terminology verbatim. "It has become increasingly apparent," the document stated, "that the prevention of further Soviet penetration of the Near East . . . depends on the degree to which the United States is able to work more closely with Arab nationalism"—Eisenhower's term for *wataniyya*. When referring to Nasser's *qawmiyya*, the document used an entirely different term: "radical pan-Arab nationalism." "In the eyes of the great mass of Arabs," it stated, "considerable significance will be attached to the position which the United States adopts regarding the foremost current spokesman of radical pan-Arab nationalism, Gamal Abdel Nasser."

If one reads this document on its own, without reference to the president's personal guidance, then one can easily mistake "Arab nationalism" and "radical pan-Arab nationalism" for synonyms. In that case, some passages indeed make it sound as if Eisenhower was advocating a strategic alignment with Nasser. If, however, one holds the president's distinction firmly in mind, then the document describes an entirely different strategy: divide and rule.

Dillinger and Capone

When the new policy was finally ratified, it reflected the guidance that the president had given at the outset, on July 25. During the drafting process, however, staffers tried to edit the document in ways that contradicted Eisenhower's basic thinking—ways that would have set the United States on a new, pro-Nasser orientation. At an NSC meeting on October 16, for example, the national secu-

rity advisor informed Eisenhower that the State Department and
the CIA were arguing in favor of defining Nasser as the leader of
the Arab world. They called for a rapproachement with him, and,
moreover, insisted that the new friendship must be visible to the
man on the street in the Arab world. Like a demon in a horror film,
Byroadism rose again from the dead.

In the meeting, it was Dulles who made the first attempt to
slay the demon, saying that he "did not think we should go as far
in our policy as to treat Nasser as the leader of the Arab world."
The president then chimed in, explaining, with concrete examples, why the pursuit of a strategic understanding with Nasser
would be self-destructive. In the Gulf, he explained, it would undermine allies. The oil-producing states "had a natural antipathy
toward Egypt, which was not, strictly speaking, an Arab state."
They guarded their oil revenues zealously. "[W]e certainly don't
want to be the agent through whom Nasser secures control of all
these oil revenues." In Syria, he continued, a policy of accommodating Nasser would close off opportunities to weaken him. "If
we could somehow bring about a separation of Syria from Egypt
and thereafter a union of Syria with Iraq, this might prove very
useful." [30]

Regarding the fundamental question of whether to reach an accommodation with Nasser, the president left no room for ambigu-
ity. "Certainly," he said, "there was no reason for the United States
to go on and treat Nasser as the head of the whole Arab nationalist movement. If we did this . . . Nasser would become the biggest
blackmailer this country ever faced."

Yet again, Eisenhower killed Byroadism. The United States,
the final version of the strategy stated, would adopt a correct relationship with Nasser, due to his special status as "the foremost
current spokesman of radical pan-Arab nationalism." However, the
strategy also qualified this judgment. "[A]spects of the drive toward
Arab unity, particularly as led by Nasser," the document noted, "are

strongly inimical to our interests." Therefore, the United States must conduct relations with Nasser "without destroying our freedom of action in dealings with other Arab leaders" and "without resigning the United States to an acceptance of the inevitability of Nasser's undisputed hegemony over the whole of the Arab world."[31] The new policy, in other words, explicitly called for using the innately fissiparous character of Arab politics to weaken Nasser's power indirectly. If Eisenhower was resurrecting old thinking, then he was returning to the Omega strategy of March 1956, not to a policy of courting Egypt.

During the waning years of Eisenhower's administration, however, the president's deep distrust of Nasser was not always obvious. The coup in Iraq led to a reemergence, in 1959, of the Iraq-Egypt split, which generated a bitter personal rivalry between Nasser and Qasim. As the new Iraqi leader migrated into the Soviet orbit, Nasser's relations with Moscow came under strain. Due to dramatic change in the strategic landscape, Eisenhower found it expedient to engage with Nasser, as he did, for example, in the fall of 1960, when the two men even met personally during a meeting of the UN General Assembly. A photo from the encounter, which captured Eisenhower and Nasser in genial conversation at New York's Waldorf-Astoria hotel, has reinforced the erroneous view that the president converted back to Byroadism.

In fact, a divide-and-rule mind-set now governed his every move. That mind-set was on sharp display at an NSC meeting in 1959, when the president and his staff first discussed the strategic significance of the Qasim-Nasser conflict—a rivalry that, of course, Eisenhower had forecast when he insisted on the *qawmiyya-wataniyya* distinction. During a debate about whether, under the circumstances, it made sense to help Nasser against Qasim, Eisenhower said this was a case of choosing between "Dillinger or . . . Capone." In a world dominated by gangsters, Eisenhower advocating managing the rivalry between them, not choosing sides.

Israel, Asset

The revolutionary wave that swept the Middle East after the Suez Crisis gave Eisenhower an intensive course in the complexity of inter-Arab conflict. The wave produced a long series of crises— one day in Syria, the next in Jordan, and the day after that in Lebanon—none of which had the slightest connection to imperialism or Zionism. As a result, Eisenhower learned that, because the Arabs were perpetually at each other's throats, no effort to organize them into a single bloc had a chance of success. Even Nasser himself, for all of his unrivaled authority, did not have the power to unite the Arabs.

When all was said and done, Nasser was simply the leader of an anti–status quo coalition—an alliance that was effective at tearing down the existing order, not at building a new one. A significant portion of the coalition's popularity derived from the murderous rage that showed its face on the streets of Baghdad during the Iraqi Revolution. Once the desecration of the dead leaders was over, the coalition disintegrated, as its constituent elements pursued contradictory political visions. In Eisenhower's eyes, Nasser was operating a protection racket. The best the United States could expect was that, in return for payment, he would temporarily refrain from destructive acts. A strategic alignment was impossible, because, sooner or later, Nasser would make a new threat and demand a new payment.

Eisenhower absorbed these elementary facts of life faster and more completely than the Arabists on his staff. Ideologically wedded to the honest broker paradigm, they forever fantasized about a grand bargain between the United States and all Arabs, led by Nasser. Because the differences between the president and his experts were a matter of fundamental perspective, they reemerged time and again in a variety of different arenas.

One particularly interesting case in point was a debate that took place in late October 1958 over policy toward the Arab-Israeli conflict. Eisenhower noted that the planning for an outbreak of violence was outdated. American planners, he explained, were mistakenly assuming that the United States would work through the United Nations to contain Israel—precisely as it had done in the Suez Crisis. The next war, however, would likely result from the destabilization of Jordan. In such a scenario, the primary interest of the United States would be to protect King Hussein of Jordan from Nasser and his Syrian partners in the UAR. Eisenhower turned to General Nathan Twining, the chairman of the Joint Chiefs of Staff, and asked whether the military had "ever war-gamed a situation in which the Egyptians and Syrians had moved against Jordan and the Israelis had replied by attacking first Syria and then Egypt."[32] Israeli power, Eisenhower clearly implied, would benefit the United States by helping the Jordanian government to fend off Nasser and his allies.

Dulles, for his part, had already reached the same conclusion. Two months earlier, he had told the Turkish foreign minister that Israel was a valuable counterweight to Nasser. "It might be a good thing," he said, "that the UAR was afraid of Israel."[33] Around the same time, he also approved the sale of arms to the Jewish state: antitank rifles and Sikorsky helicopters. These weapons were a minor factor in the overall military balance, but they represented a major change—a revolution, no less—in the secretary of state's thinking. For Dulles, as for Eisenhower, Israeli power had become an asset in the Cold War.[34]

Frankenstein's Monster

If Eisenhower parted company with the Arabists over policy, he also disagreed with them over the interpretation of recent history. The key point of dissension was the question, "Why did the post-Suez strategy fail?" Under the influence of Byroadism, the Arabists put the blame squarely on the Eisenhower administration's containment reflex. The urge to diminish Nasser had dominated American policy in March 1956, with the advent of the Omega strategy. Although it had abated during the Suez Crisis, it had returned with a vengeance in the form of the Eisenhower Doctrine. The attempt to contain Nasser, the Arabists argued, was futile, because it placed the United States at odds with Arab popular will. The price for that folly was, among other things, the fall of the Iraqi monarchy, which had foolishly attempted to stand against the Nasserist wave.

Shortly after the Iraqi Revolution, Foster Dulles vigorously rejected that interpretation of history. During an NSC session devoted to drafting a new regional strategy, he rebutted the Arabists' belief that Nasser drew his power from the will of the masses. His power was, Dulles argued, nothing less than a gift from the United States. "Secretary Dulles felt," the notetaker recorded,

> that the vogue of Nasserism in the area did not reflect an authentic pan-Arabism, but instead reflected the fact that Nasser seems to be the first successful leader of the Arab world in a thousand years. He has become the hero of the masses because he has enjoyed an unbroken series of successes, due largely to our support. In the past, U.S. support has not prevented Nasser from pursuing his ambitions. Nasser's unbroken series of successes include getting the British out of the Suez bases, taking over the Suez Canal Company, taking over Syria, getting the United Kingdom, France and Israel to suspend hostilities against Egypt, and having the government of Iraq overthrown. In connection with the British-French-Israeli attack on Egypt, Secretary Dulles noted that Egypt had been saved because the United States had upheld the principles of the Charter [of the United Nations] and in March of 1957 had almost single-

handedly persuaded the Israelis to withdraw by making a statement about sanctions. Our actions had enabled Nasser to
emerge as a great hero, who seemingly took on the great powers and came out with a victory.[35]

Nasser was Frankenstein's monster. His great achievements, the
triumphs on which his reputation was built, were entirely made in
America.

The post-Suez travails of the Eisenhower administration resulted, Dulles implied, not because containing Nasser had been a
fool's errand, but because the United States had failed to devise an
effective containment policy before it was too late. By the time the
Americans recognized that Nasser was a threat, they had already
turned him into a mythic figure. The implication of Dulles's analysis was obvious: the single greatest mistake of the administration
was handing Nasser an historic triumph in the Suez Crisis.

Eisenhower was present in the meeting as Dulles expounded
this interpretation of history. He listened quietly and raised no objections. Did his silence imply agreement? The evidence suggests
that it did. Indeed, on at least three occasions in his postpresidency,
Eisenhower expressed remorse about his management of the Suez
Crisis.

The first came in 1965, when Max Fisher visited Eisenhower
on his farm in Gettysburg, Pennsylvania. Fisher was a successful
businessman from Michigan, a leading member of the American
Jewish community, and a prominent Republican fund-raiser. As the
conversation between the two started to wind down, it turned to
the events of 1956. "You know, Max, looking back at Suez, I regret what I did," Ike said. "I never should have pressured Israel to
evacuate the Sinai."[36] As Fisher was leaving the house, Eisenhower
added, "Max, if I'd had a Jewish adviser working for me, I doubt I
would have handled the situation the same way. I would not have
forced the Israelis back."[37]

Fisher's account is uncorroborated, but less than two years later Eisenhower made a related statement to Avraham Harman, the Israeli ambassador to the United States. That conversation, by contrast, was documented. Harman visited the former president in Gettysburg in the spring of 1967, when Egypt brought Israel to the brink of war. In mid-May Nasser had suddenly reoccupied the Sinai militarily, then quickly expelled the UN peacekeepers from Gaza and Sharm el-Sheikh, while closing the Straits of Tiran to Israeli shipping. With these steps, Nasser reversed the only concessions that he had made to Eisenhower in 1957.

At that time, Ben-Gurion had complained bitterly about the absence of safeguards to prevent Nasser from doing just that. In response, Eisenhower had pledged American support for Israeli freedom of passage through the Straits of Tiran. But his promise had never been made public. Now, when the Israelis turned to the White House and requested that it honor Eisenhower's pledges, the Johnson administration was seized with amnesia. Pledges? What pledges? Harman drove up to Gettysburg to ask Eisenhower for help in refreshing President Johnson's memory by making the guarantees public. Eisenhower agreed, and the following day he held a press conference at which he was as good as his word.

In the midst of taking care of business with Harman, Ike expressed regret about his handling of the Suez Crisis. The ambassador told colleagues about Eisenhower's misgivings, and he also mentioned the subject in a cable to Jerusalem. That report, however, focused on the immediate crisis, so the discussion of Eisenhower's regret is maddeningly short, only one sentence in total. "In his reflections on the past," Harman wrote, "he still regretted the fact that they had failed to establish a clear status with respect to the Suez Canal as they had done with respect to the straits."[38]

This sentence is as revealing as it is short. Not only does it authenticate the story that Harman later told; it also indicates that Eisenhower regretted his failure to force Nasser to compromise on the Suez Canal dispute. Under the circumstances in 1956, the only way to have extracted significant concessions from Nasser would have been to reduce the level of the American opposition to the British, French, and Israelis.

Ike's Regret

Harman's story received further corroboration from Richard Nixon, who placed the fullest account of Eisenhower's regrets on the record. In 1988, Nixon revealed that Eisenhower had personally confided in him that Suez was "his major foreign policy mistake." In 1967, several months after the Six-Day War, Nixon recounted, he and Eisenhower reviewed the events of Suez. Ike gritted his teeth. "Why couldn't the British and French have done it more quickly?" he asked, lamenting the failure of the Europeans to topple Nasser. To this, Eisenhower then added words of self-criticism. "[S]aving Nasser at Suez didn't help as far as the Middle East was concerned. Nasser became even more anti-West and anti-US." Eisenhower also agreed with Nixon's assertion "that the worst fallout from Suez was that it weakened the will of our best allies, Britain and France, to play a major role in the Middle East or in other areas outside Europe."[39]

But Eisenhower never aired these sentiments in public. In early July 1967, a few months before his conversation with Nixon, he had met with C. L. Sulzberger, the legendary foreign correspondent of the *New York Times*, who asked what he would do differently if he could replay the Suez Crisis over again. Ike admitted no mistake. If he had it to do all over again, he said, then he would work harder to bring Israel, France, and Britain around to his viewpoint.

However, Eisenhower's apparent confidence in the wisdom of his Suez policy was not consistent with his attitude toward the Six-Day War, which had ended just one month before the Sulzberger interview. In 1956, Eisenhower had demanded restraint from the

Israelis; they should rely on the United Nations, not the unilateral exercise of their military power, to keep the peace. Now, by contrast, he praised their boldness, going so far as to marvel at the number of planes they had mowed down. "[T]hat sure was some harvest the Israelis got," he exclaimed. "I never had a harvest like that in World War II—340 planes in one night."

Even more telling, however, was his enthusiastic defense of Israel's preemptive action. "I don't know," he said, "what [the Israelis] could have done except [to attack], with all those Arab armies on their borders and Nasser talking of a total war to drive Israel into the sea." He invited Sulzberger to draw an analogy to the United States. "Supposing I had been president and some combination of enemies, much bigger than us, had been gathered on the seas and in Canada and Mexico promising our extinction. If I hadn't attacked first while I had the chance I would have been tried for treason."[40]

While this empathy for Israel was certainly striking, Eisenhower's decision not to place his regrets about Suez on the record still left room for skeptics—such as, for example, the historian Stephen Ambrose. In 1994, a few months after Nixon's death, Ambrose cast doubt on the late president's account of his 1967 conversation with Eisenhower. "Perhaps Eisenhower did say that to Nixon," Ambrose wrote, "but in my own interviews with Eisenhower in the mid-1960s, the former president said just the opposite. He was proud of what he had done with regard to Suez and insisted that he had been right to support Egypt."[41] We now know, however, that Ambrose greatly exaggerated his intimacy with Ike. His claim that Eisenhower confided in him about Suez is, therefore, highly suspect and entirely uncorroborated.

Nixon's testimony, by contrast, is amply corroborated—by Max Fisher and Avraham Harman. At least as powerful as the testimony of witnesses, however, is the simple fact that by mid-1958, Eisenhower and Dulles had discarded the basic assumptions about the Middle East that had compelled them to drive the British, French, and Israelis out of Egypt in 1956. In addition, Dulles, for one, bemoaned having handed the Egyptian leader a political triumph. Eisenhower clearly harbored identical views—and why wouldn't he? After all, he was a stone-cold realist. When he saved Nasser in 1956, he did not do so out of love for the Egyptian leader; he was, rather, placing a straightforward bet, wagering that stopping the war would be less damaging to the West than supporting America's traditional allies. That bet came up craps. By 1958, it was already a spectacular loser; by 1967, it was a political embarrassment.

Like all politicians, Eisenhower was loath to admit publicly that he had blundered, but the brutal truth hung before his eyes like a corpse on a rope.

Conclusion

To shut the Soviets out of the Arab world: that was Eisenhower's goal when he took office in 1953. The best method, he believed, was to broker an accommodation between the United States and Arab nationalism, and he identified Nasser as the primary partner in this effort. In order to win the Egyptian leader over to the West, Eisenhower provided him indispensable assistance in ousting Britain from the Suez Canal Zone in 1953–54. Once Nasser had thrown the British out, however, he had little use for the Americans; he gravitated instead toward the Soviets, who shared his top priority, namely, destroying the Baghdad Pact. Nasser was playing for supremacy in the Arab world, and the American agenda, which emphasized pro-Western alliances and peace with Israel, would have forced him to forfeit his ambitions. Thanks to Nasser's strategic pivot, the Soviets made deep inroads into the Arab world, so deep that by 1959 they had penetrated not just Egypt but Iraq and Syria, too.

As Eisenhower absorbed these facts, his understanding of the Middle East changed. At first, he had seen its political landscape as divided between the Arabs, on the one hand, and Britain, France, and Israel, on the other. The United States, for its part, was caught in the middle—a position that gave it no choice but to play the honest broker, to mediate between the two sides with an eye to reaching an understanding with the Arabs. Over time, however, the president discovered that the Arabs were forever at each other's throats, and no effort to organize them into a single bloc had the slightest chance of success. He therefore discarded the mental image of the honest broker and adopted instead a picture of the United States as a manager of inter-Arab conflict.

Mental images of this kind are consequential—as Max Weber, the father of modern sociology, reminds us. According to Weber, interests, not ideas, drive the behavior of states. But leaders, even the most pragmatic among them, cannot pursue interests effectively without first developing a mental picture of how the world works. Such pictures rest, ultimately, on ideas. "[T]he 'world images,' Weber writes, "that have been created by 'ideas' have, like switchmen, determined the tracks along which action has been pushed by the dynamic of interest."[1]

Weber's metaphor invites us to think of Eisenhower's paradigm shift as a change of personnel: as the replacement of the honest broker switchman with a new man. This thought, in turn, suggests an intriguing counterfactual question: What if the Ike of 1958 had appeared sooner—before the Suez Crisis? Down which alternative tracks might he have sent American policy? And with what long-term results?

Empowering Nasser

It was the Soviet-Egyptian arms deal of September 1955 that first raised serious doubts in Eisenhower's mind about Nasser. Should the United States respond to the deal, the president asked, with the carrot or the stick? He chose the carrot, in the form of funding for the Aswan High Dam, and he chose quickly, almost without a debate—a surprising fact, given that his administration was habitually accused of seeing a communist under every rock. The eagerness to forgive and forget owed much, perhaps everything, to the preeminence of the honest broker mindset. Not only did it foster receptivity to Nasser's claim that the arms deal was merely a response to Israeli aggression; it also generated defensiveness regarding the accusation that the United States supported Israel to keep the Arabs weak. As a rebuttal to this indictment, the offer of funding for the Aswan High Dam had much to commend itself. It showcased the American concern for the economic welfare of the average Egyptian and, more broadly, the average Arab. Could a power so magnanimous truly be imperialist?

But the effort to advertise the good intentions of the United States missed the point: Nasser was branding himself, not America. The arms deal was a classic example of propaganda by action. Nasser was presenting a vision of the Arab future, unveiling a new model of political and military development based on cooperation between pan-Arabism and the communist bloc. Egyptian propaganda presented the model that the West was offering, the Baghdad Pact, as an imperialist plot designed to divide and subjugate the Arabs, to prevent them from making common cause to destroy Israel. Therefore, the Arabs should unite behind Egypt, throw off the yoke of Western domination, and remake the world in accordance with their own values and aspirations. This heady message transformed the Middle East. It fueled dreams of erasing the borders drawn by the imperialists, and, in the process, of wiping Israel off the map. When Nasser challenged the West, Ike responded by offering him an expensive present.

The Ike of 1958, if he had appeared at this junction, would have recognized that failure to impose severe costs on Nasser for the arms deal strengthened him. The gift of the funding for the Aswan High Dam failed to refute the arguments of Nasser that truly mattered. The Ike of 1958 would have developed an alternative strategy that combined some or all of the following elements: adherence to the Baghdad Pact by the United States; slowing or halting the British withdrawal from the Canal Zone; supporting a vigorous Israeli military action against Egypt in response to Fedayeen raids; detaching Riyadh from Cairo; and imposing economic sanctions on

Egypt. In fact, it would be another six months before Eisenhower
gave any thought to these options. By that time, Nasser had already
pushed Jordan to the brink of revolution and turned the Baghdad
Pact into an empty shell.

A Mediator with Interests

The Suez Crisis offered the United States another major opportunity to change course. By the time the crisis erupted, Eisenhower
had already begun to question the honest broker paradigm. He had
concluded that Nasser was an inveterate blackmailer, that the Arab-
Israeli conflict could not be solved on his watch, and that American policy should contain Egypt, not court it. But even at that late
stage, the honest broker policy continued to block any track that
led to direct confrontation with Egypt or to overt cooperation with
Britain and Israel—out of fear that the whole Arab world might
unite against America.

It was precisely this fear that convinced Eisenhower, when war
erupted, to force Britain, France, and Israel to evacuate Egypt unconditionally. The result, however, was to inflate Nasser's image
beyond his wildest dreams. In reality, of course, it was American
economic pressure that forced the Europeans to beat a hasty retreat. What made the deepest impression on Arab audiences, however, was the Soviet threat to hit the British, French, and Israelis
with nuclear-tipped missiles.

The top priority of the Ike of 1958, therefore, would have been
to smash the illusion of Nasser's inevitable triumph. This is not to
suggest that the Ike of 1958 would have directly supported the military operations against Egypt. He would, rather, have recalibrated
his opposition to America's allies. The right moment for a recal-
ibration was November 7, 1956, when Eden telephoned and requested an invitation to visit Washington together with Mollet. It
was at that moment that Eisenhower made his most fateful deci-

sion of the Suez Crisis: to stand against the British, French, and Israelis in manner that was relentless, ruthless, and uncompromising. In effect, Eisenhower decided that Nasser must win the war, and that he must be seen to win. Behind this decision stood, of course, the honest broker approach.

Ike's aides convinced him to call Eden back and rescind the invitation to visit Washington, lest it "give the impression that we are teaming with the British and French."[2] The president accepted this argument. He immediately disinvited Eden; then, in the days and weeks that followed, he took further harsh steps. He refused Britain oil supplies from the Western Hemisphere. He denied it economic aid to prop up its faltering financial system. And he demanded, with single-minded purpose, the total and unconditional British, French, and Israeli evacuation from Egypt. These steps, not the original decision to oppose the war, were the key factors that gave Nasser the triumph of his life.

The Ike of 1958, by contrast, would have ensured that Nasser lost, and that he was seen to lose. To realize this goal, he would have covered the French, British, and the Israelis as they hunkered down for a long negotiation. He would have allowed them to refuse to evacuate until Nasser had buckled and made concessions, such as verifiable force limitations in the Sinai and international oversight of the Suez Canal. What the West needed most was an agreement that would have prevented Nasser from plausibly claiming that he had won an historic victory. This seems to be the idea that Eisenhower expressed at Gettysburg in 1967, when he told Harman, the Israeli ambassador, that he should have compelled Nasser to accept some form of international regime for the Suez Canal.

It was the approach that Nixon and Kissinger followed in the 1973 war. In contrast to Eisenhower's behavior in 1956, they did not force Israel to withdraw without first receiving binding guarantees from Egypt. Nixon never saw the United States as an honest broker. For him, it was an interested mediator, a power that was certainly willing to help the Egyptians manage Israel, but on the condition that they adopt an orientation in the Cold War beneficial to the United States. Israeli military might, in Nixon's view, augmented American power: it was an asset, not a liability. Nixon learned this approach, one assumes, while standing beside Eisenhower as he underwent a paradigm shift.

An Undependable Ally

If the Ike of 1958 had appeared earlier, would he have really made a difference? After all, the Middle East was located on major fault lines: the rise of the superpowers, the fall of imperialism, the advent of populist nationalism. Wasn't an earthquake inevitable? While an early arrival of the Ike of 1958 would not have pacified the Middle East, it might have reduced the extent of the upheaval, and it certainly would have created better options for managing it—options for the United States, to be sure, but especially for its allies, such as the Hashemites of Iraq, who paid a price in blood for Nasser's meteoric rise.

But Eisenhower and Dulles were largely oblivious to the vexation that they caused Iraq. In 1954, Dulles had insisted that Nuri al-Said defy Egypt and sign the Turco-Iraqi Pact—a demand that painted a target on Nuri al-Said's back and placed him squarely in Nasser's crosshairs. When the Egyptian leader began firing, however, Dulles did not come to the Iraqis' aid. On the contrary, he gave the State Department explicit orders to build up Nasser—to strengthen, that is, the very leader who was vilifying an ally of the West for obeying a direct demand from the secretary of state to participate in a major American initiative, Dulles's *personal* initiative. It is difficult to imagine a more whimsical response. But the whimsy did not end there. No sooner had the British signed on to the Baghdad Pact than Dulles came to regard it, as if through

Nasser's eyes, as a tool of imperialism. Given this cockeyed perspective, is it any wonder that, during the Suez Crisis, Eisenhower and Dulles never considered the harm that an Egyptian victory would have on Iraq?

Eisenhower's Suez policy effectively placed the power and influence of the United States behind all of the anti–status quo forces in the Hashemite states. It changed forever the political calculus of men like Qasim, the leader of the Iraqi Revolution, who learned from Suez that he could topple the monarchy without the British forces stationed in Iraq mounting a counteroffensive. Suez also showed him that he could cozy up to the Soviet Union without the United States intervening. But most important of all, it taught him that the future belonged to Nasser, not the Hashemites. The Nasserist wave that followed Suez was thus the self-fulfilling prophecy of officials, in the Henry Byroade mold, who for years had argued that Nasser was the foremost representative of deep and inexorable historical forces. For such officials, a policy that supported Nasser's Arab rivals was a foolish effort to swim against the raging current of history.

Such thinking was by no means confined to American officials. Consider, for instance, a newspaper column by Anthony Nutting in 1958. Nutting, who had resigned from Eden's government in protest over Suez, read the Jordanian intervention of that year as a hopeless effort to revive the dead thinking that had produced Eden's collusion with France and Israel. For Nutting, King Hussein of Jordan was, like Nuri al-Said, a relic of a bygone age. "However much one may admire the courage of this lonely young king," Nutting advised in a newspaper column, "it is difficult to avoid the conclusion that his days are numbered. . . . The best service Britain can now render Hussein seems to be, therefore, to offer to fly him to Cyprus when she withdraws her troops."[3]

The only thing that can be said in defense of this prognostication is that it was true in the most literal sense. Hussein's remaining days were indeed numbered—14,801, to be exact. For more than forty years he labored to disprove Nutting's prediction, but the long and strenuous effort eventually killed him. It did demonstrate, however, that Nutting was entirely wrong about everything of substance: wrong about Hussein being a has-been; wrong about British support being the kiss of death; wrong about the intervention being an act of supreme folly; and wrong about the inevitable triumph of Nasserism. But what if history had played out differently? Suppose some ambitious army officer, a Jordanian answer to Qasim in Iraq, had murdered the king just as the British troops were departing his country. In that case, Nutting would have lamented, more in sadness than in anger, the shortsightedness of those foolhardy souls who had argued that a Western military intervention in the Middle East could actually prove beneficial.

But Hussein survived and thrived. His longevity raises an uncomfortable question: Could the Ike of 1958, if he had appeared earlier, have saved the Iraqi regime as he likely saved the Jordanian monarchy? The question is unanswerable. No one can say with certainty that an early move to contain Nasser would have prevented the revolution in Iraq. Nevertheless, one must admit that Eisenhower, by hobbling Britain and empowering Egypt, fostered a revolutionary atmosphere in Baghdad, and that, more generally, the honest broker worldview instilled in Western officials a perverse desire to shun friends and embrace enemies.

Ike's Finest Hour?

If the honest broker approach has generated bad policy, it has distorted our view of the history. Through a variety of channels, the flawed assumptions of officials of the 1950s have flowed into contemporary thinking about the past. Especially noteworthy in this process of transmission is the role of two men: Henry Byroade and Kermit Roosevelt. Both coached the journalists who

wrote the earliest accounts of Eisenhower's road to Suez. Roosevelt, who died in 2000, lived long enough to guide a number
of historians when the official archives first opened. But it is the
historical documents themselves, especially the cables of Henry
Byroade, that have done the most to preserve the honest broker
perspective and, like a bacillus in a time capsule, to transmit it
across generations.

Ironically, the "inside story" of the Eisenhower administration's Middle East policy comes to us not from Eisenhower and
Dulles but from Byroade and Roosevelt—the very men, that is,
who were most personally invested in the courtship of Nasser,
and who fought against all efforts to abandon it. In fact, they
first began weaving their story line as part of the policy debate in
1955—in order, that is, to change the minds of Eisenhower and
Dulles as they began to sour on Nasser and pan-Arabism. Since
the 1950s, journalists and historians have produced countless
glosses on the Byroade-Roosevelt version of the story. No two
writers have presented it in precisely the same way, but the basics
of the story are nearly always the same, and they go something
like this.

Relations with Nasser were progressing well until February
1955, when Israel launched the Gaza Raid. By killing scores of
Egyptian soldiers, the raid exposed Nasser to attacks from hawkish
officers in his inner circle. To cover his nationalist flank, Nasser cut
the arms deal with the Soviet Union, but in his heart of hearts, he
believed that the natural place of Egypt was in the Western camp.
At first, Eisenhower and Dulles recognized that attempts to pressure Nasser would simply drive him closer to the Soviet Union.
Before long, however, restraint gave way to impatience, and they
adopted a strategy designed to contain Nasser—Omega—which
led Dulles to deny funding for the Aswan High Dam in a manner
calculated to offend. This ham-fisted power play enraged Nasser,
who reacted by nationalizing the Suez Canal. After the United

States blundered into the crisis, Eisenhower, who had been ill, took firm control. By supporting the rights of Egypt against Britain, France, and Israel, he put America's better angels in charge of policy. But the worst impulses of the administration quickly returned. The Eisenhower Doctrine, a vain attempt to force the Middle East to conform to the demands of Washington, resulted in the occupation of Lebanon, a needless military adventure. After the invasion, however, Eisenhower faced facts and returned to the same policy of accommodating Nasser that he had pursued in 1955.

Many of the authors who have repeated this story have been far removed in time from Byroade and Roosevelt, and therefore have rarely been fully aware of just how tendentious a tale it is. This is a story that delivers a strong moral: the application of force is counterproductive. The most aggressive actions of Nasser, we learn, were justifiable reactions to provocations: the Gaza Raid, and Dulles's decision to renege on funding the dam. Muscular Western policies, we learn, will almost always backfire. Of course, this story also vindicates Byroade and Roosevelt. It leads us by the nose to the conclusion that courting Nasser was the right move in the first place, and abandoning it was a gross error in judgment. If Eisenhower had listened from the start to the wise counsel of his Middle East advisors, then he could have saved himself much pain and aggravation.

The inside story also holds up the Suez Crisis as Ike's finest hour. He stood up for principle when it counted most, backing a weak country against two powerful allies of the United States. It is this supposed idealism that gives the story an enduring appeal. To all those who harbor reservations about Western interventionism in the Middle East, Eisenhower's behavior at Suez is more than just a bright spot in the past; it is also a beacon that illuminates the path forward into the future. Thus, for example, before becoming secretary of defense, Chuck Hagel reportedly bought three dozen copies of a study lauding Eisenhower's management of the Suez Crisis and distributed them to, among others, President Barack Obama, Secretary of State Hillary Clinton, and then Secretary of Defense Leon Panetta. Hagel's advice was clear: follow Eisenhower and stop the military adventurism.[4]

In addition to standing up for principle, Eisenhower also faced down Israel in the midst of an election. The inside story is therefore also appealing to all those who believe that American support for Israel is excessive—a view that received its classic expression in the 1992 book *The Passionate Attachment*, written by George Ball, a former deputy secretary of state, and his son Douglas Ball. "Eisenhower deserves great credit for being the last president for thirty years to stand up to the pressures and importunings of the Israeli government and its American supporters," the Balls write. "By doing so he demonstrated conclusively that if it chose to, an American government could effectively influence even such a powerful leader as Ben-Gurion." Eisenhower's successors, the Balls lamented, showed none of his fortitude. "They succeeded only in accelerating the American retreat from principle."[5]

But Ball and his son got it entirely wrong. It was Eisenhower himself who sounded the retreat. He did so, moreover, because the policy to which the Balls cling like barnacles failed to serve the national interest. A true realist with no ideological ax to grind, Eisenhower came to recognize that his Suez policy of sidelining the Israelis and the Europeans simply did not produce the promised results. The policy was, as he told Nixon, a blunder. Unfortunately, his reluctance to publicize this assessment has allowed those who are inspired by his management of the Suez Crisis to lay claim to his legacy.

Ike's True Lessons

Suppose Eisenhower had been more forthcoming. Suppose that during his July 1967 interview with C. L. Sulzberger he had shared

with the reporter the same regrets about Suez that he expressed to
Nixon a few months later. And suppose, further, that Sulzberger
then asked him to record, for the benefit of his successors, the key
lessons of his experience. In that case, Eisenhower might have responded by summarizing, in the five following points, the guiding
ethos of the Ike of 1958.

First, when making policy toward the Middle East, recite often
the motto of the First Marine Division of the Marine Corps: "No
better friend, no worse enemy." The United States has no standing
alliances in the Middle East to guide her behavior there—no regional equivalent to NATO in Europe, or to the series of bilateral
treaties that exist in Asia. There is, that is to say, no set of formal
legal commitments that helps the president sort friend from foe.
Each president must conceive the region anew as a conscious intellectual act. As Eisenhower discovered, the wild political crosscurrents of the Middle East make the task more complex than it might
at first sound. Friends of long standing sometimes adopt policies
that antagonize the United States, while traditionally hostile states
whisper beguilingly that they hold the solution to its problem.

Second, a president must reject advice based on the notion that
the Arab-Israeli conflict is the central strategic challenge in the
Middle East. Regional experts fall into two groups: those who see
Israel as a liability, and those who regard her as an asset. For the
former, the Arab-Israeli conflict is the core problem in the Middle East, and settling it is the master key to regional stability. "If
we can solve the Palestine problem," they say, "then our situation
throughout the Middle East will improve dramatically." For the
latter group, the conflict is truly significant only in its neighborhood. The second group has it right, but the weightiness of the Israel question in domestic politics, among other factors, can easily
trick a president into believing the exaggerated claims regarding its
broader significance. Eisenhower and Dulles fell into this trap in
1955 when they subordinated their entire strategy to the fanciful

goal of solving the Egyptian-Israeli conflict. While they were busy chasing a mirage, Nasser fleeced them.

Third, pay close attention to inter-Arab politics. Fixated as they were on the Arab-Israeli questions, Eisenhower and Dulles missed the importance of the inter-Arab struggle over the Baghdad Pact. By the time they realized that the fate of their own strategies turned on the outcome of this conflict, the damage was already done.

Fourth, adopt a tragic perspective. The Middle East is in the throes of an historical crisis, a prolonged period of instability. American policy can exacerbate or ameliorate the major conflicts, but it can rarely solve them. Americans, however, frequently seek to place themselves "on the right side of history"—as if an earth-quake has a direction. In 1953–54, this aspiration lured Eisenhower and Dulles into the trap of believing that solving the Canal Zone dispute had ended the conflict between the West and Egypt. While solving the dispute was a wise move, the Americans failed to en-tertain the possibility that Nasser's newfound power might simply fuel his ambition. In the Middle East, it is prudent to assume that the solution to every problem will inevitably generate new prob-lems. Like Sisyphus, the United States has no choice but to push the boulder up a hill whose pinnacle remains forever out of reach.

Finally, remember that a picture is worth a thousand words. "Why do men make mistakes?" asked Walter Lippmann, the fa-mous political commentator. "Because an important part of human behavior is reaction to the pictures in their heads."[6] Lippmann's debt to Weber is obvious. "[M]en react to their ideas and images, to their pictures and notions of the world, treating these pictures as if they were reality," Lippmann cautioned. When he penned those words, in 1955, he was not referring to Eisenhower's Middle East policy, but his analysis perfectly describes its principal defect. Ike's travails resulted not from lack of information, but from the false things that he regarded as true.

Eisenhower was not personally responsible for the mistaken

image of the Middle East that he had in his head, which was the product of a collective American delusion. In a number of circles (on both sides of the political spectrum) the delusion persists. Eisenhower's lessons, therefore, are as timely today as they are consequential.

ACKNOWLEDGMENTS

To consider just how many people offered invaluable assistance in the writing of this book is a humbling experience. I owe thanks, above all, to Roger Hertog, who first suggested that I write about Eisenhower. At every stage of the project, he and Susan Hertog, his wife, provided me with generous support and advice, as did Eric Cohen and the Tikvah Fund. I am also indebted to the Bradley Foundation, and, especially, to Luis Tellez of the Witherspoon Institute, who helped me keep body and soul together.

Lee Smith, Tony Badran, Adam Garfinkle, Zvi Sobel, Eliot Cohen, Mike O'Hanlon, Steve Rosen, Paul Carrese, John Walters, Jesse Ferris, and Arthur Herman commented on all or part of the manuscript and offered many other forms of assistance. As he has done on countless occasions for me and many others, Neal Kozodoy performed feats of magic. Peter Rough read, reread, and then reread some more, but he also cut, cut, and cut—ruthlessly.

My former colleagues at the Brookings Institution, Martin Indyk and Tamara Wittes, were unfailingly supportive. At the Hudson Institute, Ken Weinstein and John Walters have been as patient as they have been helpful.

I record a special debt to those who helped with research: Andrew Regenstreich, Ashleigh Whelan, Andrew Coffey, Laura Mooney, Mateo Aceves, and Daniel Swartz. Zack Gold sifted through haystacks, tirelessly searching for needles. Avnet Kleiner's investigations were worthy of Philip Marlowe. Will Inboden did more for me in one conversation than he will ever know. Professor

Tom Kolsky generously provided me access to his personal document collection.

At Simon & Schuster, Emily Loose set the project sailing with infectious enthusiasm, while Bob Bender, with the aid of Johanna Li, steered it to port with quiet mastery—teaching me, along the way, that less is more. Many thanks to Tom Pitoniak for his sharp-eyed copyediting.

My agent, Larry Weissman, not only assured me that I had a story to tell but also instructed me about how to tell it.

But my deepest gratitude goes to the brightest points on my compass: my daughters—and, of course, my wife, to whom this book is dedicated.

NOTES

CHAPTER 1. A NEW PRESIDENT

1. John Colville, *The Fringes of Power: 10 Downing Street Diaries, 1939–1955* (New York: Norton, 1985), 663.
2. U.S. Department of State, *Foreign Relations of the United States* [abbreviated hereinafter as *FRUS*] 1948, V, Part 2, 975.
3. Colville, *The Fringes of Power*, 663.
4. Ibid., 664.
5. Ibid., 661–62.
6. Richard Nixon, *RN: The Memoirs of Richard Nixon* (New York: Grosset & Dunlap, 1978), 198.
7. *The Eisenhower Diaries*, Robert H. Ferrell, ed. (New York and London: Norton, 1980), 224.
8. Ibid., 223.
9. Robert Rhodes James, *Anthony Eden: A Biography* (New York: McGraw-Hill, 1987), 157.
10. Anthony Gorst and Lewis Johnman, *The Suez Crisis* (London: Routledge, 1997), 28–29.
11. Ian Fleming, *Casino Royale* (New York: Penguin Group, 1953), 79.
12. Dwight D. Eisenhower, "Speech at London, England, June 12, 1945 (Guildhall Address)," http://www.eisenhower.archives.gov/all_about_ike/speeches/pre_presidential_speeches.pdf.
13. Ferrell, *Eisenhower Diaries*, 224.
14. Ibid., 223.
15. Hugh Wilford, *America's Great Game* (New York: Basic Books, 2013), 113–32.

CHAPTER 2: COLLISION

1. No. OPS/835, April 23, 1953, British Public Record Office, Kew [abbreviated hereinafter as PRO] PRO/FO371/102847/JE11914/10; and Joel Gordon, *Nasser's Blessed Movement* (New York: Oxford University Press, 1992), 169.

2. Dwight D. Eisenhower, *The White House Years: Mandate for Change, 1953–56* (Garden City, NY: Doubleday, 1963), 155–56.

3. Peter G. Boyle, ed., *The Churchill–Eisenhower Correspondence, 1953–1955* (Chapel Hill: University of North Carolina Press, 1990), 25.

4. *FRUS*, 1952–54, IX, Part 2, 1966–67.

5. *FRUS*, 1952–54, IX, Part 2, 1997–99.

6. Kay Summersby Morgan, *Past Forgetting: My Love Affair with Dwight D. Eisenhower* (New York: Simon & Schuster, 1977), 168.

7. *FRUS*, 1952–54, IX, Part 2, 1999.

8. Evelyn Shuckburgh, *Descent to Suez* (London: Weidenfeld & Nicolson, 1986), 75.

9. Ibid., 75.

10. "Egypt: The Alternatives," February 16, 1953, PRO/CAB 129/59.

11. Shuckburgh, *Descent to Suez*, 75.

12. Washington to FO, March 6, 1953, PRO/FO371/102796/JE1192/35.

13. Washington to FO, March 6, 1953, PRO/FO371/102796/JE1192/35.

14. Robert Rhodes James, *Anthony Eden: A Biography* (New York: McGraw-Hill, 1987), 360.

15. Washington to FO, March 9, 1953, PRO/FO371/102796/JE1192/130.

16. New York to FO, March 10, 1953, PRO/FO371/102796/JE1192/130.

17. New York to FO, March 11, 1953, PRO/FO371/102796/JE1192/130.

18. Creswell to Allen, March 19, 1953, PRO/FO371/102803/JE1992/155G; and Creswell to Allen, October 28, 1953, PRO/FO371/102820/JE1192/595; Lakeland interview, April 4, 2010, http://models.street-artists.org/wp-content/uploads/2010/07/Lakeland-interview-final.pdf.

19. *FRUS*, 1952–54, IX, Part 2, 2012.

20. Ibid.

21. Ibid.

22. No. 1236, FO to Washington, March 15, 1953, PRO/FO371/102798/JE1192/61.

23. No. 1270, FO to Washington, March 18, 1953, PRO/FO371/102796/JE1192/130.

24. No. 605, Washington to FO, March 18, 1953, PRO/FO371/102796/JE1192/130.

25. No. 645, Washington to FO March 25, 1953, PRO/FO371/102803/JE1192/134.

26. *FRUS*, 1952–4, IX, Part 2, 2026.

27. Shuckburgh, *Descent to Suez*, 86.

28. Dwight D. Eisenhower, "The Chance for Peace," April 16, 1953, http://www.eisenhower.archives.gov/all_about_ike/speeches/chance_for_peace.pdf.

29. *FRUS, 1952–1954,* 971.

30. Ibid., 975–76.

31. Ibid., 976.

32. Ibid., 977.

33. Ibid., 978.

34. Ibid., 980–981.

35. *FRUS, 1952–54*, IX, Part 2, 2057–58.

36. Ibid., 2060.

37. No. 2063, FO to Washington, May 9, 1953, PRO/FO371/102807/JE1192/264.

38. No. 1005, FO to Washington, May 9, 1953, PRO/FO371/102807/JE1192/265.

39. No. 2070, FO to Washington, May 11, 1953, PRO/FO371/102807/JE1192/265.

40. *FRUS, 1952–54*, VI, Part 1, 984.

41. *Chronology of International Events and Documents* 9 (10), 293–322, http://www.jstor.org/stable/40545353.

42. BBC, *Summary of World Broadcasts* [abbreviated hereinafter as *SWB*], No. 357.

43. BBC, *SWB*, No. 350.

44. No. Orbat/MI.4(b)/13, May 14, 1953, PRO/FO371/102869/JE1202/7.

45. Creswell to Allen, March 30, 1953, PRO/FO371/102803/JE1192/157.

46. *FRUS, 1952–54*, IX, Part 1, 5.

47. *Hansard*, 515, 883–98.

48. *FRUS, 1952–54*, VI, Part 1, 985.

CHAPTER 3: A PATIENT SULKY PIG

1. Hankey's notes, May 22, 1953, PRO/FO371/102765/JE1052/121G.

2. *FRUS, 1952–54*, IX, Part 1, 25.

3. *FRUS, 1952–54*, IX, Part 2, 2076.

4. *FRUS, 1952–54*, IX, Part 2, 2076.

5. On Mayer's request and Eisenhower's response, see Editorial Note 409,

FRUS, 1952–54, VI, Part 1, 984; and Editorial Note 318, *FRUS*, V, Part 2, 1710–11.

6. *FRUS, 1952–54*, IX, Part 2, 2077.

7. Ibid., 2079.

8. *FRUS, 1952–54*, IX, Part 1, 380–81, 385.

9. *FRUS, 1952–54*, IX, Part 2, 2088–89.

10. Ibid., 2089.

11. Ibid., 2094–95.

12. John Colville, *The Fringes of Power: 10 Downing Street Diaries, 1939–1955* (New York: Norton, 1985), 668.

13. Martin Gilbert, *Winston S. Churchill: Never Despair* (London: Heinemann), 846; Kenneth Clark, *The Other Half* (London: Harper & Row, 1977), 128.

14. Lord Moran, *Churchill: The Struggle for Survival, 1940–65* (New York: Carroll & Graff, 2006), 153.

15. Ibid., 157–59.

16. *FRUS, 1952–54*, VI, Part 1, 992–93.

17. *FRUS, 1952–54*, IX, Part 1, 395.

18. Ibid., 124.

19. Ibid., 400.

20. *FRUS, 1952–54*, IX, Part 2, 2107; Boyle, ed., *The Churchill–Eisenhower Correspondence, 1953–1955* 82–83, dated July 1, 1953.

21. *FRUS, 1952–54*, IX, Part 2, 2110.

22. Ibid., 2111–12.

23. Ibid., 2116–17.

24. *FRUS, 1952–54*, V, Part 2, 1638.

25. Ibid., 1636.

26. No. 1468, Washington to FO, July 11, 1953, PRO/FO371/102731/JE10345 /15.

27. *FRUS, 1952–54*, V, Part 2, 1680–81.

28. No. 1516, Washington to FO, July 14, 1953, PRO/FO371/102732/JE10345 /21.

29. No. 1517, Washington to FO, July 14, 1953, PRO/FO371/102732/JE10345 /22.

30. *FRUS, 1952–54*, IX, Part 2, 2121–22.

31. Ibid., 2140.

32. Ibid., 2142.

33. *Times*, October 12, 1953, p. 11.

34. *Times*, October 8, 1953, p. 2.

35. *FRUS, 1952–54*, IX, Part 2, 2165.

36. Ibid., 2164–66.

37. Colville, *The Fringes of Power*, 685–86.

38. *FRUS, 1952–54*, V, Part 2, 1758.
39. Colville, *The Fringes of Power*, 683.
40. Moran, *Churchill*, 228.

CHAPTER 4: IKE'S FIRST BET

1. Evelyn Shuckburgh, *Descent to Suez* (London: Weidenfeld & Nicolson, 1986), 120.
2. FO Minute (Bromley), December 18, 1953, PRO/FO371/102824/JE1192/689.
3. *FRUS, 1952–4*, IX, Part 2, 2184 n.2.
4. Ibid.
5. Ibid., 2184.
6. Churchill to Eden, December 28, 1953, PRO/FO371/108413/JE1192/8.
7. Eden to Churchill (Draft), PRO/FO371/108413/JE1192/8.
8. Shuckburgh, *Descent to Suez*, 125.
9. *FRUS, 1952–54*, IX, Part 1, 446.
10. *New York Times*, September 20, 1953, p. 19.
11. Minute by Eden, January 12, 1954, PRO/FO371/110819/V1193/21A.
12. Makins to FO, January 25, 1954, reproduced in: PRO/CAB129/66 /C(54)53, February 15, 1954.
13. Shuckburgh, *Descent to Suez*, 157.
14. *FRUS, 1952–54*, VI, Part 1, 1046–47.
15. Ibid., 1047.
16. Ibid., 1051–52.
17. *Daily Express*, July 28, 1954, p. 4.
18. *Hansard*, 531, 737.
19. *Times*, July 30, 1954, p. 8.
20. *Hansard*, 531, 726.
21. Ibid., 743–44.
22. Lord Moran, *Churchill: The Struggle for Survival, 1940–65* (New York: Carroll & Graff, 2006), 303.
23. *Hansard*, 531, 750.
24. *FRUS, 1952–54*, VI, Part 1, 1052.
25. "A Speech at the Lord Mayor's Guildhall Banquet," November 9, 1953, in Winston S. Churchill, *The Unwritten Alliance: Speeches, 1953–1959* (London: Cassell, 1961), 79–82.
26. Moran, *Churchill*, 296.
27. Jean Edward Smith, *Eisenhower in War and Peace* (New York: Random House, 2012), 612.
28. Lawrence Wright, *In the New World: Growing Up with America from the Sixties to the Eighties* (New York: Vintage, 2013), 105.

CHAPTER 5: ANATOMY OF A MISCALCULATION

1. No. 269, Eden to Churchill, February 21, 1955, PRO/FO371/115492/ V1073/289.
2. BBC, *SWB*, No. 547.
3. No. 269, Eden to Churchill, February 21, 1955, PRO/FO371/115492/ V1073/289.
4. *FRUS, 1955–57*, XII, 15.
5. Burdett to Byroade, June 25, 1955, United States National Archives [abbreviated hereinafter as USNA], 611.74/6-2255.
6. Shuckburgh minute, January 11, 1955, PRO/FO371/115484/V1073/26.
7. *FRUS, 1952–54*, IX, Part 1, 88.
8. Dulles to Eisenhower, May 29, 1953, Dulles Papers, Box 73, Mudd Library, Princeton University.
9. *FRUS, 1952–54*, IX, Part 1, 380–81.
10. Interview with Parker T. Hart, *The Foreign Affairs Oral History Collection of the Association for Diplomatic Studies and Training*, January 27, 1989, Library of Congress, Manuscripts Division, http://hdl.loc.gov/loc.mss/ mfdip.2004har14.
11. *New York Times*, June 2, 1953, p. 4.
12. CIA, National Intelligence Estimate, January 15, 1953, http://www.foia.cia .gov/sites/default/files/document_conversi ons/89801/DOC_0000119704 .pdf.
13. *FRUS, 1952–54*, IX, Part 1, 21.
14. Khalid Muhi'l-Din, *Wa'l-an atakallim* (Cairo: Markaz al-ahram lil-tarjamah wa-l-nashr, 1992), 194.
15. *FRUS, 1952–54*, IX, Part 2, 2086.
16. Gamal Abdel Nasser, "The Philosophy of the Revolution (Part 3)," *Akhir Sa'ah*, January 6, 1954, as translated by William Lakeland in Caffery to State, January 20, 1954, USNA 674.00/1-2054.
17. *FRUS*, 1952–54, IX, Part 1, 516.
18. Kenneth Osgood, *Total Cold War* (Lawrence: University Press of Kansas, 2006), 138–40.
19. BBC, *SWB*, No. 494.
20. Patrick Seale, *The Struggle for Syria* (Oxford: Oxford University Press, 1965), 204.
21. BBC, *SWB*, No. 126.
22. Caffery to State, August 27, 1954, USNA, 674.87/8–2754
23. *FRUS, 1952–4*, IX, Part 2, 2387.

CHAPTER 6: THE ALPHA CONTRADICTION

1. *FRUS, 1955–57*, XII, 36.
2. *FRUS, 1955–57*, XXIV, 629–30.
3. *FRUS, 1952–54*, IX, 1685.
4. Makins to FO, November 5, 1954, PRO/FO371/111095/VR1079/2G.
5. Evelyn Shuckburgh, *Descent to Suez* (London: Weidenfeld & Nicolson, 1986), 211.
6. Shimon Shamir, "The Collapse of Project Alpha," in William Louis and Roger Owen, eds., *Suez 1956: The Crisis and its Consequences* (Oxford: Clarendon Press, 1989), 92.
7. *FRUS, 1955–57*, IV, 102.
8. Ibid., IV, 70.
9. Ibid., IV, 71.
10. Ibid., IV, 70.
11. *FRUS, 1955–57*, IV, 118.
12. *FRUS, 1955–57*, XII, 47.
13. Bailey to Rose, February 28, 1955, PRO/FO371/115495/V1073/385.
14. BBC, *SWB*, No. 547.
15. Cairo to State, January 27, 1955, USNA/682.87/1–2755.
16. *FRUS, 1955–57*, XII, 43.
17. *FRUS, 1955–57*, IV, 118.
18. On this phone call and the issues it raises, see Nigel John Ashton, "The Hijacking of a Pact: The Formation of the Baghdad Pact and Anglo-American Tensions in the Middle East, 1955–1958," *Review of International Studies* 19, no. 2 (April 1993): 123–37.
19. *FRUS* 1958–60, XII, 8.
20. Shuckburgh, *Descent to Suez*, 247.
21. Ibid., 243.
22. Ibid., 211–13.
23. Ibid., 212–13.
24. This biographical sketch and all quotes come from "Oral History Interview with Henry Byroade," September 19, 1988, Truman Library and Museum, https://www.trumanlibrary.org/oralhist/byroade.htm.
25. Ibid.
26. Shuckburgh, *Descent to Suez*, 249.
27. *FRUS, 1955–57*, XIV, 78.
28. Cairo to State, March 1, 1955, *FRUS, 1955–57*, XIV, 78.
29. Cairo to State, March 8, 1955, *FRUS, 1955–57*, XII, 31.

30. State to Damascus, March 18, 1955, *FRUS, 1955–57*, XII, 39.

31. "Oral History Interview with Henry Byroade," September 19, 1988, Truman Library, https://www.trumanlibrary.org/oralhist/byroade.htm.

32. BBC, *SWP*, No. 549.

CHAPTER 7: DECEPTION

1. Mordechai Bar-On, *The Gates of Gaza* (New York: St. Martin's, 1995), 16–17.

2. Patrick Seale, *The Struggle for Syria* (Oxford: Oxford University Press, 1965).

3. Ibid., 235–36.

4. The documents appear in Guy Laron, "Cutting the Gordian Knot: The Post-WWII Egyptian Quest for Arms and the 1955 Czechoslovak Arms Deal," Woodrow Wilson International Center for Scholars, 2007. See also Guy Laron, *Origins of the Suez Crisis: Postwar Development Diplomacy and the Struggle over Third World Industrialization, 1945–1956* (Baltimore: Johns Hopkins University Press, 2013).

5. Laron, "Cutting the Gordian Knot," pp. 47–49.

6. Ibid., 47.

7. *FRUS, 1955–57*, XIV, 355–58.

8. *FRUS, 1955–57*, XIV, 356 n.5.

9. Laron, "Cutting the Gordian Knot," 56.

10. *FRUS, 1955–57*, XIV, 114–15.

11. Ibid., 117.

12. *FRUS, 1955–57*, XIV, 116.

13. Ibid., 120–25.

14. Ibid., 129–33.

15. Ibid., 141.

16. Ibid., 234, n.10.

17. Ibid., 220–22.

18. Ibid., 237–40.

19. Ibid., 262–63.

20. Ibid., 274.

21. Ibid.

22. Ibid., 353–54.

23. Laron, "Cutting the Gordian Knot," 58.

24. *FRUS, 1955–57*, XIV, 263–66.

25. For complete text, see *New York Times*, August 27, 1955, p. 2.

26. *FRUS, 1955–57*, XIV, 398–99.

27. BBC, *SWB*, No. 601.
28. *FRUS, 1955–57*, XIV, 402–3.
29. Ibid., 497–98.

CHAPTER 8: K AND BIG BROTHER

1. *FRUS, 1955–57*, XIV, 509–10.
2. Dwight David Eisenhower, *Mandate for Change* (New York: Doubleday, 1963), 536.
3. Jim Newton, *Eisenhower: The White House Years* (New York: Anchor, 2012), 196.
4. Miles Copeland, *The Game of Nations* (New York: Simon & Schuster, 1969), 159–60.
5. Ibid., 138.
6. Kermit Roosevelt, "The Partition of Palestine: A Lesson in Pressure Politics," *Middle East Journal* 2, no. 1: January 1948, 1–16.
7. Virginia Crocheron Gildersleeve, *Many a Good Crusade: Memoirs* (New York: Macmillan, 1954), 412.
8. For a pathbreaking discussion of AFME, see Hugh Wilford, *America's Great Game* (New York: Basic Books, 2013).
9. Muhammad al-Tawil, *La'bat al-umam wa 'abd al-nasir* (Cairo: Al-Maktab al-Misriyy al-Hadith, 1986), 398–400.
10. *FRUS, 1955–57*, XIV, 612–13.
11. Shuckburgh–Allen Dulles memorandum of conversation, September 29, 1955, PRO/FO371/113678/JE1194/289.
12. *FRUS, 1955–57*, XIV, 521.
13. Ibid., 520.
14. Copeland, *The Game of Nations*, 157.
15. Ibid., 158.
16. Ibid., 159.
17. Ibid., 162.
18. Ibid., 163.
19. Ibid., 164–65.
20. *FRUS, 1955–57*, XIV, 520–22.
21. Ibid., 522–23.
22. Ibid., 526.
23. Ibid., 518–19.
24. Ibid., 527.
25. Copeland, *The Game of Nations*, 165.
26. Miles Copeland, *The Game Player: Confessions of the CIA's Original Political Operative* (London: Aurum, 1989), 168.

27. Noble Frankland, ed., *Documents on International Affairs, 1956* (London: Oxford University Press, 1959), 93.

28. Ibid., 93.

29. Copeland, *The Game of Nations*, 167.

30. Donald Neff, *Warriors at Suez* (New York: Linden, 1981), 95.

31. Copeland, *The Game of Nations*, 168.

32. Frankland, *Documents*, 93–94.

33. Ibid., 94.

34. *FRUS, 1955–57*, XIV, 552.

35. Ibid., 540.

CHAPTER 9: BLOWBACK

1. Kellas to Levant Department, October 8, 1955, PRO/FO371/115536/V1075/9.

2. For resolutions of the conference, see: PRO/FO371/115536/V1075/9.

3. Glubb signal, PRO/FO371/115905/VR1092/324.

4. Glubb signal, PRO/FO371/115905/VR1092/324.

5. Damascus to FO, November 25, 1955: PRO/FO371/115910/VR1092/434; and Glubb signal, PRO/FO371/115910/VR1092/440.

6. Miles Copeland, *The Game Player: The Confessions of the CIA's Original Political Operative* (London: Aurum, 1989), 167.

7. Paul M. A. Linebarger, *Psychological Warfare* (Landisville, PA: Coachwhip, 2010), 8.

8. Robert B. Satloff, *From Abdullah to Hussein: Jordan in Transition* (Oxford: Oxford University Press, 1994), 83.

9. Glubb signal, PRO/FO371/104789/ER1091/385.

10. BBC, *SWB*, IV, No. 409.

11. Tel Aviv to FO, October 10, 1953, PRO/FO371/115905/VR1092/326.

12. Hadow minute, October 20, 1955, PRO/FO371/115905/VR1092/324.

13. *FRUS, 1955–57*, IV, 804.

14. Glubb signal, PRO/FO371/115909/VR1092/409B.

15. Glubb signal, PRO/FO371/115909/VR1092/411.

16. Glubb signal, PRO/FO371/115909/VR1092/409B.

17. Paul M. A. Linebarger, *Psychological Warfare*, 78.

18. Glubb signal, PRO/FO371/115653/VJ1051/24.

19. Duke to Shuckburgh, November 10, 1955, PRO/FO371/115653/VJ1051/22.

20. Shuckburgh, *Descent to Suez*, 297.

21. Macmillan to Eden, November 25, 1955, PRO/FO371/115532V1073/1336A.

22. Behçet Kemal Yeşibursa, *The Baghdad Pact: Anglo-American Defence Policies in the Middle East, 1950–59* (New York: Frank Cass, 2005), 144.

23. W. Scott Lucas, *Divided We Stand* (London: Hodder & Stoughton, 1991), 75.

24. BBC, *SWB*, No. 629, December 13, 1955.

25. Report by Templer, December 16, 1955, PRO/FO371/115658/UJ1051/127.

26. Anwar el-Sadat, *In Search of Identity: An Autobiography* (New York: Harper & Row, 1978), 136.

27. Mason to Rose, December 31, 1955, PRO/FO371/121476/VJ10310/3.

28. On Saudi bribery, see, for example, Macmillan to Eden, November 25, 1955, PRO/FO371/115532/V1073/1336A; and Fouracres to Goodison, December 29, 1955, PRO/FO371/121241/V1071/8. On Egyptian subversion, see Chapman-Andrews to Duke, January 18, 1956, PRO/FO 371/121465/VJ1015/106; and Cairo to FO, January 29, 1956, PRO/FO371/121242/V1071/68. See also: John Bagot Glubb, *A Soldier with the Arabs* (New York: Harper & Brothers, 1957), 391–412. For a corroborating American report, see *FRUS, 1955–57*, XIII, 13.

29. Glubb, *A Soldier with the Arabs*, 399.

30. King Hussein of Jordan, *Uneasy Lies the Head* (New York: Bernard Geis Associates, 1962), 112.

31. Cordwainer Smith, *Quest of the Three Worlds* (New York: Ace, 1966).

32. Ibid., 5.

33. Linebarger, *Psychological Warfare*, 8.

CHAPTER 10: THREE-DIMENSIONAL CHESS

1. Evelyn Shuckburgh, *Descent to Suez* (London: Weidenfeld & Nicolson, 1986), 345.

2. Robert H. Ferrell, ed., *The Eisenhower Diaries* (New York: Norton, 1981), 323.

3. *FRUS, 1955–57*, XII, 249.

4. *FRUS, 1955–57*, XV, 354–65.

5. Anthony Nutting, *No End of a Lesson: The Story of Suez* (New York: Clarkson N. Potter, 1967) 34–35. In the text, Nutting uses the word *destroyed*, not *murdered*. In 1986 he corrected the record in a communication to author Keith Kyle. See Keith Kyle, *Suez* (London: Weidenfeld & Nicolson, 1991), 99 and 581 n.53.

6. Shuckburgh, *Descent to Suez*, 346.

7. Ibid., 356–57.

8. *FRUS, 1955–57*, XV, 28–36.

9. Ibid., 302–7.

10. Ibid., 311.

11. Ferrell, *Eisenhower Diaries*, 342.

12. Ibid., 319.

13. *FRUS, 1955–57*, XV, 419–21.

14. Ibid., 326–27.

15. *Eisenhower Diaries*, 323–24.

16. *FRUS, 1955–57*, XV, 547, 735.

17. Ibid., 556–60.

18. Ibid., 560.

19. Ibid., 759.

20. Ibid., 793–97.

21. Ibid., 832–35.

22. *New York Times*, June 10, 1956, p. 24.

23. *FRUS, 1955–57*, XV, 732.

24. William J. Burns, *Economic Aid and American Policy toward Egypt, 1955–1981* (Albany: State University of New York Press, 1985), 89.

25. *FRUS, 1955–57*, XVI, 57.

26. *FRUS, 1955–57*, XV, 866.

27. Ibid., 868.

28. Burns, *Economic Aid*, 214.

29. Noble Frankland, ed., *Documents on International Affairs, 1956* (London: Oxford University Press, 1959), 111.

30. Ibid., 110–11.

31. Ibid., 111.

32. Donald Neff, *Warriors at Suez: Eisenhower Takes America into the Middle East* (New York: Linden, 1981); Kennett Love, *Suez: The Twice-Fought War* (New York: McGraw-Hill, 1969).

33. Evan Thomas, *Ike's Bluff: President Eisenhower's Secret Battle to Save the World* (New York: Little, Brown, 2012), 217.

34. *FRUS, 1955–57*, XVI, 57.

35. Frankland, *Documents*, 111.

CHAPTER 11: THE END OF EMPIRE

1. *FRUS, 1955–57*, XVI, 61.

2. Ibid., 63.

3. Ibid., 64.

4. Ibid., 77–78.

5. Ibid., 11–12.

6. Ibid., 98–100.

7. Ibid., 94–97.

8. Keith Kyle, *Suez: Britain's End of Empire in the Middle East* (London: I. B. Tauris, 2011), 195.

9. *FRUS, 1955–57*, XVI, 227.

10. Robert Menzies, *Afternoon Light: Some Memories of Men and Events* (London: Cassell, 1967), 168.

11. Transcript of press conference, August 31, 1956, http://www.presidency .ucsb.edu/ws/index.php?pid=10586.

12. Menzies, *Afternoon Light*, 167–68.

13. *FRUS, 1955–57*, XVI, 434–35.

14. Ibid., 434–35.

15. Anthony Gorst and Lewis Johnman, *The Suez Crisis* (London: Routledge, 1997), 78.

16. *FRUS, 1955–57*, XVI, 472–73.

17. *Hansard*, 558, 11–12.

18. *FRUS, 1955–57*, XVI, 491.

19. Ibid., 491.

20. *Department of State Bulletin*, September 24, 1956, pp. 476–83.

21. *Hansard*, 558, 219.

22. Anthony Eden, *Full Circle* (London: Cassell, 1960), 483–48.

23. Ibid., 498–99.

24. *FRUS, 1955–57*, XVI, 437.

25. Kyle, *Suez*, 228.

26. Mordechai Bar-On, *The Gates of Gaza* (New York: St. Martin's, 1995), 235.

27. Moshe Dayan, *Story of My Life* (New York: Da Capo, 1992), 219.

28. Bar-On, *The Gates of Gaza*, 238–40.

29. Ibid., 243.

30. Robert Rhodes James, *Anthony Eden: A Biography* (New York: McGraw-Hill, 1987), 532.

31. *FRUS, 1955–57*, XVI, 835.

32. *New York Times*, November 1, 1956, p. 14.

33. *FRUS, 1955–57*, XVI, 906.

34. Ibid., 912.

35. Ibid., 909–10.

36. Ibid., 915.

37. Ibid., 910.

38. Ibid., 911.

39. Ibid., 873.

40. Ibid., 874.

41. Nikita Khrushchev, *Khrushchev Remembers*, trans. and ed. by Strobe Talbot (Boston: Little, Brown, 1970), 434–35.
42. Noble Frankland, ed., *Documents on International Affairs, 1956* (London: Oxford University Press, 1959), 289.
43. S. I. Troen and M. Shemesh, eds., *The Suez-Sinai Crisis 1956: Retrospective and Reappraisal* (New York: Columbia University Press, 1990), 321.
44. Chester L Cooper, *The Lion's Last Roar: Suez 1956* (New York: Harper & Row, 1978), 182.
45. *FRUS, 1955–57*, XVI, 1077.
46. Kennett Love, *Suez: The Twice-Fought War* (New York: McGraw-Hill, 1969), 387.
47. *FRUS, 1955–57*, XVI, 1027.
48. Ibid., 1040.
49. Ibid., 1042.
50. Ibid., 1044.
51. Associated Press report, carried in *Ellensburg Daily Record*, December 14, 1956, p. 1.

CHAPTER 12: IKE'S SECOND BET

1. Keith Kyle, *Suez: Britain's End of Empire in the Middle East* (London: I. B. Tauris, 2011), 258.
2. *FRUS, 1955–57*, XVI, 835.
3. Ibid., 885.
4. Richard M. Nixon, *Six Crises* (New York: Allen, 1962), 161.
5. Text of radio and television address, October 31, 1956, http://www.presidency.ucsb.edu/ws/index.php?pid=10685&st=&st1=.
6. Text of address, November 1, 1956, http://www.presidency.ucsb.edu/ws/?pid=10686.
7. Herman Finer, *Dulles over Suez: The Theory and Practice of His Diplomacy* (Chicago: Quadrangle Books, 1964), 397.
8. Isaac Alteras, *Eisenhower and Israel: U.S.-Israeli Relations, 1953–1960* (Gainesville: University Press of Florida, 1993), 246.
9. *FRUS, 1955–57*, XVI, 1064.
10. *Keesing's Record of World Events*, vol. 10, November, 1956, 15217.
11. *FRUS, 1955–57*, XVI, 1095.
12. Ibid., 1344.
13. *FRUS, 1955–57*, XVII, 142–44.
14. Ibid., 179.
15. Text of statement following meeting with King Saud, February 8, 1957, http://www.presidency.ucsb.edu/ws/?pid=10976.

16. Text of radio and television address, February 20, 1957, http://www.presidency.ucsb.edu/ws/?pid=10980.
17. Mordechai Bar-On, *Moshe Dayan: Israel's Controversial Hero* (New Haven, CT: Yale University Press, 2012), 105.
18. *FRUS, 1955–57*, XVI, 1297.
19. Anthony Eden, *Full Circle* (London: Cassell, 1960), 634.

CHAPTER 13: REGRET

1. Dwight David Eisenhower, *Waging Peace: 1956–1961* (New York: Doubleday, 1965), 265.
2. *FRUS, 1958–60*, XI, 213.
3. Ibid., 215.
4. Eisenhower, *Waging Peace*, 274
5. *FRUS, 1955–57*, XII, 438.
6. Ibid., 608.
7. *FRUS, 1955–57*, XIII, 646.
8. Salim Yaqub, *Containing Arab Nationalism: The Eisenhower Doctrine and the Middle East* (Chapel Hill and London: University of North Carolina Press, 2004), 162.
9. Eisenhower, *Waging Peace*, 203.
10. Yaacov Ro'i, *From Encroachment to Involvement: A Documentary Study of Soviet Policy in the Middle East, 1945–1973* (New York: Halsted, 1974), 245.
11. *FRUS, 1958–60*, XIII, 403–4.
12. Muhammad Hasanayn Haykal, *Nasser: The Cairo Documents* (New York, Doubleday, 1973), 127–28.
13. *FRUS, 1958–60*, XII, 728.
14. Ibid., 728.
15. *FRUS, 1958–60*, XI, 269.
16. Ibid., 276.
17. Ibid., 288–89.
18. Ibid., 298.
19. Ibid., 213.
20. Ibid., 212–13.
21. Ibid., 214–15.
22. Eisenhower, *Waging Peace*, 271–72.
23. *FRUS, 1958–60*, XI, 220.
24. Eisenhower, *Waging Peace*, 274.
25. *FRUS, 1958–60*, XI, 220.
26. Ibid., 426.

276 *NOTES*

27. Fawaz Gerges, *The Superpowers and the Middle East: Regional and International Politics, 1955–1967* (Boulder, CO: Westview, 1994), 124.
28. *FRUS, 1958–60*, XII, 116.
29. Ibid., 127.
30. Ibid., 178.
31. Ibid., 189.
32. Ibid., 184.
33. Yaqub, *Containing Arab Nationalism*, 263.
34. Abraham Ben-Zvi, *Decade of Transition: Eisenhower, Kennedy and the Origins of the American-Israeli Alliance* (New York Columbia University Press, 1998).
35. *FRUS, 1958–60*, XII, 128.
36. Peter Golden, *Quiet Diplomat: A Biography of Max M. Fisher* (Detroit: Cornwall, 1992), xviii.
37. Ibid., xix.
38. Israeli Archives, 5986/3, May 24, 1967.
39. Richard Nixon, "My Debt to Macmillan," *Times*, January 28, 1987, p. 16. I owe my knowledge of this and other sources on Eisenhower's regret to: Peter Rodman, *Presidential Command: Power, Leadership, and the Making of Foreign Policy from Richard Nixon to George W. Bush* (New York: Vintage, 2009).
40. C. L. Sulzberger, *An Age of Mediocrity: Memoirs and Diaires, 1963–1972* (New York: Macmillan, 1973), 357–58.
41. Stephen E. Ambrose, Review of *Nixon: A Life* by Jonathan Aitken. *Foreign Affairs* 73, no. 4 (July/August 1994): 168.

CONCLUSION

1. Quoted in Judith Goldstein and Robert O. Keohane, *Ideas in Foreign Policy: Beliefs, Institutions, and Political Change* (Ithaca, NY: Cornell University Press, 1993), 11–12.
2. *FRUS, 1955–57*, XVI, 1044.
3. Anthony Nutting, "A Mid-East Settlement Is Imperative," *New York Herald Tribune*, July 31, 1958.
4. David Ignatius, "What Suez Crisis Can Remind Us about U.S. Power," *Washington Post*, January 25, 2013, https://www.washingtonpost.com/opinions/david-ignatius-what-suez-crisis-can-remind-us-about-us-power/2013/01/25/e3a3ca5e-6682-11e2-85f5-a8a9228e55e7_story.html.
5. George Ball and Douglas B. Ball, *The Passionate Attachment* (New York: Norton, 1992), 49.
6. Walter Lippmann, *The Public Philosophy*, (New York: Little, Brown, 1955), 92.

INDEX

and U.S.'s Northern Tier plan, 57–58,
  69–70
U.S.'s special relationship with, 2–3,
  4, 64–65
see also British Empire; Foreign
  Office, British
Gromyko, Andrei, 221
Guatemala, coup in, 214

Hagel, Chuck, 254–55
Hammarskjöld, Dag, 200, 201, 208,
  209–10
Hankey, Robin, 36
Harkabi, Yehoshafat, 147
Harman, Avraham, 240–41, 242, 249
Hart, Parker, 75
Hashemite monarchy, 12, 70, 86, 87,
  149, 150, 215–16, 222, 250, 251
Head, Antony, 63
Hebron hills, 147–48
Hitler, Adolf, 6
Hoover, Herbert, Jr., 166–67, 201
Hull, John, 22, 23
Humphrey, George, 129, 201
Hungary, 191–92, 197, 199
Hussein, Ahmed, 110, 111, 132–34,
  169–70, 174
  Eden's Suez scheme denounced by,
    184–85
Hussein, King of Jordan, 149, 150–51,
  152, 154, 155, 157, 162, 237
  assassination plot against, 226
  Iraq coup and, 217
  and merger of Egypt and Syria, 225
  Nasser opposed by, 226, 231
  Nutting's disdain for, 251–52
Husseini, Hajj Amin al-, 143

India, 15, 62
Iran, 13, 46, 227
  coup in, 124, 214, 220

Iraq, 8, 55, 58, 59, 88, 145, 162, 222,
  223, 251
  in Arab League, 82
  in Arab Union, 225–26
  Baghdad Pact and, 152–53
  British basing rights in, 188
  Dulles's policy on, 74–75, 76, 86–87
  Eden's policies on, 69–70
  Egypt's split with, 235
  Nasser's propaganda against, 70
  in Northern Tier, 73, 84
  in pact with Turkey, *see* Baghdad
    Pact
  revolution in, 12, 215–18, 226, 235,
    236, 238, 251
  Syrian plans to federate with, 85,
    86–87
  U.S. aid to, 58
Israel, 12, 13, 237
  Arab resentment of, 9, 43, 74
  and Baghdad Pact, 113
  in border clashes with Egypt, 115,
    119–20
  British-U.S. desire for ceding of
    land by, 91–92
  Churchill on, 4
  in closing of airspace to U.S., 230
  creation of, 150
  Egyptian terrorism against, 148,
    150–52
  and Egypt-Soviet arms deal, 129–30
  Egypt's peace negotiations with, 118
  Gaza Raid of, 93, 94, 102, 103, 104,
    105, 107–8, 112, 116, 253
  Jordan attacked by, 145–46, 147–49
  Kermit Roosevelt's desire to tack
    away from, 126, 129
  Nasser's desire for border war with,
    159–60
  in 1973 war, 249–50
  proposed sanctions on, 209, 211–12